IN A ROMAN KITCHEN

IN A ROMAN KITCHEN

Timeless Recipes from the Eternal City

JO BETTOJA

FOREWORD BY
MICHAEL BATTERBERRY

PHOTOGRAPHY BY
PAOLO DESTEFANIS

WILEY

JOHN WILEY & SONS, INC.

This book is printed on acid/free paper. ♾

Copyright © 2003 by Jo Bettoja. All rights reserved

Published by John Wiley & Sons, Inc., Hoboken, New Jersey
Published simultaneously in Canada

No part of this publication may be reproduced, stored in a retrieval system, or transmitted in any form or by any means, electronic, mechanical, photocopying, recording, scanning, or otherwise, except as permitted under Section 107 or 108 of the 1976 United States Copyright Act, without either the prior written permission of the Publisher, or authorization through payment of the appropriate per/copy fee to the Copyright Clearance Center, Inc., 222 Rosewood Drive, Danvers, MA 01923, (978) 750/8400, fax (978) 750/4470, or on the web at www.copyright.com. Requests to the Publisher for permission should be addressed to the Permissions Department, John Wiley & Sons, Inc., 111 River Street, Hoboken, NJ 07030, (201) 748/6011, fax (201) 748/6008, e/mail: permcoordinator@wiley.com.

Limit of Liability/Disclaimer of Warranty: While the publisher and author have used their best efforts in preparing this book, they make no representations or warranties with respect to the accuracy or completeness of the contents of this book and specifi/ cally disclaim any implied warranties of merchantability or fitness for a particular purpose. No warranty may be created or extended by sales representatives or written sales materials. The advice and strategies contained herein may not be suitable for your situation. You should consult with a professional where appropriate. Neither the publisher nor author shall be liable for any loss of profit or any other commercial damages, including but not limited to special, incidental, consequential, or other damages.

For general information on our other products and services or for technical support, please contact our Customer Care Department within the United States at (800) 762/2974, outside the United States at (317) 572/3993 or fax (317) 572/4002.

Wiley also publishes its books in a variety of electronic formats. Some content that appears in print may not be available in electronic books. For more information about Wiley products, visit our web site at www.wiley.com.

Interior design and layout: Joel Avirom and Jason Snyder
Design assistant: Meghan Day Healey

Library of Congress Cataloging/in/Publication Data:

Bettoja, Jo.
   In a Roman kitchen : timeless recipes from the Eternal City / Jo Bettoja.
       p. cm.
Includes index.
 ISBN 0/471/22147/3
 1. Cookery, Italian. 2. Cookery—Italy—Rome. I. Title.
 TX723 .B4696 2003
 641.5945—dc21

                                        2002015345

Printed in the United States of America

10 9 8 7 6 5 4 3 2 1

CONTENTS

An Appreciation

CUISINE IS THE EXPRESSION OF HISTORY, culture, and traditions that are often antique and complex. Yet from the cooking of a region, one can understand much of a people, maybe in a more profound manner than through theoretical studies. Indeed, the aromas, tastes, color, and form of prepared foods convey tactile knowledge and allow others to "feel" and taste the place where they were prepared.

Roman cuisine has something special to offer because it contains the history, culture, and traditions of one of the oldest cities in the world. It encompasses simplicity and complexity, poverty and wealth, strong and delicate tastes. And this is what the readers of this book will find in the recipes here, reported with an attention to detail and loving care by Jo Bettoja, in the traditional pasta *all'amatriciana, alla carbonara, al cacio e pepe,* and *all'arrabiata,* and in the cheeses, vegetables, and all the other dishes of the Roman table.

There has been much debate about the amount of knowledge contained in cooking. It is interesting that the Italian language, the language of a people notoriously known for loving their own food, has two words with the same root: *sapera* (knowledge) and *sapore* (taste). As Mayor of Rome I am happy to bring attention to the connection between this collection of recipes and the knowledge of the city. In this way, even people who read this book thousands of miles from Rome will have the opportunity to enjoy a taste of the Eternal City; and those who know the city may well find new surprises.

My *Buon appetito* goes with best wishes to the readers of this book. It is from one who not only has the difficult job of governing the city, but also from a Roman who loves his city deeply—for her history, her culture, and, therefore, for her *cucina.* It is also a wish that you will accept the invitation these recipes offer and make a future visit to Rome to appreciate directly its unique tastes, amplified by its hospitality and *simpatia,* "good will."

WALTER VELTRONI, MAYOR OF ROME

FOREWORD

MICHAEL BATTERBERRY

THE VICTORIANS LIKED TO KEEP ALBUMS they called memory books, bulging with pictures, letters, Valentines, pressed souvenirs, to preserve, as in amber, old pleasures and affections. These were touchstones meant to bridge the gap between the flatlands of daily life and shining peaks of times gone by. Reading the manuscript of Jo Bettoja's *In a Roman Kitchen*, a work of love and great depth, has induced much the same effect.

Swiftly delivered, the promise of the book's subtitle, *Timeless Recipes from the Eternal City*, triggered instant flashback. Even before grazing through Jo Bettoja's vibrant Roman recipes, I was transported by the first sentence of her introduction: "My home is in Rome, not far from the Trevi Fountain, just a short walk from the marketplace." In point of fact, in my early twenties, so had been mine. I can still catch the perfume of ripe white peaches and chunks of rose madder watermelon lilting skyward from vendors' pushcarts below my rooftop apartment. Just as I can still hear the leonine roar of the coin-glittered fountain.

Jo Bettoja and I, both Americans, each went to live in Rome during the aptly epitaphed "sweet life" Dolce Vita era. Although we periodically met—socially, Rome shrank to a village in winter—we wouldn't develop a friendly rapport until a couple of decades later, shortly after she and her partner Anna Maria Cornetto had launched, in the late 1970s, their groundbreaking and, transatlantic food gossip had it, hotly fashionable cooking school. They called it Lo Scaldavivande, after a traditional terra cotta cooking pot.

Fashionable, you ask? The seventies represented a dark passage for Rome, indeed for all of Italy, a time of danger and social disruptions personified by the dreaded Red Brigade. Many Romans accustomed to employing live-in cooks saw them march off into the populist sunset. Even *principesse* with closet loads of palazzo pajamas found themselves culinarily bereft. At the same time, as in America, numbers of high-powered men decided to learn how to cook for fun. Jo and Anna Maria rose to answer the call. All of this roughly coincided with the cofounding in America of *Food & Wine* magazine by my wife Ariane and myself. Professional curiosity prompted us to dispatch an editor to Rome to report on the team's culinary doings. Among the trophies was a fresh-faced recipe for a fennel and orange salad which, we're convinced, was responsible for its now universal ubiquity.

Back before we knew each other, Jo and I, both resolute Italophiles, had moved in overlapping Roman circles. Although soft-spoken by Eternal City standards, she was hard to miss, a sought-after Vogue model born in Millen, Georgia, a cotton country town near Savannah. Two years after her arrival, she wed Angelo Bettoja, a distinguished owner of Italian luxury hotels. This signaled the start of a gradual Ovidian metamorphosis from expat Southern belle into an authoritative Roman matron and mother of three children, Maurizio, Roberto, and Georgia. This turn of events at the altar would immediately root us in two different Roman camps, the married and the unmarried. Nevertheless, the sensuous cycles of Roman sun and moon kept us all on common ground.

Breakfasts of fragrant caffe lattes and Rome's omnipresent rosette-slashed rolls taken on deliriously flowering terraces high above the Fiat tides. Canopied lunches on cool cobble-stones at rickety, pasta-laden tables spread with not unpleasantly damp white cloths. Lunches in bathing suits on the reed-shaded sands of Ostia's beachside *stabilimenti*; usually scalding hot bowls of midget clams in brothy tomato sauce, picked at with sea salty fingers and washed down with floods of iced Frascati doused with Pellegrino and squirts of lemon. Round-the-clock dollcup caffeine breaks in clattery espresso bars and intrigue-breeding cafés. Possibly a gelato or a small pastry or two. Or a couple of Rosati's or Doney's chocolates. Then maybe just one more Negroni. Then time to change for dinner!

Dinner often was cause for drama. *Poi, dové andiamo?* So, where shall we all go? Here's where smiles became fixed. Or faded altogether. Scratch a Roman at twilight and you'll find a *ristorante* — no make that *trattoria* — critic. Roman classics, as you'll learn in this pro-foundly, definitively informed book, are not only the domain of Latin scholars. Romans believe their recipes, like papal inscriptions, deserve to be carved in marble. The question of which establishments reproduce which of these best had been known to cause superficial scarring of friendships. Not uncommon, in my own experience, have been evenings when preprandial wranglings have dragged on so long, they'd be closing the doors when we got there. I'm glad to report that many of the Roman dishes most hotly debated at nightfall over the years have been calmly collected by Jo for her book. This should be helpful in quelling future partisan disputes should they arise.

Just recently, I had a long-distance chat with Jo, to congratulate her on her manuscript. We talked about Roman cooking boiling down to the quality of its ingredients. Of the ease with which Romans, on the spur of the moment, will set extra places at the table, just as she'd been brought up to do in the American South. About how most Roman dishes, again as in the South, are expressive of warm family life. We toyed with other Rome/South affinities: putting one's best foot forward when entertaining, the common love of pork, chicken, greens. Then, more specifically, about the subtly delicious spaghetti sauced with wild hops, a fleeting seasonal marvel Ariane and I tasted not long ago at the Bettojas' sixteenth/century hunting lodge in the Roman countryside, the recipe for which I'm grateful to find in the book.

Seasonal vegetables have become to modern Romans what cream is to their armies of cats. Let me give an example. Years ago I had the good luck to witness a performance of a demented epicureanism worthy of the young Caligula. In the plushly carpeted second floor sanctum of a restaurant off the fashion/prone Via Veneto, a local count, notable for his decoration of the abodes of the famous, used to entertain friends and clients. His lavish patronage was perpetually rewarded with possession of the most prestigious central round table. Like Jefferson and Washington, who annually competed with their Virginia neighbors to see who could rush the first spring pods to table, the count had a known passion for young peas, among other things.

One day early in March, the silk-lapeled captain began his recitation of off-the-menu dishes with *piselli e prosciutto*, green peas flavored with prosciutto. Not possible, sniffed the count, it's too early. No, the man bowed, I promise you, *caro Conte*, the chef himself told me. All right, he replied, unconvinced, but if they're not fresh, I will do something terrible. The peas arrived, suspiciously drab. The count took one taste, pronounced them canned, rose from his chair and, stone-faced, circled the table, evenly sprinkling the offending pellets onto the carpet. Then, like a demonic flamenco dancer, he proceeded to stamp them into the Persian rug. Reclaiming his seat, he calmly called for a second look at the menu.

In Rome, such fanatical concern for the fresh condition of seasonal foods must by no means be seen as the cranky preserve of spoiled aristocrats. Let me give a more earthy example. My second Roman apartment, blessed with a fountain and vine-tented garden, an oasis for entertaining, I came to share with Francesco Ghedini, a precocious and wickedly funny screenwriter-journalist, a Bolognese *marchese* whose inherited love of good food would lead to his writing, with his American bride, a landmark book in English on Northern Italian dishes. Sharing the rent, I gained a resident tutor in Italian cuisines. That is until the invasion of Eleonora, a freeform Roman housekeeper who abruptly commandeered the apartment's narrow kitchen. In the ferocious tones and tough across-the-Tiber accent of Anna Magnani, Eleonora professed to know everything about everything, including cooking. Roman cooking, she ranted, was the world's best, and let's not forget it.

Eleonora insisted on choosing the menus. Who had the strength to argue? She was an amazonian shopper. Just down the street, she announced, some distant cousins had opened a little greengrocer shop. Eleonora grandly demanded that they deliver. It was curtains if they didn't fork over their best. On one occasion, drawn by an all too recognizable bellow, I tracked her down to her cousins' door, arms laden with what she denounced as *porca miseria!*—swinishly miserable excuses for artichokes and blood oranges. She was demanding her lire back and instructing her combative relatives where the returned produce should be rudely repositioned. The next day we found a conciliatory gift basket, actually an old orange crate, of flawless fruits and vegetables by the door.

Dear vanished Eleonora, Jo Bettoja's witchily descriptive recipes have, in a flash, summoned you up in the flesh. I hope that you finally married that boyfriend you used to allude to proudly as *ingegnere*, "engineer" in English, an honorific conferred, I suspect, because he drove a gladiatorial motorcycle and not a paparazzo's wimpy Vespa. If so, I hope he deserved your insistent weekly provision of veal scaloppine transformed into saltimbocca alla Romana, following, from what I recall, the same recipe plan of action cited by Jo in her book. (I still can sniff the pungent sting of prosciutto, fresh sage, and white wine spiraling out of the kitchen.) And I hope he fully appreciated the mint and garlic breath of your artichokes alla Romana. Your winily fragrant stuffed peaches. Your inflammatory *penne all'arrabbiata*. Speaking of which, didn't you, with Roman thrift, add zing to that spicy tomato, pancetta, and hot red pepper sauce by cooking it down with heels of cheese rind? I'll have to discuss that with Jo. On the strength of her nourishing text, on its truths and integrity, on the kitchen epiphanies gathered from Roman chefs, chic hostesses, vegetable vendors, and a food-fixated taxi driver (three of whose recipes she's pleased to present), Jo is certainly the one who will know.

Acknowledgments

JO BETTOJA

Thank you to my friend and agent Irene Skolnick for her patience with me and my fax . . . and to my friend and editor Susan Wyler for her help and understanding.

These friends and aquaintances all gave me recipes and helped in various ways, with recipes, Romanisms, and encouragement:

Luciano Archangeli, Signora Ascarelli, Elisabetta and Memma Beretta, Maria Gaetana Bettoja, Sally Castelnovo, Ninetta Cecacci Mariani, Donatello Cecchini, Anna Maria Cornetto Bourlot, Landing Diedhiou, Ginetta Bettoja Forges D'Avanzati, Ippolita Gaetani D'Aragona, Assunta and Giovanni Grossi, Rossana Guidi, Giulia Lazzaroni Fiastri, Signor Nibbi, Vera Panzera, Ada Parasiliti, Mina Romana, Irene Bettoja Speciale Picciche, Angela Saratti Ziffer, various Roman taxi drivers, and people from my market.

INTRODUCTION

My HOME IS IN ROME, not far from the Trevi Fountain, just a short walk to the marketplace. The city's open-air markets fill the ancient squares and line the narrow streets, offering an embarrassment of seasonable produce amid scenes of bustling daily life, at once uniquely Roman and utterly universal.

As I write this it is May. The *bancarelle*, the vendors' old pushcarts, are heavy with mounds of fresh greens—broccoli rabe, chard, spinach—all crisp and glistening with dew, their pronounced perfumes already mingling with the heady bouquets of Mediterranean herbs: rosemary, sage, and thyme. Here are peas, swelling in their tender shells, one of the great blessings of spring; the famous Roman artichokes, with or without prickly points; fava beans, calling for laborious, but highly worthwhile, shelling and peeling. There are the green-pointed, primeval-looking broccoflower Romano; bunches of tall asparagus, cultivated or wild; new potatoes bursting in their flaky spring jackets; golden blushing apricots from the sunny inland hillsides; strawberries by the crateload; and cherries of all sizes, tastes, and shades: tart red, pinkish and tangy, or black as wine and lusciously sweet. This abundant goodness is a feast for the eyes, deftly arranged and rearranged with great talent and genetically acquired flare, all sheltered from the elements by broad canvas canopies that flap in the breeze, reflecting back at the sky the baking sunshine.

The vendors (some third-generation) know their clients if not by name, then by their passions and preferences. They're great characters, these *fruttivendoli*, all crust and wit and song, always more than happy to strut their great expertise by offering recipes and limitless variations on any given gastronomic theme. Their suggestions are not highly structured recipes as found in books, but more like culinary fugues, ideas or departure points for experienced cooks who can go the route blindfolded once they're shown the way. I always visit the same stand. They earned my habitual patronage when they met the odd challenge of finding sweet potatoes (*Introvabili!*—"Unfindable!") for my Christmas Georgia sweet potato soufflé. Here's a Roman shopping lesson I learned the hard way: If you see something that tempts you, you'd better get it then and there, as you're not always likely to find it again.

The butchers, with their locally bred beef, veal, and pork, are in the same square as the poultry sellers, who carry naturally plump chickens, feathery game (in the autumn, mostly), and rabbits for marvelous eating. Not far from the Trevi Fountain we have a wonderful *salsamenteria*, and that's where I buy my cheeses, prosciutto, salamis, and crusty Roman breads.

Romans still shop for one day's eating at a time, and that's the way I've come to live as well. It was, indeed, the rhythms of daily life in the Eternal City that impressed me so strongly when I first arrived from my small Georgia hometown over forty years ago. I came for Rome's art and architecture but remained because of the Roman people, so like my fellow Southerners—talkative, eccentric, generous, friendly, and *very* fond of food.

Rome, founded in 753 B.C., is in Lazio, one of Italy's twenty diverse regions, each a nation in itself, with its own habits and passions, which constitute a separate culture. Lazio's hospitable coastal plains and hills, temperate and fertile, were once inhabited by the enigmatic Etruscans. The southern parts, where the hills fall away to the sea, are low and misty in their depths. Over the years the marshes have been largely drained to solve the once widespread malaria problem, but there are still enough wetlands for the buffalo, whose milk makes the best mozzarella cheese.

In the region's central mountains, sheep safely graze under the watchful eyes of shepherds and their *maremmani*, big, shaggy, mercurial white dogs of ancient origin. The shepherds still alternate pastures according to season: hills in the summer, plains in the winter. Not so long ago the woolly flocks were led right through the center of Rome at night on their way to fresh grazing land. Even today you're likely to spot them just outside the city gates. Lazio's famed fruits and vegetables are deeply loved by the Romans, who, despite the recent arrival of imported produce from all over the agricultural world, prefer seasonal foods, home grown. I, too, jealously seek out *roba nostrane*, our own local products.

Roman eating habits have changed over the years: no more long dinners in the middle of the day with hours of family chat over pasta, meat, two or more vegetables, salad and fruit, sometimes even cheese. (My husband's ninety-six-year-old aunt always said that Gorgonzola could be served only at midday.) Traditionally, a one- or two-hour siesta followed this ritual feast, but then off went the men, fortified and eager, back to work until seven-thirty or eight o'clock in the evening. The Romans know how to live, but they're hard workers, too.

Supper, on the other hand, was traditionally light: soup, then perhaps greens—spinach, Swiss chard, or broccoli rabe, lightly dressed at the table with oil and lemon, salt and pepper—the sort of eating that leaves you well adjusted and long lived. Sometimes there would be eggs. Or there might have been fish, grilled or poached, or cheeses fresh from the shepherds' hillside huts; then maybe a pudding or cooked fruit. Of course, this was how Romans ate when there was just the family around. If there were guests, it was quite another matter. Rice might have been served in the evenings, but never pasta. Fish was a likely first course, with meat as a second, accompanied by at least three vegetables. The generous, symphonic repast would reach its crescendo with a rich dessert served to oohs and ahs, and then there would be coffee, of course, and spirits. The way one sets a table and what is served is an extension of one's whole personality; Romans pride themselves on their largesse and grandeur at mealtime.

But daily life is changing. Nearly everybody's out all day long now, working for a living, no longer coming home at midday for a big meal and then a nap. You no longer find good, devoted cooks in every household, as everpresent and stalwart as a fine old stove. Not so long ago there was always a spare room for grandmothers and maiden aunts, once worth their weight in gold to the bigger Roman families; now we all live in mini-apart-ments, the real estate equivalent of the divisions and subdivisions that have altered the family unit as it used to be. These changes of habits have shortened considerably the amount of time people spend in the kitchen. Still, the Romans always find a way around things. As the saying goes, *Fatta la legge, trovato l'inganno* (Make a law, then find a way around it).

And the way around it in this case is that the men, who'd always been good backseat drivers in the kitchen, now cook—an entirely unexpected turn of events. In cooking schools, they often outnumber the lady students. Enthusiastically encouraged by their partners, they're focused and concentrated, even persnickety, you could say, especially about ingredients.

The substantial midday meal—pasta, meat, vegetables, fruit, and cheese—has now evolved into lunch, often just pasta and a salad. Dinner has taken the lead. And why not? That's the way the rest of the working world lives. But despite all the shortcuts taken, Romans are steady and true to their food. Their cooking retains its pastoral origins, always seasonal, uncomplicated, and simply prepared, which makes sense when exceptional ingredients are the rule.

Surely the best baby lamb in all of Italy comes from Lazio, as do the best salamis, *coppa* (head cheese), sausages, and *porchetta* (suckling pig). The very best artichokes in all of Europe come from the Roman countryside, as does the best sheep's milk ricotta, (first brought here, it is said, by Saint Francis). Lazio's pecorino Romano, together with the famous French Roquefort, was one of the first two DOC (Denominazione di Origine Controllata) cheeses in Europe. The region's wonderfully aromatic olive oils are from Canino and the Sabina area, where the oldest olive tree in Europe stands, wizened and proud. (It takes the arms of ten men to circle it.) The best ripe figs, peaches, cherries, and other fruits, the best hazelnuts—the list goes on. If Rome didn't already have its great cultural wealth, these things alone would make it the envy of any urban center anywhere.

Romans' love of offal, with its peculiar, strong flavors, is unique, as is their penchant for simple, companionable polenta and daily breads. Romans worship their own food with unflagging loyalty; when traveling abroad, they'll wander around for hours looking for an Italian restaurant. And even though they are more sophisticated now and will even go so far as to eat foreign foods, they would never admit that anyone cooks as well as Romans do.

A few of the recipes I've gathered here are from old cookbooks, but most are from private Roman households, big and traditional, or small and modern. In spite of the changing times, Romans will always love their food. Home cooks, I'm confident to predict, will continue to prepare the classic Roman specialties I've grown to love. There will always be those occasions that demand good eating: Sundays, baptisms, first communions, engagement parties, birthdays, weddings, comings of age, graduations, first job appointments, or promotions—any celebration, really, big or small. After all, who needs much of an excuse to eat well? *Tutte le feste finiscono a tavola*, they say. (All feast days end at the table.) As for me, I'll always think of Rome as one big feast, one in which I've had the most glorious time!

Indove se magnuca, Er celo ce conduca.

May heaven deliver us to wherever we can eat.

ANTIPASTI

A magna' e a gratta', tutto sta a incomincia'.

Eating is like stealing, it's all in how you start.

In his introduction to Luigi Carnacina's *Roma in Cucina*, a seminal Italian cookbook, culinary historian Vincenzo Buonassisi says that a Roman of two thousand years ago wouldn't feel at all out of sorts confronting the Roman foods of today. Some of the ancient Roman's favorite things might be missing, of course, but there would be lots of dishes or ingredients familiar to him. Olive oil, pancetta, ricotta, the wild herbs of the fields, dried fava beans, chickpeas, and lentils — all these foodstuffs of long ago remain in use now. The winter vegetables of ancient times were turnips and cabbage, and we still eat those. We serve chestnuts cooked in milk and taste the same sheep cheeses they knew and loved.

The ancient Roman ate very little meat: an occasional wild boar or some small game, what the hunter could find and what the fisherman caught. Oxen were beasts of burden, who pulled the carts and plowed; therefore, they were not to be eaten. Cows produced more calves and gave milk; they, too, were too valuable to offer up as food.

LUIGI CARNACINA is author of a number of Italian cookbooks. Though much older than we — he was born in 1888 — Carnacina was a friend of mine and of my husband, Angelo. Like the great Italian cookbook writer Ada Boni, Carnacina was Roman, and both his book and Boni's are classics of Roman food. Probably his best book is *Roma in Cucina*, in which he lovingly explains the simple Roman dishes his mother and grandmother made and remembers with nostalgia the fried street food sold in Rome when he was a boy.

Carnacina was only twelve years old when he started work in a Roman *osteria* and fourteen when he left Italy for foreign glories. He worked for Escoffier at the Savoy in London and did stints at many of the grand hotels in Europe and America. When he returned to Italy, Carnacina collaborated on books with Vincenzo Buonassisi, a culinary historian, who wrote the introduction to *Roma in Cucina*, and with Luigi Veronelli, also a culinary historian and a wine expert.

FAVA BEANS AND PECORINO

(*Fave e Pecorino*) THE MOST ROMAN of all antipasti is this combination of raw fava beans served with small chunks of pecorino Romano cheese. The *fave* are heaped in the middle of the table alongside platters of pecorino Romano pieces cut from a wedge using a small, wedge-shaped Parmesan cheese knife. Each person shells and eats his or her *fave*, traditionally seven small beans at a time with a piece of pecorino and a glass of cool white Frascati wine from the Castelli Romani. When fava beans are in season, you can see people in the trattoria having a glorious time, with mountains of bean pods in front of them.

Eighteen hundred years ago, a Roman named Giovenale, a well-to-do man of letters, prepared the following meal for a friend. With only one exception, it could be a Roman meal of today. The antipasti consisted of hard-boiled eggs, anchovies, lettuce, mint, arugula, and other salads, followed by hog's breast marinated with tuna (the exception). The second course was grilled kid and baby lamb chops, fava beans, cabbage (probably served as a salad), chicken, and prosciutto. To end the meal, there was fresh fruit. These are the typical ancient meals that gave birth to the Latin proverb *ab ovo usque ad mala*, "from eggs to apples," referring to the Roman manner of beginning all meals of importance with eggs and ending them with apples.

Truthfully, the Romans in general are not big antipasto eaters, but here is an assortment of the kinds of small foods with which they often do begin a meal:

Prosciutto, with or without melon or peeled figs

Anchovies or sardines, with bread and butter

Olives

Baby artichokes packed in oil

Hard-cooked eggs

Lettuces, radishes, tomatoes, and roasted peppers

Salamis of all kinds

Bruschetta (page 13)

Another favorite antipasto is simply fresh fennel, a palate cleanser, which readies you for your pasta. But it has other virtues, too; fennel is stimulating and an aphrodisiac, or at least so the Romans say. Typical of bawdy Rome, this antipasto is called *cazzimperia,* which means "imperial phallus."

Put a large flat platter in the middle of the table with fennel that has been washed and dried and cut into fourths or eighths. Leave on the feathery fennel fronds. Put a small bowl in front of each person. Have extra virgin olive oil, salt and a pepper mill on the table. Each person mixes oil, salt, and pepper in his or her bowl and dips the fennel into the dressing before eating it. Celery can be used, too. Very delicious and very refreshing.

MARIA'S BREAD SALAD

Panzanella di Maria

SERVES 4

1 pound firm Italian bread, 1 or 2 days old, thickly sliced (450 g)

———

1 medium white onion, finely chopped

———

4 ripe but firm medium-large tomatoes, cut into small dice

———

1 celery heart, thinly sliced

———

1 small cucumber, peeled, quartered lengthwise, and thinly sliced

———

20 basil leaves, torn if large

———

Salt and freshly ground black pepper

———

¾ cup extra virgin olive oil (180 ml)

———

¼ cup white wine vinegar (60 ml)

———

Panzanella, which is prepared very simply, can be a light midday meal or a starter.

When Anna Maria Cornetto and I had our cooking school, Lo Scaldavivande, a woman called Maria was always there to lend us a hand. Born in the Borgo, a part of Rome near Saint Peter's, she was as Roman as they get. She had a lovely Borghiciano accent, and she was very strong willed, the backbone of her household, in fact. She was devoted to the school and freely offered her opinion on everything. This is her recipe for panzanella. Not that Maria originated the idea — all Romans know it. According to her, the dish was created in Rome and was only much later adopted by the Tuscans, who wrongfully claim it as their own.

1 Soak the bread in cold water for 20 minutes. Squeeze the bread and crumble it coarsely into a bowl.

2 Meanwhile, soak the onion in cold water for 15 minutes; drain and reserve.

3 Mix together the bread, onion, tomatoes, celery, cucumber, and basil leaves. Season with salt and pepper to taste. Beat together the oil and vinegar and pour over the bread mixture. Toss to mix the panzanella thoroughly. Serve at room temperature.

BRESAOLA WITH ARUGULA AND PARMESAN CHEESE

Bresaola, Rughetta, e Parmigiano

SERVES 4 AS A STARTER

½ pound arugula, tough stems removed (225 g)

7 ounces bresaola, very thinly sliced (200 g)

Parmesan curls*

4 lemon wedges

Extra virgin olive oil

Freshly ground black pepper

* To make Parmesan curls, run a potato peeler over a large cut from a wedge of the cheese. For best results, the cheese should be just out of the refrigerator.

Although not a classic Roman dish, this very modern salad can be found at lunch and dinner parties everywhere in the city; it's even on many restaurant menus. Although technically an antipasto, it makes an excellent first course, a particularly good choice when you're in a rush. The arugula can be washed ahead of time, dried, and stored in the refrigerator in a plastic bag until needed, and the Parmesan curls can be precut, covered, and refrigerated. Each person should trickle a little olive oil and squeeze a bit of lemon juice over the completed assembly; a crank of the pepper mill adds just the right finishing touch. If bresaola is not available, thinly sliced prosciutto can be substituted, but it is not quite the same thing.

1 Rinse and dry the arugula. If prepared ahead, store in the refrigerator until needed.

2 When ready to serve, if the arugula is tender and fresh, arrange it on plates, with the stem ends toward the center and the tips of the leaves toward the plate's rim. If the arugula is not perfect, chop it coarsely and make a bed of the greens on the plates.

3 Divide the bresaola among the plates, laying the slices in a circle on top of the arugula. Put the Parmesan curls on top and set a lemon wedge in the center of each plate. Serve with olive oil and a pepper mill.

BRESAOLA WITH ARUGULA AND GRAPEFRUIT SECTIONS

Prepare the arugula and bresaola as above but omit the Parmesan cheese and put grapefruit sections, with pith and peel removed, on top of the bresaola. Dress directly with extra virgin olive oil and lemon juice, in the proportion of 1 tablespoon olive oil to 2 tablespoons lemon juice per plate. Grind black pepper over each plate at the table.

BRESAOLA WITH FRESH ARTICHOKES AND PARMESAN CHEESE

In place of the arugula, substitute 4 tender, fresh artichokes, trimmed to the heart and rubbed with lemon. Slice the raw artichoke hearts very thin and distribute the slices over the bresaola together with the Parmesan curls. Serve with the lemon wedges, extra virgin olive oil, and freshly ground black pepper.

BRUSCHETTA

1 loaf crusty Italian bread

Cloves of garlic, cut in half

Extra virgin olive oil

Salt

Here is the Roman version of garlic bread, which is toasted first and then perfumed with a rubbing of raw garlic and a drizzle of good oil. It is delicious with 1 or 2 slices of prosciutto.

Cut crusty Italian bread into ½-inch slices. Toast the bread and rub the warm slices lightly with a cut clove of garlic. Trickle extra virgin olive oil over the toast and season with salt.

CROSTINI WITH MOZZARELLA AND ANCHOVIES

Crostini con Mozzarella e Alici

SERVES 4

⅔ pound fresh mozzarella
cheese (300 g)

---

4 slices of Italian bread,
sliced ½ inch thick

Salt and freshly ground
black pepper

---

6 tablespoons unsalted butter,
melted (90 g)

---

5 anchovy fillets

⅓ cup hot milk (80 ml)

These hot skewers of toasted bread and good fresh mozzarella, drenched in a rich anchovy sauce, are very popular in Rome. We serve the dish as a serious antipasto — it is not light — or as a lunch dish accompanied perhaps only by a salad.

1 Preheat the oven to 375°F (190°C).

2 Slice the mozzarella about ⅜ inch thick and cut the slices into 1½-inch squares. Remove the crusts from the bread and cut the slices into squares just a little larger than the cheese.

3 Season the mozzarella lightly with salt and pepper. Beginning and ending with a square of bread, thread the bread and cheese onto 4 thin metal skewers, pressing the cheese so that it adheres to the bread. Paint with half the melted butter.

4 Suspend the skewers in a baking dish and bake for about 20 minutes, or until light brown.

5 In a small saucepan, dissolve the anchovies in the remaining melted butter over low heat, mashing them with a wooden spoon. Stir in the hot milk.

6 When the crostini are done, transfer the skewers to 4 plates and drizzle the anchovy sauce over them. Serve at once.

CAPRESE SALAD

Insalata Caprese

SERVES 4 TO 6

3 large ripe red beefsteak tomatoes, sliced about ¼ inch thick

---

18 to 24 fresh basil leaves

---

1 pound fresh mozzarella cheese, sliced about ¼ inch thick (450 g)

¼ cup extra virgin olive oil (60 ml)

Salt and freshly ground black pepper

No one seems to know where this simple, summery starter originated, but it was not on the island of Capri. It is eaten all over Italy and only requires finding ripe tomatoes and good mozzarella. Needless to say, because it is so simple, you must have the best of ingredients for this dish. I like to present my salad in a single row on a long, narrow platter, but, of course, it can be formed in a ring on a round plate if that is more convenient.

NOTE: In Rome, a Caprese salad is never dressed with vinegar, only a light drizzle of the best extra virgin olive oil to highlight the tomatoes and cheese.

Lay out a slice of tomato on a platter. Place 1 large or several small basil leaves on top of the tomato. Place a slice of mozzarella on the tomato, overlapping so it covers only half the slice. Add more basil leaves and continue layering until you have used all the cheese, tomatoes, and basil. Each person pours oil over the salad and seasons it with salt and pepper to taste.

FRESH MOZZARELLA

In Italy, true fresh mozzarella means *mozzarella di bufala*, which is rarely used in Rome for cooking. *Bufalo* mozzarella is eaten as is, with salt, pepper, and maybe a drop of olive oil. Purists insist that for best taste and texture, the cheese must be consumed within three hours of the time it is made. Of course, even in Rome it is difficult to find mozzarella that fresh.

The cheese is made exclusively with water buffalo milk. The buffalo are milked twice a day, morning and evening. The evening and the morning milk are mixed with whey from the previous day, and with rennet, and fermented. It is then reheated and put into another vat, where it ferments again for a few hours and is churned and boiled. Finally, the balls of mozzarella are formed, by hand or machine, and put into brine. And then you start counting a maximum of three hours, after which time, according to the producers, the cheese starts losing its character. However, even day-old mozzarella is delicious.

For cooking, we use *fior di latte*, a mozzarella-type cheese made from cow's milk, which is the cheese sold as fresh mozzarella in America. It, too, can be very good, especially if it is exceptionally fresh.

In Rome, I have been buying my mozzarella from Michele Avenati for many many years. He has beautiful big cheeses, which weigh a kilo, about 2 ¼ pounds, and small bite-size ones for salads. Avenati says also that mozzarella should be eaten as soon as it is made, but that it can be kept in its serum (milky, watery liquid) up to three days in a very cool place, not in the refrigerator. Avenati sells smoked *provola di bufala*, scamorza, caciocavallo, *burrata pugliese, nodini pugliesi, fiore sardo*, pecorino Romano, and ricotta Romana, to name a few.

The shop is kitty-corner to the Palazzo delle Esposizioni on Via Nazionale, one of Rome's best art exhibition buildings with varied shows, recently a spectacular one on Rome's seventeenth century; one on Nero's famous palace, the Domus Aurea; one on ecclesiastical art; as well as photographic shows and the like. Via Nazionale, the street of the Palazzo delle Esposizioni, is a midpriced shopping area, and very popular.

Michele Avenati, Via Milano 44, 00187 Roma, telephone 06 4882681

POOR MAN'S CAVIAR

Caviale dei Poveri

MAKES ABOUT 1¼ CUPS

1 pound oil-cured black olives,
pitted (450 g)

2 tablespoons capers, rinsed and
dried

1 clove of garlic, coarsely
chopped

2 anchovy fillets packed in oil,
drained and cut into pieces

Freshly ground black pepper

1 to 2 tablespoons lemon juice,
or to taste

Extra virgin olive oil

Very thin lemon slices, without
peel or pith, quartered (optional)

Olives for this savory spread are the wrinkled, oil-cured kind, which have a smoky, slightly bitter taste. They are usually dried in front of the fireplace, as we do in the country, or slowly in an oven. If eaten whole, the olives are dressed with garlic, a little lemon juice, olive oil, and, sometimes, dried red peppers (see Marinated Olives, page 23). The *caviale* here has substantially the same flavors, but is chopped and served on rounds of brown bread with a tiny piece of lemon on top. Jars of *simple caviale*, similar to French tapenade, without the capers, garlic, and anchovies, are also sold in shops and often used to add a special taste to dishes.

I like to serve this spread on rounds of brown bread. If you do so, garnish each canapé with a quarter slice of lemon on top. Prepare the garnish by removing all the yellow peel and white pith from the lemon; slice the lemon very thin and cut each slice into 4 pie-shaped wedges.

Put all the ingredients except the oil and lemon slices in a blender or a food processor and process until coarsely chopped. Add the oil in a trickle, as for mayonnaise. Do not add too much oil; the olives must have time to absorb it. And do not overprocess; the finished spread must be the consistency of caviar or tapenade.

NOTE: A blender works better than a food processor for this. Stop to scrape down the sides when necessary. If preparing the spread well in advance, add the lemon juice just before serving to maintain the fresh flavor.

GOLDEN BREAD

Pandorato

SERVES 6 TO 8

Firm-textured white bread, about 1½ pounds (675 g)

1½ pounds mozzarella cheese (675 g)

1 cup tepid milk (230 ml)

Flour, for dredging

3 eggs or more, as needed

Salt

Olive oil or lard, for frying

The *panifici romani*, Roman bread bakeries, usually sell just that: bread and not pastries. (For sweet pastries, you have to go to a *pasticceria*.) But the kinds of bread seem endless. There's a loaf for every taste. First of all, there is the Roman *rosetta*, small or large; then there are puffed-up flowerlike individual rolls, and *ciriole* and *fruste*, like small baguettes. There are loaves called *pane casareccio*, a coarse country bread, and there are *ciavatte*, which translates to "slippers," and *ossi*, which means "bones." *Pane francese* is like a French baguette, and there are more refined loaves from Terni, with or without salt. There are squared-off loaves of sandwich bread, white or brown. Best of all, you can usually order the kind of bread you want for tomorrow, if it is not available today. And let's not forget the midmorning pizza, white or red, which everyone eats around eleven o'clock.

With all this bread, it's hardly surprising that the Romans would find creative ways to use it. Originally *pandorato* was fried in lard, though now olive oil is most often used, the light alternative in this case. Anchovies packed in salt, cleaned, rinsed, and dried, can be added, as can thinly sliced prosciutto. *Pandorato* is delicious as a hot antipasto or, cut into smaller pieces than indicated in this recipe, as a nibble with drinks.

1 Trim the crusts from the bread and cut into ¼-inch-thick slices about 2 by 3 inches. Slice the mozzarella cheese the same size as the bread and form into sandwiches. Sprinkle the sandwiches with the tepid milk and dip the edges rapidly in milk in a saucer. Put flour in a soup bowl and dredge the sandwiches in the flour, being careful to flour the ends. (This will help prevent the mozzarella from seeping out.)

2 Put the sandwiches in a baking dish that can hold them in a single layer. Beat the eggs in a small bowl, season with salt, and pour the beaten eggs over the prepared sandwiches, turning them so that they absorb the egg on both sides. There will be some egg left in the bottom of the dish. Let stand for about 1 hour, turning the sandwiches once or twice, so that they absorb the remaining egg.

3 Heat 1¼ inches olive oil or lard in a deep frying pan until hot but not shimmering. Fry the sandwiches a few at a time over moderately high heat, turning several times, until they are golden. Drain on paper towels, season again with salt, and serve at once.

CRUSTY BREAD WITH MUSHROOMS

Crostone con Funghi

MAKES 8 TOASTS

1 pound fresh mushrooms,
preferably porcini (450 g)

¼ cup extra virgin olive oil
(60 ml)

1 clove of garlic, peeled

Salt and freshly ground
black pepper

8 slices of Italian bread,
about ½ inch thick

1½ tablespoons butter,
at room temperature (20 g)

8 very thin slices of lemon
(optional)

1 tablespoon chopped parsley

Although crostone are best made with porcini mushrooms, they can be prepared with other mushrooms, even simple cultivated ones. If porcini are unavailable or prohibitively expensive, a mix of white button and wild mushrooms would be nice. But the bread must be crusty Italian bread, lightly toasted and served warm.

1 Clean the mushrooms and cut them into slices about ¼ inch thick.

2 Heat the olive oil in a large skillet and brown the whole garlic clove lightly over moderate heat. Add the mushrooms, season with salt and pepper to taste, and cook until light brown.

3 While the mushrooms are cooking, toast the bread and butter it. If using cultivated mushrooms, put a thin slice of lemon on each slice of toast. Discard the garlic and put the mushrooms on top of the toast slices. Sprinkle parsley on top and serve the crostone hot.

NOTE: If desired, garlic can be rubbed lightly over the bread before the mushrooms are added.

EGGPLANT, MOZZARELLA, AND ANCHOVY ROLLS

Antipasto Estivo

MAKES 15 OR 16 ROLLS

1½ pounds eggplant, preferably
the long narrow kind, thinly
sliced, about ¼ inch thick
(675 g)

Coarse salt

Extra virgin olive oil (optional)

1 pound yellow and red bell
peppers (500 g)

6 ounces fresh mozzarella
cheese, cut into thin 1-inch
strips (170 g)

1 ounce anchovy fillets, drained
and halved (30 g)

Basil leaves or fresh oregano

Pitted black olives, Gaeta
or oil-packed

Freshly ground black pepper

The Italian name of these savory bites translates literally as "summer antipasto," but I think it is more helpful — and tempting — to know what goes into them. The reason for the simple name is that in Rome, as in all of Italy, we use ingredients in season, and certain summer combinations are classic.

The components for this little antipasto can be prepared in advance and assembled at the last moment. It is served at room temperature, or the little rolls can be placed seam down in a lightly oiled ovenproof dish and baked in a moderate oven until they are heated through and the mozzarella is melted. Either way, it is the essence of the famous Mediterranean *cucina*.

1 Layer the eggplant in a colander, salting each layer, and let stand for 1 hour. Rinse the eggplant in cold water and pat dry on paper towels. If grilling, paint them sparingly with extra virgin olive oil. Salt lightly and set aside on paper towels after grilling or frying.

2 Roast the peppers in a 400°F (200°C) oven until the skins are blackened, turning once, about 40 minutes in all. Remove the peppers from the oven and wrap them in foil until they are cool enough to handle. Seed and skin the peppers and cut them into ½-inch strips.

3 Cut the eggplant into strips about ¾ inch wide. Lay the eggplant strips out on a work surface and set a strip of pepper on each. Then layer on a strip of mozzarella, a piece of anchovy, a leaf of basil or a pinch of oregano, and an olive half. Salt lightly and season with pepper to taste. Roll up carefully and fasten each roll with a toothpick.

OCTOPUS WITH BAY LEAVES AND RED PEPPER

Polipo in Antipasto

SERVES 6 TO 8

1⅔ pounds octopus, cleaned
(750 g)

———

2 tablespoons white wine vinegar

———

Extra virgin olive oil

———

3 bay leaves, or more, to taste

———

2 dried peperoncini, or more
to taste, broken into pieces

———

Oregano

———

As with so many Italian recipes, the flavor of this dish improves after a day. The octopus is also good with drinks at *aperitivo* time. Serve in bite-size pieces, with toothpicks on the side, and accompany with small squares of Italian bread.

1 Check that the octopus has been cleaned properly. Wash it in cold water and drain. (In the unlikely event that you have fished the octopus yourself, you probably already know that you must beat the meat for several minutes with a wooden bat to tenderize it.)

2 Put the octopus in a pan that closes hermetically, without water, and cook over low heat. After 30 minutes, test the octopus with a kitchen needle. If necessary, continue cooking until the octopus is tender, adding a very small amount of water only if it seems too dry.

3 When the octopus is ready, remove it from the heat and pour on the vinegar. Let cool, then cut into bite-size pieces. Arrange the octopus in layers in a container, dressing each layer with olive oil, bay leaves, peperoncini, and oregano. Cover and refrigerate for up to several days. Let return to cool room temperature before serving.

MARINATED OLIVES

Olive Accondite

1 pound Greek or oil-cured black olives (450 g)

3 cloves of garlic, cut into tiny slivers, or larger pieces (which are easier to avoid)

¼ teaspoon hot red pepper flakes, or to taste

1 teaspoon dried oregano

½ teaspoon crushed fennel seeds

⅓ cup extra virgin olive oil (80 ml)

2 to 3 tablespoons lemon juice

Thin lemon slices, cut into small triangular pieces

Olives are grown all over Italy, and each part of the country has its own way of dressing them, Rome being no exception. They are served with aperitifs, along with salted almonds, and rarely, in a home, is anything else offered with your glass of wine before a meal — there is too much still to come.

Put the olives in a bowl and sprinkle the garlic, red pepper flakes, oregano, and fennel seeds over them. Dress the olives with olive oil and lemon juice. Let stand at room temperature, tossing every now and then, until you are ready to serve them. Garnish with the lemon pieces.

NOTE: If you truly like garlic, finely chop together the garlic and hot pepper flakes, mix, and then add all the other ingredients.

SUMMER SALAD WITH TUNA AND FAVA BEANS

Insalata Estiva

Serves 6 to 8

2 small heads of lettuce of your choice, whichever is freshest

4 small ripe but firm tomatoes, cut into 4 wedges each

1 cup (½ pound) pitted black olives, halved (225 g)

1 large yellow bell pepper, cut into narrow strips

1 small cucumber, peeled and thinly sliced

2 white bunching onions, or 1 small white or red onion, thinly sliced and separated into rings

8 anchovy fillets, cut into small pieces

1 can (5 ounces) oil-packed tuna, drained (165 g)

1½ pounds fresh fava beans, shelled and peeled (675 g)

Think of this as a Roman salade niçoise: a bright summer salad chock full of fabulous fresh vegetables, tuna fish, and eggs, lightly dressed with lemon juice and olive oil. We usually present *insalata estiva* as a starter, because it stimulates your appetite as an antipasto should, but it can also be served as a light main course. If quail eggs are available, they make a charming substitute for hen's eggs; since they are so small, you'll need 8.

3 raw artichoke hearts, very thinly sliced and rubbed with lemon (optional but desirable)

Lemon Vinaigrette (recipe follows)

4 hard-cooked eggs, cut into 4 wedges each

1 Prepare all the ingredients for the salad. Make sure your salad greens are dry.

2 Toss the greens with some of the vinaigrette in the salad bowl. Add all the other ingredients, except the eggs. Toss and pour the remaining dressing over the salad. Arrange the egg wedges on top of the salad and serve at once.

LEMON VINAIGRETTE

Salsa al Limone

MAKES ABOUT ¾ CUP

3 tablespoons fresh lemon juice

1 teaspoon powdered mustard, preferably Colman's

½ cup plus 1 tablespoon extra virgin olive oil (135 ml)

1½ tablespoons chopped fresh basil, oregano, or tarragon, or a combination of herbs

Salt and freshly ground black pepper

In a small bowl, beat the lemon juice with the mustard until blended. Gradually whisk in the olive oil until the dressing is emulsified. Stir in the herb of your choice and season with salt and pepper to taste.

ROASTED SWEET PEPPERS WITH ANCHOVIES AND BASIL

Peperoni in Antipasto

SERVES 4 TO 6

3½ pounds large red and yellow
bell peppers (1.575 kg)

3 tablespoons salt-packed capers

4 salt-packed anchovies

Extra virgin olive oil

Small handful of fresh basil,
broken into pieces by hand, or
parsley chopped fine, or a pinch
of dried oregano

An excellent starter, these peppers are of the one-calls-for-another school — that is, it's impossible to eat just one. Good bread is necessary with these, too. They can be prepared ahead and refrigerated but should be served at room temperature.

1 Preheat the oven to 400°F (200°C).

2 Wash and dry the peppers. Roast them in the hot oven for 20 minutes. Turn the peppers over and roast for another 20 minutes. Immediately seal the peppers in a paper sack or wrap them in foil until cool. Their skin can then be peeled away easily and discarded. Put the peppers on a cutting board and cut into them slices about 1 inch wide.

3 Meanwhile, rinse the capers well and soak them in a bowl of cold water for 20 minutes to remove excess salt. Drain on paper towels.

4 Scrape any excess salt off the anchovies. Split them lengthwise and remove the center bones. Rinse and dry the fillets, then halve each anchovy lengthwise. (You will have 4 fillets for each anchovy.)

5 To assemble the antipasto, arrange the pepper slices on a large platter, interspersing them with the anchovy fillets. Sprinkle the capers over the top and drizzle olive oil over the peppers. Just before serving, garnish with the basil or other herb.

HOW TO CLEAN SALT-PACKED ANCHOVIES

USING YOUR THUMBNAIL, open up the anchovy and remove and discard the entrails, bones, and fins. Divide the fish into two parts and rinse off the salt under cold running water. Drain on paper towels.

WINTER SALAD WITH ARTICHOKES AND FENNEL

Insalata Invernale

SERVES 4 TO 6

2 tablespoons salt-packed capers

4 salt-cured anchovy fillets,
rinsed and dried, cut into
½-inch pieces

2 large artichokes

1 lemon, cut in half

2 medium-small fennel bulbs,
thinly sliced

¾ cup black olives packed in oil,
pitted (150 g)

Salt

½ teaspoon powdered mustard,
preferably Colman's

⅓ cup extra virgin olive oil
(80 ml)

Freshly ground black pepper

2 large handfuls of arugula,
washed, trimmed, and dried

Wedge of Parmesan cheese

Here's an alternative salad we prefer in winter. As is true all over Italy, in Rome we like to eat with the seasons, choosing ingredients that are best and most flavorful at each time of year. Serve this as a first course with warm bruschetta (page 13).

1 Rinse the capers. Rinse the anchovy fillets and soak them in a small bowl of cold water for about 20 minutes to remove excess salt. Drain them well and dry on paper towels.

2 Meanwhile, trim the artichokes down to the hearts as described in box on page 211. Rub them all over with the cut lemon.

3 When ready to prepare the salad, drain and dry the artichokes and cut them into very thin slices. In a salad bowl, combine the artichokes, capers, fennel, anchovy fillets, and olives. Toss to mix well.

4 Squeeze the juice from the remaining lemon half into a small bowl and add a pinch of salt. Beat with a fork to dissolve the salt; beat in the mustard. Gradually whisk in the olive oil until the dressing is emulsified. Season with pepper and more salt to taste, keeping in mind that there are several salty ingredients in the salad.

5 Divide the arugula among 4 to 6 salad plates. Pour the dressing over the salad in the bowl and toss well. Divide the salad among the plates, arranging it on top of the arugula. With a swivel-bladed vegetable peeler, shave thin slices from a chunk of Parmesan cheese and arrange across the top of each salad.

PASTA and RICE

Panza mia, fatti capanna.

This old Roman proverb advises one's belly to become a warehouse
so it can hold more good things to eat. In other words, Romans are
known for eating themselves silly.

IN ROME, PASTA ALWAYS STARTS A MEAL; not a day goes by without it. We eat simple pastas every day, and we prepare special pasta dishes for holidays and celebrations. When a house gets a new roof, the owner invites all the builders to a feast in which pasta is the star. In the eighteenth century, to celebrate the covering of the roof of the Palace of the Consulta, the Italian supreme court, Pope Clement XII gave each workman a *libbra* (about ⅔ pound) of macaroni, plus a generous quantity of wine, bread, salami, and cheese. So it should come as no surprise that this is the longest chapter in the book.

Pasta is a serious matter in all of Italy, and there is nothing worse than overcooking it. I have known people to throw away 2 pounds of pasta that turned out too soft and to start all over again. Most Italians like their pasta *al dente* — literally, "to the tooth," meaning there is still some resistance to the bite. In Rome, we prefer it *in piedi*, "standing up," which indicates very al dente, offering a fair amount of resistance. In other words, Roman pasta is very chewy, a real texture food. Stories about foreigners tossing spaghetti at a wall to see if it sticks — meaning it is ready — horrify Romans. It is their ability with pasta that provides them with another sign that they are simply the best cooks in Italy — or, for that matter, in the whole world.

Italians use less sauce on their pasta than Americans do, because the taste of the pasta itself is important to them. I once heard of a roaring fight between a musical conductor and a writer over which pasta went best with a particular sauce. They were at a formal dinner party, and the argument became so heated that one of them got up, took his chair into another room, and finished his dinner out there. Given that fine artisan pastas are now much more readily available all over, you might want to try cooking your pasta a little less than you used to and tossing it with a bit less sauce to allow the pasta to shine through. The result may surprise and delight you.

NOTE: For all the recipes in this chapter, when the yield for a pasta recipe is 4 to 6, it means 4 as a main course or 6 as a first course.

COOKING PASTA

How to Cook Dried Pasta

For every pound (450 g) of dried pasta, you need 4 to 5 quarts (4 to 5 l) of water and 2 tablespoons coarse salt. Bring the water to a rolling boil in a large stockpot, add the pasta, and stir with a wooden fork to separate the pieces. Lower the heat to a regular boil and cook until the pasta is al dente, or slightly less if you want to eat it Roman style. Most brands give exact times on the package, but it is always a good idea to taste when you are a couple of minutes away from the optimum time and to keep tasting every 30 to 60 seconds, until the pasta is perfectly done.

How to Cook Fresh Pasta

Again, you need abundant boiling salted water, but here, since the cooking is so fast, it is essential that you keep tasting the pasta as it cooks to achieve exactly the right texture. You'll find the timing varies according to the freshness of the pasta. Fettuccine, lasagne noodles, tagliatelle, and stuffed fresh pastas such as ravioli, agnolotti, tortellini, and cappelletti all have different cooking times. If you buy your pasta from a shop, the vendor may be able to suggest an approximate time. As a rule of thumb, fresh pasta cooks in as little as 2 to 3 minutes, which is why it is essential to keep testing it.

ROMAN TOMATO SAUCE WITH PASTA

Salsa di Pomodoro alla Romana

SERVES 4 TO 6

¼ cup olive oil (60 ml)

2 cloves of garlic, peeled and crushed

2 small or 1 medium dried peperoncino

1 medium onion, very thinly sliced

3¼ pounds ripe firm tomatoes, peeled and sliced ½ inch thick (1.45 kg)

2 teaspoons tomato paste

Coarse salt and freshly ground black pepper

1¼ pounds long or short pasta (500 g)

4 tablespoons butter, optional (60 g)

2 tablespoons chopped fresh parsley, oregano, marjoram, or basil

Every hamlet in Italy has its own tomato sauce. This is Rome's. While many pasta dishes call for cheese, Romans usually do not serve it with this sauce, but, of course, you can put out a bowl of grated pecorino Romano or Parmesan cheese, if you wish.

1 Heat the olive oil in a large deep skillet or flameproof casserole over moderately high heat. Add the garlic and peperoncino and sauté until the garlic is a light brown and the peperoncino dark; then discard them. Add the onion to the pan and cook, stirring often and adding a few tablespoons water every now and then to prevent burning, until the onion is golden, about 5 minutes.

2 Raise the heat to high and add the tomatoes. Cook for a few minutes, breaking up the tomatoes into pieces with a wooden spoon. Put the tomato paste in the center of the pan and mix into the tomatoes. Season the sauce with salt and black pepper to taste. With the heat still on high, cook the sauce, continuing to break up the tomatoes and stirring often, for about 15 to 20 minutes, or until the sauce has thickened. If it looks as if the tomatoes are beginning to scorch, reduce the heat slightly.

3 Warm a large pasta serving bowl. Cut up the butter, if using, into small pieces, directly into the bowl.

4 In a large pot of boiling salted water, cook the pasta until it is al dente. Drain the pasta well and transfer to the serving bowl. Pour half the tomato sauce over the pasta; toss to mix. Add the rest of the sauce and toss again. Garnish with your favorite herb and serve at once with a pepper mill on the table.

SPAGHETTI WITH ARUGULA

Spaghetti con Rughetta

SERVES 4 TO 6

1 pound spaghetti or other
long pasta (450 g)

⅔ pound arugula (300 g)

3 tablespoons butter (45 g)

2 tablespoons extra virgin
olive oil

1 scant cup heavy cream
(200 ml)

Salt and freshly ground
black pepper

½ cup walnuts, finely chopped
but not pulverized (60 g)

⅔ cup freshly grated Parmesan
cheese (70 g)

Today Romans prefer their pasta with vegetables; there is much less meat sauce served, and even less pasta with seafood. Because there is never any time, they have devised an infinity of pastas based on herbs and cream, quick and easy to prepare. I ate this *spaghetti con rughetta* at a ladies' luncheon, another new fashion here in Rome. Not too long ago, no one would have thought of having only women to lunch.

1 In a large pot of boiling salted water, cook the spaghetti until it is al dente.

2 While the pasta cooks, prepare the sauce: Rinse the arugula well and trim off the tough stems. Set aside a few leaves for garnish. Chop the remainder coarsely.

3 In a large skillet, heat the butter and olive oil over moderate heat. Add the arugula and cook, tossing, until it is wilted, 2 to 3 minutes. Pour in the cream, bring to a simmer, and cook for 2 to 3 minutes longer. Season with salt and pepper to taste. Stir in the chopped walnuts.

4 Drain the pasta well and add to the pan with the hot arugula. Toss over low heat, sprinkling on the cheese as you turn the pasta. Pour the pasta into a warmed serving dish and top with a grinding of black pepper. Garnish with the reserved arugula and serve at once.

PASTA WITH BROCCOLI

Pasta con i Broccoli Siciliani

SERVES 2 OR 3

1 pound fresh broccoli (450 g)

½ pound spaghetti or other long pasta (225 g)

¼ cup extra virgin olive oil (60 ml)

⅓ cup freshly grated pecorino Romano or Parmesan cheese (35 g)

Salt and freshly ground black pepper

Don't be misled by the Italian name of this recipe. It is a Roman, not a Sicilian, dish. In Italy we have *cavolfiore* (cauliflower), *broccolo romano* (broccoflower, similar to cauliflower but with a pointed head that is pale green at the tips), and *broccoli siciliani* (the same plain green broccoli that's eaten in America). All three of these vegetables marry perfectly with pasta, and they have the extra benefit of good nutrition, being full of vitamins, calcium, and potassium. They are delicious on their own, but even better with pasta. What isn't? — a good Roman would ask.

Note the two-to-one proportion of vegetable to pasta, a distinctive feature of this dish. Perhaps it should be called "Broccoli with Pasta." For a larger group, this recipe doubles easily.

1 Put on to boil a pot of salted water large enough to cook the broccoli and pasta together.

2 Clean the broccoli florets and trim the larger florets so that they are all more or less the same size. Peel the stems and cut them into pieces about the same size as the florets. When the water boils, add the broccoli and boil for 6 minutes. Add the pasta and cook until it is al dente; drain.

3 Put 1 tablespoon of the olive oil in a large pasta bowl. Add the drained pasta and broccoli to the bowl. Pour in the remaining 3 tablespoons olive oil and mix thoroughly, sprinkling on the cheese as you mix. Season with salt to taste and a generous grind of black pepper.

4 Serve the broccoli and pasta at once, hot, with extra cheese and a pepper mill at the table.

SPAGHETTI WITH CHEESE AND BLACK PEPPER

Spaghetti Cacio e Pepe

SERVES 4 TO 6

⅓ cup freshly grated Parmesan cheese (35 g)

———

⅓ cup freshly grated sheep's milk caciotta cheese (35 g)

———

⅓ cup freshly grated cow's milk caciotta cheese (35 g)

———

⅓ cup freshly grated pecorino Romano cheese (35 g)

———

¼ cup milk (60 ml)

———

⅓ cup extra virgin olive oil (80 ml)

———

Freshly ground black pepper

———

1 pound spaghetti (450 g)

———

This classic Roman pasta is normally made only with pecorino Romano and black pepper. The version here, which uses four cheeses for a much more sophisticated and complex flavor, was given to me by my friend Angela, a superb cook and an authority on Roman food.

Caciotta cheese is usually prepared in the winter and can be a mixture of cow's milk and sheep's milk, but more often is one or the other. The cheese is made in round forms and can be mild or sharp. The cheeses may be varied according to taste, but the pecorino Romano–Parmesan taste should dominate.

1 In a bowl, mix the Parmesan, the 2 caciottas, and the pecorino Romano cheese. Stir in the milk. When the milk is absorbed, add the oil, stirring until well mixed. Add a very generous grinding of black pepper, so much, in fact, that the mixture looks gray — or so Angela says. (Some people pound peppercorns in a mortar for this pasta.)

2 In a large pot of boiling salted water, cook the spaghetti until it is al dente. Scoop out and reserve ¼ cup of the pasta cooking water. Drain the pasta and mix in half of the cheese mixture, tossing with a fork and spoon. The cheeses tend to lump, so add 2 tablespoons of pasta water. When the spaghetti and cheese are mixed, add the rest of the cheese, tossing, and the remaining 2 tablespoons of pasta water, if necessary. Grind more pepper over the spaghetti and serve at once.

PEPERONCINO, a small hot pepper, in Rome is usually dried and always red. There are hotter ones and less hot ones; you have to know your peperoncino. Usually it is gently sautéed with garlic and then both garlic and peperoncino are discarded . . . but not always. You rarely find hot red pepper flakes here; the peppers are sold whole. It is a personal thing, but most often the peperoncino taste is mildly spicy, really hot for only a few dishes, like *aglio, olio, e peperoncino* (below), or *penne all'arrabiata* (page 70).

PASTA WITH GARLIC, OIL, AND HOT RED PEPPER

Pasta con Aglio, Olio, e Peperoncino

SERVES 4

1 pound long pasta: spaghetti, trenette, or spaghettini (450 g)

½ cup extra virgin olive oil (120 ml)

4 cloves of garlic, peeled and crushed

1 dried peperoncino, or hot red pepper flakes to taste

2½ tablespoons finely chopped fresh parsley

Romans are naturally sociable. If forced always to eat alone, they would likely starve to death. They are also natural improvisers: this thrown-together pasta is proof of that. Oil, garlic, peperoncino, pasta, and good friends, coupled with a voracious appetite, are all you need. Needless to say, this pasta is most often prepared for two, late at night. The recipe can easily be halved — or doubled. If you don't have peperoncino, lots of freshly ground black pepper is almost a substitute. Cheese is not eaten with this dish, to which the Italians attribute almost magical powers. They say it settles your stomach, among other things, and restores your strength.

1 Cook the pasta in a large pot of boiling salted water until it is just al dente.

2 While the pasta is boiling, put the olive oil in a skillet large enough to contain the cooked pasta. Add the garlic and peperoncino or hot pepper flakes; this dish must be spicy. Cook over moderately low heat until the garlic is a blond color, 2 to 3 minutes.

3 As soon as the pasta is ready, drain and add it to the skillet with the garlic and peperoncino. Mix thoroughly and rapidly, while sprinkling the parsley over the pasta. Serve at once, with a pepper mill on the table.

SPAGHETTI WITH GORGONZOLA AND MASCARPONE

Spaghetti con Gorgonzola e Mascarpone

SERVES 2 TO 4

½ pound spaghetti (225 g)

2 ounces gorgonzola cheese, at room temperature (60 g)

2 ounces mascarpone, at room temperature (60 g)

½ cup finely chopped walnuts, plus 2 tablespoons coarsely chopped, for garnish (60 g)

3 tablespoons freshly grated Parmesan cheese

Salt and freshly ground black pepper

Rich and easy are the bywords of this dish. Although made with a northern Italian cheese (gorgonzola), this pasta is very popular in Rome because it makes a fast and easy one-dish meal. All that's needed is a lightly dressed salad of bitter greens and, perhaps, fresh fruit for dessert. In small portions, it doubles as an elegant first course at dinner parties. Extra nuts scattered over the pasta just before serving finish the dish nicely. This recipe can be doubled, or even tripled, easily.

1 In a large pot of boiling salted water, cook the spaghetti until it is al dente.

2 While the pasta is cooking, prepare the sauce: Put the gorgonzola in the bowl in which you will be serving the pasta. Add the mascarpone and blend with a fork. Scoop out ¼ cup of the pasta cooking water and stir it into the cheeses a little at the time, until the sauce is creamy but not too runny; you may not need it all. Add the finely chopped nuts and Parmesan cheese. Season lightly with salt and pepper to taste.

3 Drain the pasta (not too thoroughly) and turn it into the bowl with the cheeses and nuts. Toss all together. Serve at once with the extra nuts sprinkled over the finished pasta and a pepper mill on the table.

QUICK SUMMER PASTA

Pasta Estiva Svelta

SERVES 3 TO 4

2½ tablespoons extra virgin olive oil

⎯⎯

1 clove of garlic, peeled and crushed

⎯⎯

1 dried peperoncino, or hot red pepper flakes to taste

⎯⎯

1 pound ripe tomatoes, peeled, seeded, chopped, and drained (450 g)

⎯⎯

8 sun-dried tomatoes (about ½ cup), very finely chopped

⎯⎯

⅓ cup pitted oil-cured black olives, halved if large (75 g)

⎯⎯

⅔ pound spaghettini or other long pasta (300 g)

⎯⎯

1½ tablespoons chopped basil or parsley

⎯⎯

This sauce requires no salt or pepper, because the sun-dried tomatoes are salty enough and the peperoncino is spicy enough. Of course, it can be made in the wintertime, too, but the recipe is a specialty of beach-loving Romans, who want their pasta but don't want to work too hard at it. They usually bake in the sun until about three o'clock and then rush home, starving, for their late lunchtime pasta.

1 Put on a large pot of lightly salted water to boil for the pasta.

2 Meanwhile, heat the oil in a 10-inch (25-cm) skillet. Add the garlic and peperoncino and cook over moderately low heat until the garlic is light brown. Discard both the garlic and the peperoncino.

3 Add the fresh tomatoes, dried tomatoes, and olives to the skillet. Raise the heat to moderate and simmer for 4 to 5 minutes, until the sauce comes together.

4 Cook the pasta al dente. Drain thoroughly (because the tomatoes usually release some liquid) and add the pasta to the skillet with the sauce. Mix well over the lowest heat and serve at once, with the basil sprinkled on top.

QUICK MUSHROOM PASTA

Pasta con Funghi Rapida

SERVES 2 TO 3

¼ cup extra virgin olive oil
(60 ml)

2 cloves of garlic, peeled and
crushed

⅓ cup thinly sliced white onion
(35 g)

½ pound mushrooms, trimmed,
washed, and thinly sliced
(225 g)

Salt and freshly ground
black pepper

½ pound spaghettini (225 g)

2 tablespoons chopped fresh
basil or parsley

For a Roman pasta, this one is especially light.

1 Put on a pot of salted water to boil for the pasta.

2 Heat the olive oil in a large skillet and brown the garlic lightly. Discard the garlic and add the onion to the pan. Cook for 3 minutes over moderately low heat, stirring often, until the onion is softened and translucent.

3 Add the mushrooms, raise the heat to moderately high, and cook for 3 to 5 minutes, or until the liquid the mushrooms release has almost entirely evaporated. Season well with salt and pepper.

4 Meanwhile, cook the spaghettini until it is al dente; watch carefully, as pasta this thin cooks rapidly. Drain the pasta and add it to the skillet with the sauce. Mix well and serve at once with the chopped basil sprinkled generously over the top.

BUCATINI IN TOMATO SAUCE WITH BACON AND HOT PEPPER

Bucatini all'Amatriciana

SERVES 4 TO 6

2 tablespoons extra virgin olive oil or lard

⅓ pound pancetta, cut into thin, short strips (150 g)

½ small onion, finely chopped

1 dried peperoncino, or hot red pepper flakes to taste

7 Italian plum tomatoes, drained and cut into pieces if canned; peeled, seeded, and julienned if fresh

Salt and freshly ground black pepper

1 pound bucatini, spaghetti, or vermicelli (450 g)

¾ cup freshly grated pecorino Romano cheese (75 g)

Bucatini is a long pasta with a hole in the center. It is very popular in Rome and is traditionally eaten *all' amatriciana*. This is one of those recipes that are taken very seriously, like *spaghetti alla carbonara*. In other words, you'd better be careful how you make it, and, even more, to whom you serve it, because everybody has an opinion about it. Note that lard, the original fat in this dish, is listed as an alternative to olive oil. The healthier alternative is, of course, much more popular these days in Rome, as everywhere else, but you might want to try the traditional ingredient someday to see what it tastes like.

If you've ever tried to wrap a strand of bucatini around a fork, you know it doesn't work. Especially cooked as Romans prefer it, quite al dente, the hole in the middle prevents it from becoming very malleable. So unlike most long pastas, bucatini is often broken into 2 or 3 lengths as it is added to the pasta pot.

1 In a large skillet, heat the oil. Add the pancetta and cook over moderately high heat, stirring, until light brown. Remove with a slotted spoon and keep warm.

2 Add the onion and peperoncino to the hot fat, reduce the heat to low, and cook, stirring, until the onion is lightly colored, about 5 minutes.

3 Add the tomatoes, season with salt and black pepper to taste, and simmer for about 8 minutes, no more. (The tomatoes must not be too loose or too thick.) Discard the peperoncino and return the pancetta to the skillet. Taste the sauce for seasoning. You should be able to taste the peperoncino. If not, add a pinch of hot pepper flakes.

4 Cook the pasta in a large pot of boiling salted water until it is very al dente. Drain and toss with half of the pecorino Romano cheese. Mix with two-thirds of the sauce, put onto a serving platter, pour the rest of the sauce over the pasta, and serve at once, with the rest of the pecorino Romano passed at the table.

PASTA WITH MARINARA SAUCE

Pasta alla Marinara

SERVES 4 TO 6

⅓ cup extra virgin olive oil (80 ml)

1 dried peperoncino, or hot red pepper flakes to taste

2 cloves of garlic, finely chopped

2 cups canned Italian plum tomatoes, partially drained (500 ml), or 1 pound ripe fresh tomatoes, peeled, seeded, and coarsely chopped (450 g)

½ teaspoon salt

1 pound spaghetti or linguine (450 g)

2 tablespoons finely chopped parsley

In Rome, there are two kinds of *pasta alla marinara*. In restaurants the dish almost always includes seafood, which is why the name translates as "sailor's pasta." At home, it has no fish in it and is the familiar chunky tomato sauce renowned throughout the world. Here is the home-style version.

1 Heat the oil in a large skillet with the whole peperoncino, if using it. (If using hot red pepper flakes, add them later with the tomatoes.) Add the chopped garlic and cook gently over moderately low heat until the garlic is lightly colored, about 3 minutes.

2 Discard the peperoncino and add the tomatoes. Season with the salt and cook over moderately high heat, breaking up the tomatoes with a wooden spoon, for 15 minutes, or until the sauce has thickened.

3 In a large pot of boiling salted water, cook the pasta until it is al dente; drain well and transfer to a warmed serving bowl. Pour the sauce over the pasta and toss to coat. Garnish with the chopped parsley and serve at once.

SPAGHETTI WITH PANCETTA, EGGS, AND CHEESE

Spaghetti alla Carbonara

SERVES 4 OR 5

1 pound spaghetti (450 g)
———

8 ounces pancetta, sliced about
¼ inch thick and cut crosswise
into thin strips (225 g)
———

2 whole eggs
———

2 egg yolks
———

3 tablespoons heavy cream
———

¼ cup freshly grated pecorino
Romano cheese (25 g)
———

2 tablespoons freshly grated
Parmesan cheese
———

Salt and freshly ground
black pepper
———

Another Roman pasta considered almost sacred, *una cosa seria* (that is, "a serious thing"), is *spaghetti alla carbonara*. Italian bacon, called pancetta, is the most important ingredient here. Authentic *spaghetti alla carbonara* is actually made with *guanciale*, cured hog jowls, which make it truly special, but since this is not readily available, pancetta, which is common in Italian markets in the United States and even in the deli section of many supermarkets, offers a good alternative. A fatty bacon, provided it is not smoked, is almost as good and is probably easier to find.

A few tablespoons of cream are often added in Rome to prevent the eggs from curdling, although some disagree about whether it is appropriate. A pepper mill is essential. One of my friends contends that the name of this pasta derives from the Italian word *carbone*, which means coal, because originally the dish was covered with black pepper when it was served.

1 Bring a large pot of salted water to a boil. Add the pasta and cook until it is barely al dente.

2 While the pasta is cooking, in a large, deep skillet or flameproof casserole, cook the pancetta over moderate heat until it is golden, 4 to 5 minutes.

3 In a small bowl, beat together the whole eggs, egg yolks, cream, pecorino Romano, and Parmesan cheese. Season with salt and a generous grinding of pepper.

4 Drain the spaghetti and add to the skillet with the pancetta with its rendered fat, mixing thoroughly. Pour the egg mixture over the pasta and toss rapidly over the lowest heat to coat evenly. Remove from the heat as soon as the egg begins to thicken. Continue tossing to mix well, adding another grinding of black pepper.

5 Serve at once in a heated dish with extra cheese and a pepper mill on the side.

NOTE: If you wish to make this dish for fewer or for more people, it is helpful to know that the general proportion for *carbonara* per person is usually 1½ to 2 ounces (40 to 55 g) pancetta, 1 egg, 1 tablespoon pecorino Romano cheese, and 1 tablespoon Parmesan. When the number of servings is increased, I like to use some whole egg and some egg yolk, to keep the sauce rich and silky.

PECORINO ROMANO CHEESE

PECORINO ROMANO is the quintessential Roman cheese. It is eaten all over Lazio and used, instead of the "northern" Parmesan, for pasta, as an after-dinner cheese, and for most everything else. However, today it is also used mixed with Parmesan to dress pasta when a less strong taste is desired. It is made exclusively of sheep's milk. As it ages, it develops a stronger taste. When fresh, or aged for around six months, it is a robust and good cheese to end your meal. After aging for six months to one year, it is a grating cheese. (But they all tell you a different story.) Once you have aquired a taste for this cheese, you will be able to find the right one for you. Pecorino is probably one of Italy's oldest cheeses, certainly Lazio's. It was made when Rome was a small shepherds' village, and it is still made substantially in the same way. It should be grated when needed, not in advance. In America this cheese is also called Romano.

GINETTA'S PARTY PASTA

La Pasta di Ginetta

SERVES 8 TO 10

2 cloves of garlic, peeled

2 dried peperoncini

3 tablespoons olive oil

½ pound plain pancetta, cut
into thin julienne strips (200 g)

½ pound smoked pancetta, cut
into thin julienne strips (200 g)

2 pounds penne rigate (Ginetta
always uses De Cecco brand)
(900 g)

3 tablespoons unsalted butter
(45 g)

½ cup freshly grated Parmesan
cheese (50 g)

¼ cup torn fresh basil leaves

Freshly ground black pepper

My husband's cousin Ginetta Forges D'Avanzati is an interior designer and a very good cook. Her favorite recipe is an extremely simple pasta. It is so popular among her friends that she gets frequent requests for the recipe, even from food professionals. Keep in mind, though, that because it contains so few ingredients, it demands the best pancetta and cheeses, and perfumed fresh basil.

1 Cook the garlic and peperoncino in the olive oil. Discard the garlic when it is golden and add the pancetta, frying until it is almost crisp.

2 Cook the pasta in a large pot of boiling salted water until it is al dente, drain, and turn it into the pan with the pancetta. Add the butter to the pasta and toss.

3 Transfer the pasta to a serving bowl and toss it with the Parmesan cheese and basil. Top with a generous grinding of black pepper.

ANGELICA'S PASTA WITH RAISINS AND PINE NUTS

La Pasta d'Angelica

SERVES 3 TO 4

⅓ cup extra virgin olive oil
(80 ml)

_____

1 large onion, thinly sliced

_____

3 cups canned Italian plum
tomatoes, drained, with half the
juice reserved (750 g)

_____

¾ cup flavorful black olives, such
as Gaeta, pitted and cut into
pieces (150 g)

_____

¼ cup raisins (40 g)

_____

3 tablespoons pine nuts

_____

Pinch of sugar

_____

Salt and freshly ground
black pepper

_____

12 ounces spaghetti or other
long pasta (340 g)

_____

My daughter has a beautiful and glamorous friend who works in Italian television here in Rome. Like so many professional women, she's always pressed for time. Cooking is not important to her, so she devised one easy pasta sauce she can count on anytime she has to entertain. The surprise is that it's so good, all her friends make it as well.

1 Heat the olive oil in a large sauté pan and add the onion. Cook slowly over low heat until the onion is soft and translucent, 7 to 10 minutes.

2 Add the tomatoes with their reserved juices and simmer for 10 minutes, mashing the tomatoes with the back of a wooden spoon.

3 Add the olives, raisins, pine nuts, and sugar. Season with salt and pepper to taste. Cook for 10 more minutes, or until the sauce has thickened.

4 In a large pot of boiling salted water, cook the pasta until it is al dente. Drain and add to the sauce in the pan; mix thoroughly. Serve the pasta hot.

PASTA WITH RICOTTA AND SAUSAGES

Pasta con Ricotta e Salsicce

SERVES 4 TO 6

12 ounces Italian sausages
(340 g)

1 pound spaghetti (450 g)

⅔ pound ricotta, drained
if necessary (300 g)

2 tablespoons butter (30 g)

Salt and freshly ground
black pepper

½ cup freshly grated Parmesan
cheese (50 g)

The butchers in Rome make very good sausages with fat and lean pork, adding garlic and peperoncino to taste, when the weather turns cold. Here is a meaty version of the ricotta recipe on page 57 that is usually prepared in Rome in winter, which is sausage season.

1 Remove and discard the casings from the sausages. Crumble the sausages into a skillet. Add 3 tablespoons water and cook over moderate heat, stirring, until the meat is no longer pink, about 5 minutes.

2 Meanwhile, in a large pot of boiling salted water, cook the spaghetti until it is al dente. Scoop out and reserve ⅓ cup of the pasta cooking water.

3 Warm a pasta serving bowl. Put the ricotta and the butter, cut into bits, into the bowl. Using a fork, stir in the reserved pasta water, 1 tablespoon at a time, to make a creamy sauce. Mix in the cooked sausages. Season with salt and pepper to taste.

4 Drain the pasta and add to the serving bowl. Toss to mix, sprinkling on the Parmesan cheese as you toss. Serve at once with more black pepper ground over the top.

PASTA WITH WILD HOPS

Pasta con i Nopoli

SERVES 2

½ pound nopoli (wild hops) or
pencil-thin asparagus tips
(225 g)

———

6 tablespoons extra virgin
olive oil

———

2 cloves of garlic, peeled
and crushed

———

¼ beef bouillon cube, crumbled

———

Salt and freshly ground
black pepper

———

½ pound spaghetti (225 g)

———

Nopoli is the word for wild hops in the Lazian dialect; the Italian word for the same plant is *luppoli*. This rather unusual pasta is made with the wild hops plant, which twines up fences and free-standing poles. To harvest it, you break off the new shoots at the tender part of the stalk, like wild asparagus. In fact, they look like miniature asparagus, and pencil-thin wild asparagus are also good prepared this way. Add the tender hop leaves, too. While you may not make this dish often, I wanted to include it because it is so authentically Roman.

1 Rinse the *nopoli* thoroughly, swishing them around in a large bowl of cold water to clean them thoroughly. Let soak while you prepare the pasta as follows.

2 In a large skillet, heat the olive oil with the garlic. Cook over moderate heat until the garlic is brown, about 3 minutes; discard the garlic. Lift out the *nopoli* and without draining add them to the oil in the skillet. Add the ¼ bouillon cube. Cover and cook for 10 minutes, stirring every now and then. Season with salt and pepper. Remove from the heat and cover to keep warm.

3 In a large pot of boiling salted water, cook the spaghetti until it is al dente. Drain the pasta and transfer to the skillet with the *nopoli*. Toss to mix well. Serve with a pepper mill at the table. Romans do not eat cheese with this dish.

SPAGHETTI WITH WHITE CLAM SAUCE

Spaghetti con Vongole in Bianco

SERVES 4 TO 6

2⅔ pounds baby clams (vongole)
(1.2 kg)

Coarse salt

Cornmeal

¾ cup extra virgin olive oil
(180 ml)

1 pound spaghetti (450 g)

2 cloves of garlic, peeled and
crushed

¼ teaspoon hot red pepper
flakes, or more to taste

3½ tablespoons finely chopped
parsley

Freshly ground black pepper

Spaghetti con vongole in bianco (with clams, in a sauce without tomatoes, therefore white) is a recipe from my first cookbook, *Italian Cooking in the Grand Tradition*, which I wrote with my fellow cooking teacher Anna Maria Cornetto. Since I can't improve on it, because this is the way we prepare it in Rome, I give it to you almost as it is in our book. This is eaten especially on Christmas Eve, when it is traditional in Italy to serve an all-seafood meal.

1 Scrub the clams and then rinse 2 or 3 times in cold water. Fill the sink with cold water and add 2 small fistfuls of coarse salt. Put the clams in a colander and immerse them in the water. Sprinkle a handful of cornmeal over the clams, cover the colander with a lid, and leave for at least 5 hours, or better, overnight, in the refrigerator. When ready to use the clams, rinse them 3 times in cold water and drain.

2 In a large skillet, heat 2 tablespoons of the olive oil over high heat. Add the clams. Cover the skillet with a lid and cook, shaking the pan continuously, until the clams open, 3 or 5 minutes.

3 Let the clams cool a little. Set aside a few of the clams in their shells to serve on top of the pasta. Strain the clam juice in the skillet through a single thickness of paper towel and reserve ⅔ cup of the juices. Shell the remaining clams and add them to the reserved juice.

4 In a large pot of boiling salted water, cook the spaghetti until it is very al dente.

5 While the pasta is cooking, heat the rest of the oil in a clean large skillet over moderately low heat. Add the garlic and cook slowly until light brown, 3 to 4 minutes. Quickly add the hot pepper, the clams with their juice, and 2 tablespoons of the parsley. Simmer for 1 to 2 minutes to heat through. Season with salt and pepper to taste.

6 Drain the pasta and add it to the clam sauce in the skillet. Toss rapidly and thoroughly over moderate heat. Transfer to a warm serving dish, arrange the reserved clams in their shells over the pasta, and sprinkle the remaining chopped parsley on top. Serve at once.

SPAGHETTI WITH ZUCCHINI

Spaghetti con Zucchine

SERVES 2 TO 3

¼ cup extra virgin olive oil (60 ml)

1 small onion, very thinly sliced

2 cloves of garlic, peeled

1 peperoncino (optional)

1¼ pounds fresh small zucchini, washed and sliced about ⅛ inch thick (575 g)

Salt and freshly ground black pepper

1 teaspoon dried oregano, or 2 tablespoons torn fresh basil or mint leaves

¼ cup heavy cream (60 ml)

½ pound spaghetti or other long pasta (225 g)

3 tablespoons freshly grated Parmesan cheese

Here's a simple zucchini pasta with just a bit of cream for smoothness. If you leave out the hot pepper, it is very appropriate for children and makes a good, quick family lunch.

1 Heat the olive oil in a large skillet. Add the onion and garlic with the peperoncino, if using, and cook over low heat, stirring. When the onion begins to color, raise the heat to moderately high and add the zucchini. Stir-fry the zucchini until they are tender but firm, 15 to 20 minutes.

2 Season the zucchini with salt and pepper to taste and the dried or fresh herb of your choice. Discard the garlic and peperoncino. Add the cream and reduce the heat to low. Simmer for 1 to 2 minutes.

3 Meanwhile, in a large pot of boiling salted water, cook the pasta until it is al dente. Drain well and pour the pasta into the skillet with the zucchini. Mix thoroughly, sprinkling the Parmesan cheese over the pasta as you toss, and serve at once. Pass extra Parmesan at the table.

SPAGHETTI WITH TUNA FISH

Spaghetti con Tonno

SERVES 4 TO 6

1½ tablespoons butter, at room temperature (20 g)

1 tablespoon anchovy paste

5 tablespoons olive oil

2 cloves of garlic, peeled and crushed

1⅓ pounds ripe plum tomatoes, peeled, seeded, and cut into thin strips (600 g)

Salt

1 can (6 ounces) tuna packed in oil, preferably olive oil, drained (170 g)

1 pound spaghetti or other long pasta (450 g)

2 tablespoons finely chopped parsley

Tuna packed in oil might seem an odd condiment for pasta, but it is often used in Rome. *Spaghetti alla carrettiera* (The Cart Driver's Spaghetti, opposite) and *spaghetti alla boscaiola* (woodsman's style) are other well-known pastas containing tuna. Any quick taste test will illustrate the difference between a good Italian tuna packed in olive oil and ordinary oil-packed tuna. It may seem troublesome to have to sauté the tuna separately when it would be easier to just add it to the tomato sauce, but the extra cooking step, which I first saw in Luigi Carnacina's *Roma in Cucina*, really makes a difference.

1 Mix together the butter and anchovy paste until they are evenly blended.

2 Heat 3½ tablespoons of the olive oil in a large skillet. Add the garlic and cook over moderate heat until the garlic is light brown. Discard the garlic and add the tomatoes. Season with salt to taste. Raise the heat to moderately high and cook, stirring and shaking the pan often, until the excess liquid in the tomatoes evaporates, 10 to 15 minutes.

3 In a large pot of boiling salted water, cook the pasta until it is al dente.

4 Meanwhile, put the remaining 1½ tablespoons oil in a small skillet and heat over high heat until almost smoking. Add the tuna and sauté, stirring, for 2 or 3 minutes.

5 Drain the pasta and transfer to a warmed serving dish. Toss rapidly with the anchovy butter to coat. Add the tomatoes and toss; last of all add the hot tuna. Mix well. Sprinkle the parsley on top and serve at once. Be sure to pass a pepper mill at the table.

THE CART DRIVER'S SPAGHETTI

Spaghetti alla Carrettiera

SERVES 4

*1 ounce dried porcini
mushrooms (25 g)*

*¼ cup plus 2 tablespoons extra
virgin olive oil (80 ml)*

*2 cloves of garlic, peeled
and crushed*

*1 or 2 dried peperoncini, or
hot red pepper flakes to taste*

5 canned Italian plum tomatoes

*1 can (6 ounces) tuna packed
in oil, drained (170 g)*

*Salt and freshly ground
black pepper*

12 ounces spaghetti (340 g)

2 tablespoons chopped parsley

You can tell by the name that this is a very old recipe, and the combination of dried porcini, garlic, and peperoncino is distinctly Roman. Everyone knows this pasta and everyone makes it. A number of versions given to me for *spaghetti alla carrettiera* were wildly different, but all agreed there should be little tomatoes; sometimes only tomato paste with a little water is used. It is a quick, easy pasta to prepare.

1 Soak the porcini in a bowl of tepid water until they are soft, 20 to 30 minutes. Remove, squeezing excess water back into the bowl. If the porcini seem gritty, rinse them under cold water; pat dry. Chop the mushrooms not too finely.

2 Heat ¼ cup of the olive oil in a large skillet. Add the garlic and whole peperoncini (if using hot pepper flakes, add them with the tomatoes). Cook over moderately low heat, turning the garlic, until it is golden.

3 Add the chopped porcini and cook for 3 minutes, stirring often. Add the tomatoes, mashing them with a wooden spoon. Simmer uncovered for about 10 minutes, stirring often. Discard the garlic and peperoncini.

4 Add the tuna and simmer over low heat for 2 minutes. Season with salt and a generous amount of black pepper. Remove from the heat and mix in the remaining 2 tablespoons oil.

5 In a large pot of boiling salted water, cook the spaghetti until it is al dente; if in doubt, err on the side of extra firm. Drain the spaghetti and toss with the sauce in a warmed pasta bowl. Sprinkle the parsley on top and serve at once.

SPAGHETTINI WITH MIXED SEAFOOD IN SPICY TOMATO SAUCE

Pasta con Frutti di Mare

SERVES 4 TO 6

1½ pounds mussels (675 g)

1 pound small hard-shell clams (450 g)

1 pound squid, cleaned, thinly sliced (290 g)

10 ounces extra-large shrimp, peeled and deveined, with shells reserved (250 g)

1 small onion

2 cloves of garlic, peeled

Dried peperoncino or hot red pepper flakes

⅓ cup plus 2 tablespoons olive oil (110 ml)

2½ pounds ripe firm tomatoes, peeled, seeded, coarsely chopped, and drained in a colander (1.125 kg)

While in Rome pasta is usually served as a first course, more and more we are eating it like Americans, as our main dish. With fresh tomatoes and an enticing mix of shellfish, this summery dish is really a meal in itself, needing no more than a simple salad and some fresh fruit for dessert. Hot pepper is called for, but you can decide how spicy you want to make it.

1 Remove the mussels' beards, scraping with a knife, and scrub the shells well. Rinse the mussels under cold water. Scrub the clams well and rinse 2 or 3 times in cold water. Soak in cold salted water until needed. Rinse and drain the squid.

2 Put the mussels and clams, along with the reserved shrimp shells, in a large flameproof casserole. Cover and cook over high heat, shaking the pan and stirring the shellfish up from bottom to top once or twice, until the shells open, 4 to 5 minutes. As soon as the shells open, use a strainer or slotted spoon to transfer the mussels and clams to a colander set over a bowl to catch the juices.

3 Discard the shrimp shells and any shellfish that do not open. Shuck the mussels and clams, keeping them separate. Rinse the shucked clams in the shellfish liquid in the pot to remove any remaining sand. Strain the liquid through a double layer of cheesecloth and reserve.

4 Make the *battuto*: Finely chop together the onion, garlic, and peperoncino.

*Salt and freshly ground
black pepper*

1 pound spaghettini (450 g)

2 tablespoons chopped parsley

5 Heat the olive oil in a clean large flameproof casserole. Add the *battuto* and cook over moderately high heat, stirring often, until the onion softens, 3 to 4 minutes.

6 Add the tomatoes and season with salt and a generous amount of black pepper. Cook for another 5 minutes, stirring occasionally. Add the squid and reduce the heat to low. Simmer uncovered for 15 minutes. If the sauce seems dry, stir in a few tablespoons of the reserved shellfish liquid.

7 Add the mussels, clams, and shrimp. Cook until the shrimp are pink and curled, 2 to 3 minutes. Stir in as much of the remaining liquid as needed to make a thick sauce.

8 Cook the spaghettini in a large pot of boiling salted water until it is al dente. Drain and immediately add to the casserole with the shellfish and sauce. Toss to mix well, transfer to a warmed serving platter, garnish with parsley, and serve.

IL BATTUTO

The *battuto* adds flavor to soups and sauces. It is made up of some or all of these ingredients — garlic, onion, carrot, celery, pancetta, ham fat or fat and lean ham, parsley, tomato, and, often, peperoncino. These ingredients are finely chopped together, usually with a mezzaluna, a halfmoon-shaped knife with two handles, which you hold while rolling and chopping the vegetables together. You can also use a large chef's knife or pulse in a food processor. The mixture is then slowly cooked in oil or lard and forms the flavor base of your dish. The *battuto* is particularly Roman.

SPAGHETTINI WITH SALMON CAVIAR

Spaghettini con Caviale Rosso

SERVES 2 TO 4

2 tablespoons unsalted butter
(30 g)

½ cup heavy cream (120 ml)

½ pound spaghettini or nidi
(225 g)

¼ pound plus 2 tablespoons
salmon caviar (110 g)

2½ tablespoons minced fresh
chives or scallion greens

Freshly ground black pepper

This quick and easy but elegant pasta is all the rage everywhere in Rome. It's the kind of dish that works perfectly as a before- or after-opera treat and causes gasps at the most sophisticated dinner parties. It has been made with every kind of caviar, and some cooks add vodka. Chives work best by far here, but because they are sometimes so hard to find, the green of scallions is offered as an alternative. The recipe doubles easily, but be sure to use a larger saucepan, so the cream doesn't bubble over.

1 Cut the butter into pieces directly into a pasta serving bowl. Put the cream in a small saucepan and simmer for 8 minutes, or until it has thickened.

2 In a large pot of boiling salted water, cook the spaghettini until it is al dente. Drain the pasta and put it into the serving bowl. Pour on the hot cream and toss to mix.

3 Gently mix in ¼ pound of the caviar and 1½ tablespoons of the chives. Sprinkle the remaining 1 tablespoon chives and the extra caviar over the pasta. Serve immediately, with a pepper mill on the table.

SWEET ROMAN PASTA WITH RICOTTA

Pasta con la Ricotta alla Romana

SERVES 4 TO 6

1 pound rigatoni or other short pasta (450 g)

⅔ pound ricotta, drained if necessary (300 g)

1 tablespoon sugar

1 teaspoon ground cinnamon

Pasta with ricotta sweetened with a little sugar and spiced with cinnamon is an old Roman specialty, which is not often eaten today. You may find, however, that children enjoy it a lot. On page 57, you'll find the more common savory Roman preparation.

If fresh ricotta is available, this pasta is superb. (Ricotta should be drained, even overnight, if necessary.) Good ricotta is also delicious eaten as a dessert, with sugar and rum, as in Rome, or with cocoa and sugar.

1 In a large pot of lightly salted boiling water, cook the pasta until it is al dente. Scoop out and reserve ⅓ cup of the pasta cooking water.

2 While the pasta is cooking, warm a serving bowl. Put the ricotta, sugar, and cinnamon in the bowl and add the reserved pasta water 1 tablespoon at a time, stirring, until the mixture is creamy.

3 Drain the pasta and transfer to the serving bowl. Toss to mix well. Serve at once.

FETTUCCINE WITH ARTICHOKES

Fettuccine alla Ciociaria

SERVES 4 TO 6

5 large artichokes

½ lemon

Salt and freshly ground
black pepper

7 tablespoons unsalted butter
(105 g)

1 pound dried fettuccine
(450 g)

1 cup heavy cream (230 ml)

2 tablespoons chopped fresh
mint, plus leaves to decorate
the dish

1 cup freshly grated Parmesan
cheese (100 g)

At Christmastime, shepherds make their way to Rome to play traditional Roman Christmas songs on their bagpipes. These country musicians are from La Ciociaria, in the southern part of Lazio. They wear thick, high white woolen handmade socks and flat sandal-like shoes, which lace up to their knees with leather thongs. These shoes are called cioce, from ciociaria. La Ciociaria is known for its beautiful women (Gina Lollabrigida for one!), and artists' models from there were once famous all over Italy. More pertinent to a cookbook, this area is also known for its artichokes, which are especially good, and for its wonderful cooks. This recipe is a modern version of their traditional pasta and artichoke dish.

1 Clean the artichokes, as explained on page 211. Cut the artichokes in half, lay them cut side down on a cutting board, and cut lengthwise into thin slices. Put them into a bowl of cold water. Squeeze the juice of the half lemon into the bowl and add the lemon half as well.

2 When almost ready to serve the pasta, put on to boil 5 quarts of water with 2 tablespoons coarse salt.

3 Drain the artichoke slices on paper towels. Heat 3 tablespoons of the butter in a large skillet and sauté the artichokes until they are tender but still al dente. (Start testing after 2 minutes. It's impossible to give a precise time, because it depends on the freshness of the artichokes.) Salt the artichokes while cooking them. Remove from the heat and cover to keep warm until the pasta is ready.

4 Add the pasta to the boiling salted water and cook until it is al dente. Drain well.

5 While the pasta is cooking, add the cream to the skillet with the artichokes and simmer over low heat for about 10 minutes. Pour the drained pasta into the skillet with the artichokes. Add the remaining 4 tablespoons butter, the mint, and the Parmesan cheese, mixing rapidly. Transfer to a warmed serving dish, decorate with the extra mint leaves, and serve at once, with a pepper mill and more grated Parmesan on the side.

MINA'S PASTA WITH RICOTTA

Pasta con la Ricotta di Mina

SERVES 4 TO 6

1 pound rigatoni or other short pasta (450 g)

4 tablespoons butter (60 g)

⅔ pound ricotta, drained if necessary (300 g)

½ cup freshly grated Parmesan cheese (50 g)

Salt and freshly ground black pepper

Below is my friend Mina's recipe, a savory pasta with ricotta that's one of those extremely simple comfort dishes everyone loves. A generous amount of freshly ground black pepper is an essential part of this dish.

1 In a large pot of boiling salted water, cook the pasta until it is al dente. Scoop out and reserve ⅓ cup of the pasta cooking water.

2 While the pasta is cooking, warm a serving bowl. Put the butter, cut into bits, into the warm bowl. In a separate small bowl, mash the ricotta with a fork and add the pasta water 1 tablespoon at a time, enough to make a creamy sauce. Stir in the Parmesan cheese until the sauce is blended.

3 Drain the pasta and add to the butter in the bowl. Toss until the butter melts and coats the pasta. Add the cheese sauce and toss again to mix well. Season generously with salt and pepper to taste and serve at once. Pass a pepper mill and extra Parmesan cheese at the table.

FETTUCCINE WITH PEAS AND PROSCIUTTO

Fettuccine alla Papalina I

SERVES 4 TO 6

4 tablespoons butter (60 g)

1 tablespoon extra virgin olive oil

1 small white onion, finely chopped

About 3 cups garden-fresh peas (2⅔ pounds, or 1.2 kg, in the shell)

¼ pound prosciutto in a single slice, cut into small dice (110 g)

Salt

2 eggs

¾ cup freshly grated Parmesan cheese (75 g)

1 pound dried fettuccine (450 g)

The Italian name for this dish translates as "the Pope's fettuccine." That's because the recipe was invented for Cardinal Eugenio Pacelli in Trastevere, the "other side of the Tiber" — the river that runs through Rome. After the cardinal became pope, the fettuccine, too, was elevated to papal status. Still, it remains a very simple dish.

1 Heat the butter and olive oil in a small pan. Add the onion and cook over low heat until soft and translucent, 5 to 7 minutes. Add the peas and cover the pan. Cook over low heat for about 10 minutes, or until the peas are tender but still firm. Add the diced prosciutto, salt lightly, and simmer for about 3 minutes.

2 Beat the eggs with 3 tablespoons of the Parmesan cheese in the bowl in which you will serve the pasta.

3 Cook the fettuccine in a large pot of boiling salted water until it is al dente. Drain well. Turn the pasta into the serving bowl, sprinkle on the rest of the Parmesan cheese, and mix thoroughly. Add the hot peas, toss quickly, and serve with more Parmesan and a pepper mill on the side.

NOTE: If you are worried about raw eggs, you could cook your eggs as Luigi Carnacina suggests in his book *Roma in Cucina*. Beat the eggs with the Parmesan cheese and 2 tablespoons of heavy cream. Melt some of the butter and, when it bubbles, pour in the egg mixture. As soon as the eggs begin to solidify, add the peas and prosciutto to the skillet, mix, and pour this mixture over the drained pasta, tossing rapidly. Pass extra Parmesan cheese at the table.

FETTUCCINE WITH PEAS, MUSHROOMS, AND PANCETTA

Fettuccine alla Papalina II

SERVES 4 TO 6

¼ cup extra virgin olive oil (60 ml)

1 clove of garlic, peeled

1 pound mushrooms, sliced
¼ inch thick (450 g)

2 tablespoons chopped parsley

Salt

3 tablespoons dry white wine

2 tablespoons lard or butter (30 g)

1 small white onion, very finely
chopped

3 ounces pancetta, thinly sliced,
then cut into thin julienne strips
(85 g)

1½ cups garden-fresh peas (about
1½ pounds in the shell) (675 g)

1 pound dried fettuccine (450 g)

¾ cup freshly grated Parmesan
cheese (75 g)

This is a more elaborate version of the previous pasta. It adds mushrooms and pancetta for a richer effect. Note the use of lard, which is an ancient fat. Of course, you may substitute butter, as I indicate.

1 Heat the olive oil in a large skillet. Add the garlic and cook slowly over low heat until it is just beginning to brown. Discard the garlic. Add the mushrooms to the oil and cook over moderately low heat, stirring often, until the liquid they release has evaporated. Sprinkle on the parsley, season with salt, and add the wine. Cook for another minute or 2, until most of the wine evaporates. Remove from the heat.

2 In a small saucepan, melt the lard or butter. Add the onion and pancetta and cook over low heat, stirring, until the onion is soft and translucent and the pancetta is beginning to brown. Add the peas, cover, and cook slowly over low heat for about 10 minutes, or until the peas are tender. Season the peas and pour them into the skillet with the mushrooms. Mix well.

3 Cook the pasta in a large pot of boiling salted water until it is al dente. Drain the pasta and transfer to a warmed serving bowl. Toss the pasta with the Parmesan cheese and then pour the mushrooms and peas over it. Serve at once, with extra Parmesan cheese and a pepper mill on the side.

THE JEWISH "GHETTO" OF ROME

IN ROME, the word *ghetto* is not derogatory, but simply indicates a place. Jews have lived in Rome without interruption since the second century B.C. During medieval times they were concentrated in Trastevere and the area around Castel Sant'Angelo. In 1555, Paolo IV obliged the Jews to transfer to a quarter of Rome that had walls and gates, part of the site of the present Ghetto. In 1870, with the arrival of the Piedmontese, the Ghetto was opened finally, and the Jewish population given the same rights as the Romans. There have always been mixed marriages between Jews and Catholics in Rome. Many Jews were hidden by the Romans during the German occupation, a dangerous undertaking, of course, for all the parties.

Today the Ghetto contains about 15,000 people, and it is an upscale neighborhood, famous for its wonderful restaurants with traditional Jewish-Roman dishes, which have been integrated into classic Italian cuisine—the most famous, of course, being fried whole artichokes. People who live in the Ghetto still use Roman-Jewish expressions and sell and eat their special sweets, coveted by many Romans. One bakery in particular is always packed.

Panificio Cordella Antonio is *the* bakery of the Ghetto; it is commonly referred to as *il forno del Ghetto* (the Ghetto bakery). They make a profusion of breads of all types, but consider their specialties to be pizza *rosso* and *bianca* (*rosso*, or red, with tomato sauce; *bianca*, white, with oil and kosher salt); loaves of white bread, made with pizza dough, called *ossi*, or "bones," because they are shaped like bones; sesame bread; and *bottoncini*, or "buttons," which are small rolls, with olive oil in the dough, studded with olives, walnuts, or raisins.

Panificio Cordella Antonio, Piazza Costaguti 30/31, telephone 06 688 3012

The bakery is near the Costaguti Palace, which is not open to the public, and in the heart of the Ghetto, not too far from the Temple, which was built at the end of the 1800s. At one end of the street are the ruins of the Roman period fish market and at the other end is a beautiful very old, pre-Renaissance palace, again not open to the public. There are also several good restaurants which specialize in Jewish dishes along the way. The best known is Piperno, famous for its *carciofi alla giudia* ("artichokes the Jewish way").

ROMAN FETTUCCINE WITH FRESH PEAS

Fettuccine con Piselli

SERVES 2 TO 3

3 tablespoons unsalted butter
(45 g)

1 heaping cup garden-fresh
peas, 1⅓ pounds in the shell
(600 g)

½ cup heavy cream (120 ml)

Salt and freshly ground
black pepper

½ pound dried fettuccine
(225 g)

⅓ cup freshly grated Parmesan
cheese (35 g)

2 tablespoons chopped parsley

Most lovers of Italian food are familiar with Venetian *risi e bisi*, or rice and peas, but the Romans are happy to mix fresh peas with their beloved pasta as well. With all its butter and cream, this dish might not seem particularly Roman, but it was one of the first great pastas I tasted in Rome, many years ago. It was in a restaurant called Il Pompiere in the Jewish ghetto, and the peas were fresh and unforgettably sweet. For a similar pasta with prosciutto added, see Fettuccine with Peas and Prosciutto (page 58). There is also a version with mushrooms added; see Fettuccine with Porcini Sauce (page 62).

1 Melt 2 tablespoons of the butter in a small saucepan. Add the peas, cover, and simmer over very low heat until tender but still firm, 8 to 10 minutes. Add the cream and simmer until thickened, about 5 minutes. Season with salt and pepper to taste.

2 Cook the fettuccine in a large pot of boiling salted water until it is al dente. Drain the pasta and transfer to a heated bowl that contains the remaining 1 tablespoon butter. Mix well, sprinkling the Parmesan cheese over the pasta as you toss. Add the peas and cream, mix, and serve at once, with chopped parsley sprinkled over the top.

NOTE: If using frozen peas, do not thaw them, but add them still frozen to the hot butter. Simmer, covered, until they are tender but firm. This will take a little longer than fresh peas, 12 to 15 minutes in all.

FETTUCCINE WITH PORCINI SAUCE

Fettuccine con Salsa di Funghi Porcini

SERVES 4 TO 6

1½ ounces dried porcini (40 g)

1 small onion, finely chopped

8 tablespoons (¼ pound) unsalted butter (120 g)

½ cup dry white wine (120 ml)

1 beef bouillon cube

3 tablespoons flour

2 egg yolks

⅛ teaspoon grated nutmeg

3 tablespoons chopped parsley

Salt and freshly ground black pepper

1 clove of garlic, peeled

1 pound fresh porcini, cleaned and sliced into pieces ¼ inch thick (450 g)

1 pound dried fettuccine (450 g)

1 cup freshly grated Parmesan cheese (100 g)

At our hunting lodge in upper Lazio, we gather wild mushrooms of all kinds, particularly porcini when we can find them, but also *ovoli*, which look like long, orange eggs. These are sliced thinly and eaten raw as a salad. There are lots of other types of mushrooms, of course, and each one is served with a specific pasta, long or short, or rice, which suits it. Sometimes the caps of the porcini are baked in the oven with chopped garlic, parsley, and olive oil, or even cut into chunks and sautéed with garlic and oil.

This is our favorite recipe for porcini with pasta. It uses both the fresh and dried. Since fresh porcini are hard to come by, and extremely expensive if you don't pick them, you could make this recipe with the dried porcini and another wild mushroom for the fresh. While the taste will not be truly Roman, the dish will be delicious.

1 Soak the dried porcini in 1¾ cups hot water for 2 hours. Strain the water through a coffee filter or a double thickness of paper towel and reserve it. Rinse the dried mushrooms until clean, chop them, and set aside.

2 Cook the onion in 4 tablespoons of the butter over low heat until it is soft and translucent, about 10 minutes, stirring every now and then. Add the chopped dried porcini and cook for about 5 minutes. Add the white wine, turning up the heat a little, and allowing it to evaporate almost completely.

3 In a separate pan, combine the reserved mushroom water with the bouillon cube and bring to a boil. Sprinkle the flour over the dried porcini sauce, stirring, and pour over the boiling mushroom liquid. Allow to thicken, stirring constantly. Let the sauce cool slightly, then add the egg yolks, nutmeg, and parsley. Season with salt and pepper to taste.

4 In another skillet, heat the remaining 4 tablespoons butter with the garlic. Add the fresh porcini mushrooms and sauté, stirring often, for 6 minutes. Season with salt and pepper. Mix half of the fresh mushrooms with the prepared sauce.

5 Cook the pasta in boiling salted water until it is al dente. Drain the pasta and toss with the Parmesan cheese in a warmed bowl. Toss with the sauce and sprinkle the reserved porcini on top.

6 Serve at once with a pepper mill and extra Parmesan on the side.

CLASSIC SAUCE FOR FRESH FETTUCCINE

Salsa per le Fettuccine

SERVES 10 TO 12

1 ounce dried porcini mushrooms (30 g)

1 medium onion, coarsely chopped

1 medium carrot, peeled and coarsely chopped

1 celery rib, coarsely chopped

1 small handful of parsley, coarsely chopped

1 clove of garlic, peeled and coarsely chopped

¼ pound pancetta, coarsely chopped (110 g)

7 tablespoons butter (105 g)

2 tablespoons olive oil

4 chicken livers, finely chopped

½ pound sausages, casings removed, sausage crumbled (225 g)

⅔ pound ground beef, ground twice (300 g)

While this sauce has a generic name, there is nothing run-of-the-mill about its flavor. In Rome, sauce for fettuccine means a complex meat sauce. *La salsa per le fettuccine* is prepared more or less the same way all over Rome — in private homes, restaurants, and trattorias — and it is rarely tampered with. The fettuccine should be slightly thick homemade pasta, or at least fresh store-bought. If you are not serving a large group, know that *la salsa* freezes well. This is my friend Angela's recipe.

1 Soak the dried mushrooms in a bowl of hot water until they are soft. Rinse the mushrooms and check that they are free of grit. Chop them fine and reserve.

2 Make the *battuto*: Using a mezzaluna or a large chef's knife, finely chop together the onion, carrot, celery, parsley, garlic, and pancetta, turning and mixing the ingredients as you chop.

3 Heat 3 tablespoons of the butter and the olive oil in a large flameproof casserole. Add the *battuto* and cook over low heat, stirring often, until the *battuto* is golden, about 15 minutes. Add the chopped mushrooms, chicken livers, sausages, and ground beef. Cook over moderately high heat, stirring frequently, for 15 minutes. Season with the nutmeg and salt and pepper to taste.

4 Stir in the wine and cook until the liquid is almost completely evaporated. Add the pureed tomatoes, tomato paste, and sugar and season again with salt and pepper. Lower the heat, set a wooden spoon over the edge of the pan, put on the lid, and simmer, stirring often, until the sauce is thickened (but not too dense), about 25 minutes. There will be about 6 cups of sauce.

½ teaspoon grated nutmeg

Salt and freshly ground
black pepper

½ cup dry white wine (125 ml)

4 cups pureed tomatoes,
about 2¼ pounds (1 kg)

4 tablespoons tomato paste

1 tablespoon sugar

3 pounds fresh fettuccine (1.35 kg)

5 Cook the pasta in a large pot of salted boiling water until it is al dente. Warm the dish in which you will serve the pasta. Cut the remaining 4 tablespoons butter into small pieces and add to the dish. Drain the pasta and toss with the butter and sauce. Serve at once.

NOTE: Penne rigate, rigatoni, or other dried short pasta may be used instead of fresh fettuccine. You will need 2 pounds (900 g) for first-course servings for 10 to 12.

FRESH PASTA

PRACTICALLY NO ONE makes fresh pasta at home anymore; lack of time is probably the principal reason, but the availability of fresh pasta is the other cause. You can find good freshly made pasta almost everywhere in Rome.

One of the best fresh pasta shops (if not the best) is Pasta all'Uovo Gatti Venturini, in Testaccio. My daughter is a regular customer there, and she entertains me with stories about the friendly, talkative owners, who often discuss recipes with their clients. They have very "modern" tagliolini flavored with salmon or with white truffles in the wintertime and with basil in the summertime. They make agnolotti with meat stuffing and tortellini with meat stuffing. Their delicious ravioli are filled with the freshest ricotta and parsley or spinach. They also sell various long and short pastas, quadrucci all'uova for soups, etc.

Their potato gnocchi, made only on Thursdays, are truly special and quickly sold out. (There is a Roman saying that assigns a particular dish to each day of the week, and Thursday is gnocchi day.) The owners do not make them in the summer, however, because they say the potatoes are not good then. They also eschew pumpkin and spinach gnocchi, because these watery vegetables would not hold together with the high-quality fresh potatoes they use.

Pasta all'Uovo Gatti Venturini, Via G. Branca 13, telephone: 06 574 0595

FETTUCCINE WITH FAVA BEANS

Fettuccine con le Fave

SERVES 3 TO 4

3½ pounds unshelled fava
beans (about 3 very full cups)
(1.575 kg) or 1 pound frozen
fava beans (450 g)

6 tablespoons extra virgin
olive oil

4 or 5 sliced scallions,
white part only (about ½ cup)

Salt

¼ pound boiled ham, coarsely
chopped (115 g)

1 large clove of garlic

2 tablespoons chopped
fresh mint

Freshly ground black pepper

⅔ pound dried fettuccine
(300 g)

3 tablespoons freshly grated
pecorino Romano cheese

The Romans haven't invented a pie made with fava beans yet, but they are trying hard. Here their treasured bean is combined with fettuccine for a dish that is at once elegant and homespun.

1 Shell the fava beans if they are fresh, rinse in cold water, and drain. If they are frozen, thaw and drain.

2 Heat the olive oil in a large skillet. Add the scallions and cook over low heat for about 8 minutes, until they are meltingly soft. As they cook, salt them lightly and add a tablespoon of hot water occasionally to prevent browning. Stir every now and then.

3 Add the fava beans and ⅓ cup (80 ml) hot water to the scallions. Cover the pan and cook for another 8 minutes over moderately low heat, stirring every now and then. Add the ham and cook 3 or 4 minutes longer, until the beans are tender but firm.

4 Finely chop together the garlic and mint. Add to the skillet and simmer for another 2 or 3 minutes. Season with salt and pepper to taste.

5 Cook the fettuccine in a large pot of boiling salted water until it is al dente. Drain the pasta and add to the skillet with the hot fava beans; mix well. Sprinkle the pecorino Romano cheese over the pasta, toss again, and serve at once on a heated platter, decorated with mint leaves. Pass extra pecorino Romano and a pepper mill at the table.

NOTE: If desired, pancetta can be used instead of the boiled ham. Chop it coarsely and cook with the onions over low heat until the onions are soft and translucent and the pancetta is light brown. Cook the fava beans until they are tender but firm, then follow the rest of the recipe.

PENNETTE WITH ZUCCHINI

Pennette con Zucchine

SERVES 4

½ cup olive oil (120 ml)

———

3 cloves of garlic, peeled

———

1 dried peperoncino (optional)

———

2 pounds zucchini, sliced about
⅛ inch thick (900 g)

———

1 large handful (½ cup) fresh
mint leaves, torn into pieces

———

Salt and freshly ground
black pepper

———

12 ounces pennette rigate or
similar short pasta (340 g)

———

½ cup coarsely chopped shelled
pistachios (80 g)

———

2 tablespoons pine nuts,
coarsely chopped

———

This zucchini pasta is really better if prepared and eaten right away, but in a pinch, the zucchini can be cooked ahead and reheated. It's a beautiful green dish, equally good in summer or winter, although zucchini are probably better in summer. If fresh mint is not available, dried mint may be substituted, using half the quantity called for. If only salted pistachios are available, that is fine, too; just watch the added salt. This dish is good both warm and at room temperature, which makes it perfect for a buffet.

1 Heat the olive oil in a very large skillet or flameproof casserole. Add the garlic and peperoncino and cook slowly over low heat until the garlic is golden. Discard both the garlic and the peperoncino.

2 Add the zucchini and 3 tablespoons of the mint to the hot oil. Cook, tossing, over moderately high heat until the zucchini are tender but al dente, 10 to 15 minutes. Season with salt and pepper.

3 Remove half of the zucchini to a food processor and add half the remaining mint. Process until the zucchini are finely chopped but not pureed. Return to the remaining zucchini in the pan.

4 Cook the pasta in a large pot of boiling salted water until it is al dente. Scoop out and reserve ½ cup of the pasta cooking water. Drain the pasta and mix with the hot zucchini, adding the reserved pasta cooking water slowly if the pasta seems too dry. Add half of the pistachios and all of the pine nuts; toss to mix well.

5 Sprinkle half of the remaining mint and 1 tablespoon of the remaining pistachios over the bottom of a warmed serving dish. Add the pasta with zucchini and sprinkle the rest of the mint and pistachios on top. Serve at once.

PENNE WITH PESTO AND ZUCCHINI

Penne con Pesto e Zucchine

SERVES 4 TO 6

Basil Pesto (recipe follows)

3 pounds fresh zucchini, washed and trimmed (1.35 kg)

⅓ cup extra virgin olive oil (80 ml)

Salt and freshly ground black pepper

1 pound penne rigate or plain penne (450 g)

Sprigs of fresh basil for garnish

Grated Parmesan and pecorino Romano cheeses, to pass at the table

B asil pesto is often used in Rome, principally on pasta. As the whole world knows by now, pesto is great by itself but enhanced by a simple vegetable like zucchini. Zucchini lend themselves perfectly to pasta, as shown by the numerous recipes that are passed around Rome.

1 Prepare the pesto as described below.

2 Trim the zucchini and quarter lengthwise; then cut crosswise into pieces about the same length as the penne. Heat the olive oil in a large skillet. Add the zucchini, cover, and stew over low heat, stirring occasionally, until tender but still slightly al dente, about 20 to 30 minutes. Season with salt and pepper. Drain off and reserve the oil.

3 Cook the penne in a large pot of boiling salted water until it is al dente. Drain the pasta and toss in a warmed large serving bowl with the pesto. If the pasta seems dry, add as much of the reserved oil as you need. Add the hot zucchini and mix well. Garnish the dish with basil.

4 Serve the pasta at once. Pass bowls of both cheeses at the table.

BASIL PESTO

MAKES ABOUT 1½ CUPS

⅓ cup pine nuts (60 g)

3 tablespoons peeled pistachios

2 cloves of garlic, peeled and sliced

2 ounces basil leaves (weighed after washing and drying), about 2 packed cups (60 g)

¼ cup freshly grated Parmesan cheese (25 g)

¼ cup freshly grated pecorino Romano cheese (25 g)

½ cup extra virgin olive oil (120 ml)

Salt and freshly ground black pepper

Sometimes only pecorino Romano cheese is used in pesto, but I prefer the mellower effect of a mixture of pecorino Romano and Parmesan. Also, while it is not cricket, in a pinch I have substituted walnuts for pine nuts. The flavor is very different but also good.

Put the pine nuts, pistachios, garlic, basil, Parmesan, and Romano cheese into a blender or food processor. With the machine on, gradually add the olive oil in a slow stream, as in making mayonnaise. Scrape down the sides as necessary. Season with salt and pepper to taste. Cover and reserve the pesto until needed.

SPICY PENNE

Penne all'Arrabbiata

SERVES 8 TO 12

¼ cup extra virgin olive oil

2 medium onions, chopped

4 cloves of garlic, chopped

½ pound pancetta or fat bacon
(do not use smoked bacon), cut
into thin julienne strips (225 g)

2 large cans (32 ounces each)
Italian plum tomatoes, drained
(1.8 kg)

1½ teaspoons salt, or to taste

2 dried peperoncini or
½ teaspoon hot red pepper flakes

2 pounds penne or other short
pasta (900 g)

½ pound pecorino Romano
cheese,* grated (225 g)

Chopped basil or parsley,
for garnish

*If you prefer your cheese less sharp, you
can use half pecorino Romano and half
Parmesan here.

This classic favorite is standard fare in at least half of the dinner parties thrown in Rome. For that matter, you're just as likely to find it at country suppers. The dish should be very spicy, flavored with dried hot red peppers. The Romans think that these peperoncini are "good" for you, the absolute opposite of black pepper, which is "bad" for you. I have given two versions: the first, made with canned tomatoes, is used often, but the second one, prepared from fresh tomatoes, is the classic recipe.

1 In a very large skillet or flameproof casserole, big enough to contain both the sauce and the pasta, heat the oil. Add the onions and garlic and cook over moderately high heat, stirring, until light brown, 10 to 12 minutes.

2 Add the pancetta and sauté until brown but not crisp. Add the tomatoes, salt, and peperoncini or hot pepper flakes; the sauce should be *piccante*, or spicy. Simmer uncovered, mashing the tomatoes with the back of a wooden spoon, until the sauce has thickened, about 20 minutes.

3 Cook the penne in a large pot of salted boiling water until it is al dente. Drain and add to the hot tomato sauce. Mix over low heat, adding 2 handfuls of pecorino Romano cheese as you toss. Turn the penne out onto a large platter and sprinkle with the chopped basil or parsley.

4 Serve with extra grated Romano and a pepper mill.

CLASSIC PENNE ALL'ARRABBIATA WITH FRESH TOMATOES

SERVES 6 TO 8 AS A FIRST COURSE,
4 TO 6 AS A MAIN COURSE

⅓ cup extra virgin olive oil
(80 ml)

½ small onion, very finely sliced

2¼ pounds ripe plum tomatoes,
peeled, seeded, and cut into
chunks (1 kg)

Salt

1 dried peperoncino, broken
into pieces, or ½ teaspoon hot
red pepper flakes

1⅓ pounds penne (600 g)

Here is the original Roman version of this spicy dish. Fresh tomatoes lend themselves to use in smaller quantities than do the canned ones used in the previous recipe, but the sweetness and intensity of flavor when the vegetable is in season makes it clear why this is a classic.

1 In a large skillet, heat the olive oil over moderate heat. Add the onion and cook, stirring, until soft and translucent, 3 to 5 minutes.

2 Add the tomatoes, season with salt to taste, and add the peperoncino or hot pepper flakes. Cook over brisk heat until the sauce has thickened, mashing the tomatoes with the back of a wooden spoon, about 15 to 20 minutes.

3 Cook the penne in a large pot of salted boiling water until it is al dente. Drain, mix rapidly with the hot sauce, and serve at once.

IF TOMATOES ARE green and/or not flavorful, add a teaspoon or two of good tomato paste to them. It will heighten the taste.

OVEN-BAKED PASTA

Pasta al Gratin

SERVES 8 TO 10

Béchamel Sauce (recipe follows)

1⅓ pounds penne rigate or other short pasta (600 g)

4 tablespoons unsalted butter (60 g)

1¼ cups freshly grated Parmesan cheese (125 g)

Salt and freshly ground black pepper

1 pound fior di latte or fresh mozzarella cheese, shredded (450 g)

Because this dish can be prepared ahead of time, it is perfect for casual entertaining. A typical Roman family dish, it is served most often on Sundays. Instead of true Italian mozzarella made from buffalo milk, for this pasta we use use *fior di latte*, which is made of cow's milk and is much less expensive.

For the record, this pasta is one of the reasons my telephone bills went sky-high while my daughter was studying in New York — she would always lose the recipe. Now she makes it better than I do.

1 Make the bechamel. Let it cool to room temperature before using. Preheat the oven to 375°F (190°C).

2 Cook the pasta in a large pot of boiling salted water until it is al dente. Drain the pasta and return it to the pot with the butter and two-thirds of the Parmesan cheese. Season with salt and pepper to taste. (If preparing in advance, spread the pasta out on a large platter to cool completely at this point.)

3 Mix the béchamel with the pasta, reserving a little sauce for the top of the dish. Generously grind some more black pepper over the top and add the shredded *fior di latte* or mozzarella. Toss to mix. Turn into a buttered 16-by-11-inch (40-by-28-cm) baking dish. Spoon the reserved béchamel over the top and sprinkle on the remaining Parmesan cheese.

4 Bake the pasta for 45 minutes, or until the surface is brown and crusty. This may take slightly longer if the dish has been prepared in advance. Serve hot. Refrigerate any leftover pasta but heat it, covered, before serving it.

BECHAMEL SAUCE

Balsamella

MAKES ABOUT 7 CUPS

4½ cups milk (1.1 l)

1 cup flour (110 g)

¼ teaspoon salt

⅛ teaspoon freshly ground
black pepper

8 tablespoons butter (110 g)

1 cup heavy cream (250 ml)

⅔ cup freshly grated Parmesan
cheese (70 g)

Grated zest of a small lemon,
washed (optional)

Freshly grated nutmeg

1 Put half of the milk, all of the flour, and the salt and pepper into a blender and mix for 30 seconds. Melt the butter in a large saucepan and pour in the milk mixture. Stir in the rest of the milk and the cream. Bring to a simmer, stirring, and cook, stirring constantly, until the sauce boils and thickens, about 5 minutes.

2 Remove from the heat and stir in the Parmesan cheese and the lemon zest, if you're using it. Season with nutmeg to taste. Cover the surface with plastic wrap and let the sauce cool. Refrigerate if preparing it in advance.

MOZZARELLA CHEESE

IN ITALY MOZZARELLA is only made from buffalo milk and we rarely use it for cooking. Instead, we use *fior di latte*, made from cows' milk, a cheese very similar to the mozzarella found in America. Real *mozzarella di bufala* has a special mark, usually a small buffalo, and is most often eaten as is, with only a trickle of special extra virgin olive oil, salt, and pepper. Truly, for best flavor and texture, it should be eaten within 2 to 3 hours of its making, and the people from Campania, where it is mostly produced, think even that is too long.

BAKED MACARONI WITH CAULIFLOWER

Maccheroni con Cavolfiore

SERVES 3 TO 4

2½ pounds cauliflower
(1.125 kg)

⅓ cup extra virgin olive oil
(80 ml)

1 clove of garlic, peeled and
crushed

1 dried peperoncino, or hot red
pepper flakes to taste

Salt and freshly ground
black pepper

⅔ pound pennette, maccheron-
celli, or other short tubular pasta
(300 g)

⅔ cup freshly grated pecorino
Romano cheese (65 g)

Cauliflower — as well as the Roman broccoflower (*broccolo romano*) suggested in the variation
that follows — are particularly identified with Rome
and the Roman countryside. It is said these vegetables
"marry" pasta well — a Roman way of explaining
that the two things go well together.

1 Preheat the oven to 375°F (190°C). Lightly oil an 11-by-7-inch
(28-by-18-cm) baking dish.

2 Remove the florets from the central stalk of the vegetable, cutting
them so that they are all about the same size, 1 to 1½ inches; discard
the stalk. In a large saucepan of boiling salted water, cook the florets
al dente, 2 to 3 minutes; drain.

3 Heat the olive oil in a large skillet. Add the garlic and whole
peperoncino, if using it. (If using hot pepper flakes, add with the
cauliflower.) Cook slowly over low heat until the garlic is brown;
then discard both garlic and peperoncino.

4 Add the cauliflower to the skillet and cook over moderately low
heat, stirring every now and then, for about 10 minutes, until light
brown and tender. Season with salt and pepper.

5 Meanwhile, in a large pot of boiling salted water, cook the pasta
until it is al dente; drain and return to the pot. Add ½ cup of the
pecorino Romano cheese and half of the cauliflower; toss to mix
well. Turn into the oiled baking dish and spread the remaining
cauliflower on top. Season with a generous grinding of black
pepper. Sprinkle with the remaining cheese.

Bake for about 20 minutes, or until the top is lightly colored. Traditionally, this pasta is served hot, but cold leftovers are good, too, especially very late at night.

MACARONI WITH BROCCOFLOWER

Prepare the pasta as described above, but substitute an equal amount of broccoflower, also called *broccolo romano* or *broccoli romaneschi*, for the cauliflower.

WALKING IN ROME

SAN CRISPINO is near the Trevi Fountain and near the little open air market in Via del Lavatore, on one side limited by the walls of the Quirinale (where the president of the Republic lives). It is near the Pasta Museum in Piazza Scanderbeg too. And only a short walk up to the left from the Pasta Museum is the Quirinale with its beautiful statue from Roman antiquity and a magnificent view of the Roman rooftops, church cupolas, and Roman sky. A little further along on the side of the Quirinale is Sant'Andrea al Quirinale church by Bernini and Boromini's San Carlino alle Quattro Fontane church, both absolutely breathtaking.

BAKED RIGATONI WITH SMALL TOMATOES

Rigatoni con Pomodorini

SERVES 6 TO 8

2½ pounds large cherry
tomatoes (1.125 kg)

Big pinch of sugar

½ pound onions (optional)
(225 g)

½ cup extra virgin olive oil
(120 ml)

Salt and freshly ground
black pepper

Dried oregano or chopped
fresh basil

1⅓ pounds rigatoni or other
short pasta (600 g)

The small (almost cherry) tomatoes we use for this quick and easy pasta are called *pachino*. They come from Sicily, near the town of Pachino, where evidently they got their name. The earth that produces this special tomato is said to be unusually rich volcanic soil. They are about one inch wide when halved and surprisingly flavorful, very good in pasta sauces. They are also used as a simple antipasto vegetable, cut into halves, trickled with extra virgin olive oil, and sprinkled with salt and oregano. There is a similar tomato now marketed in America; if these are not available, cherry tomatoes can be substituted.

1 Preheat the oven to 375°F (190°C).

2 Cut the tomatoes in half and dust the cut halves with a light sprinkling of sugar. Put them into an ovenproof dish with shallow sides, preferably one that can double as a serving dish. If using the onions, slice them very thin, using a mandoline if you have one. Scatter the onion slices over the tomatoes. Pour the oil over all and mix gently. Season with salt, pepper, and oregano or basil to taste.

3 Bake for 20 to 30 minutes, stirring once or twice, until the tomatoes are soft and lightly colored.

4 In a large pot of salted water, cook the pasta until it is al dente. Drain well and transfer to a warmed serving bowl. Pour the tomatoes and onions with all their oil over the pasta, toss gently, and serve.

NOTE: If the tomatoes are baked without the onions, add a handful of fresh basil torn into pieces, instead of the oregano, to the pasta as you mix it with the tomatoes.

GRATIN OF RIGATONI WITH RADICCHIO

Maccheroni al Radicchio Gratinati

SERVES 4 OR 5

¼ cup extra virgin olive oil (60 ml)

2 tablespoons finely chopped onion

1 pound radicchio di Treviso, trimmed and coarsely shredded (450 g)

Salt and freshly ground black pepper

⅓ cup red wine (80 ml)

4 tablespoons butter (60 g)

½ cup heavy cream (125 ml)

1 pound rigatoni (450 g)

½ cup freshly grated Parmesan cheese (50 g)

Although this pasta is not Roman—it is actually Senegalese—how about that?—I include it because it is a family pasta for me. The dish makes a stunning first course and I guarantee that all your friends will ask for the recipe.

1 Preheat the oven to 400°F (200°C).

2 In a large nonreactive skillet, heat the olive oil over moderately low heat. Add the onion and cook slowly until it is soft and translucent, 5 to 7 minutes. Add the radicchio, season lightly with salt and pepper, mix well, cover, and cook over low heat for 5 minutes, or until the radicchio is wilted.

3 Pour in the red wine, stir, cover again, and allow to cook gently for 5 minutes longer, or until the radicchio is soft, stirring occasionally. Season with salt and generously with pepper, and, if the wine has not evaporated, cook for a few minutes longer uncovered until the radicchio remains moist but most of the liquid is absorbed.

4 In another skillet or flameproof casserole large enough to hold the pasta too, melt the butter. Add the radicchio mixture and the cream. Simmer over moderately low heat, stirring occasionally, until the cream thickens, about 5 minutes.

5 Meanwhile, in a large pot of boiling salted water, cook the pasta until it is al dente. Drain well and add the pasta to the skillet with the radicchio. Mix, tossing with the Parmesan cheese. Transfer to a heatproof platter and bake for 5 minutes. Serve at once.

SPINACH AND RICOTTA GNOCCHI

Gnocchi di Spinaci e Ricotta

SERVES 4

1 pound fresh spinach, well rinsed (450 g), or 1 package (10 ounces) frozen spinach (280 g)

10 ounces ricotta, drained (280 g)

Salt and freshly ground black pepper

6 tablespoons freshly grated Parmesan cheese

2 egg yolks

¼ teaspoon grated nutmeg

Flour, for dredging the gnocchi

4 tablespoons butter (60 g)

9 fresh sage leaves

This is just about my favorite dish here in Rome, gnocchi made with ricotta and spinach or Swiss chard. It can be a substantial first course or a one-dish meal. Below, you'll find the classic recipe, followed by two variations. One uses fontina cheese and cream. The other one has the filling enclosed in crespelle (crepes) and baked in the oven, sometimes served with a light tomato sauce. Children love these gnocchi.

1 Cook the fresh spinach in the water clinging to its leaves after washing, until wilted but still bright green. Drain and let cool. Whether the spinach is cooked fresh or thawed frozen, drain and squeeze it to remove as much water as possible. Finely chop but do not puree. If the spinach is frozen, put into a pan without water and, on lowest heat, cook the spinach, turning, until just cooked, a few minutes.

2 Mix the chopped spinach with the ricotta and season with salt and pepper to taste. Add 3 tablespoons of the Parmesan cheese, the egg yolks, and the nutmeg. Add enough of the remaining 3 tablespoons Parmesan, 1 tablespoon at a time, until the mixture binds but remains soft. It may not take all the cheese. If prepared ahead, cover and refrigerate.

3 Bring a large pan of salted water to a simmer. Sift the flour onto a work surface or a large platter.

4 Using 2 tablespoons, form oval gnocchi about 2½ inches long and about 1½ inches wide and roll them in the flour to coat them. Using a slotted spoon, slide the gnocchi into the simmering water; do not overcrowd the pan. When the gnocchi rise to the surface, let them simmer for 3 to 4 minutes. Remove from the pan with a slotted spoon and put them into a warm dish. Cover and set in a warm place while preparing the others.

5 Melt the butter in a medium skillet over moderate heat. Add the sage leaves and sauté until light brown. Pour the butter and sage leaves over the gnocchi and serve at once. Pass extra Parmesan cheese at the table.

BAKED SPINACH AND RICOTTA GNOCCHI WITH FONTINA AND CREAM

Prepare the gnocchi as described above, but omit the butter and sage. Transfer the poached gnocchi to a buttered baking dish, preferably one that will look nice on the table. Sprinkle 5 ounces (140 g) of shredded Italian fontina cheese over the top and drizzle ⅔ cup (160 ml) fresh heavy cream over the gnocchi. Bake in a preheated 375°F (190°C) oven for 25 minutes, until bubbly and golden brown.

RICOTTA

RICOTTA IS CONSIDERED Rome's other cheese, even though, since it is made from the whey, it is not a true cheese. Like pecorino, it is made of sheep's milk and is available all year round. *Ri,* "again," and *cotta,* "cooked," explains how it is made. After the pecorino is made, the whey that is left is cooked again and the ricotta made from it. Watery at first, it is put into the traditional loosely woven willow baskets, which give it a shape while allowing the liquid to drain. It is absolutely delicious and should be eaten as fresh as possible. If necessary, it should drain all night. In northern Italy ricotta is made with cow's milk, too. Ricotta should always be kept in the refrigerator.

CREPES STUFFED WITH SPINACH AND RICOTTA

Crespelle di Spinaci e Ricotta

SERVES 6 TO 8

1 recipe Spinach and Ricotta Gnocchi (page 78), uncooked and with the butter and sage leaves omitted

½ cup milk (120 ml)

½ cup flour (70 g)

4 eggs

¼ teaspoon salt

Pinch of freshly ground black pepper

Butter, for the crepe pan

⅔ cup heavy cream (160 ml)

2½ tablespoons grated Parmesan cheese

The spinach and ricotta mixture used for gnocchi on page 78 can also be rolled up in *crespelle*, thin Italian crepes, and baked in the oven.

1 Prepare the spinach and ricotta mixture to use as filling. If made ahead, cover and refrigerate; let the filling return to room temperature before proceeding.

2 Make the *crespelle* batter: Put all the milk, flour, eggs, salt, and pepper into a blender and whirl for 30 seconds, or until the batter is smooth and creamy. Pour into a small bowl set near the stove.

3 Put a tablespoon or 2 of butter in a saucer and place near the bowl of crespelle batter. Heat and butter a 6-inch (15-cm) crepe pan and ladle in just enough batter to barely cover the bottom of the pan, quickly rotating the pan to spread the batter evenly. (A ¼-cup measure makes pouring easy.) Cook over moderately high heat, reducing the heat as necessary, until the crepe is light brown, 1 to 2 minutes. Turn over and cook briefly on the other side, which will brown in spots, 15 to 20 seconds. Repeat with all the batter. Stack the cooked crepes on a plate, separating them with squares of waxed paper. If preparing in advance, cover and refrigerate until needed.

4 When ready to serve the *crespelle*, preheat the oven to 350°F (175°C).

5 Divide the filling among the *crespelle*, rolling them up. Place them, seam side down, in a buttered shallow baking dish. Pour the cream over the crespelle and sprinkle the Parmesan cheese on top. Bake for 25 to 30 minutes, until hot throughout and light brown on top.

SEMOLINA GNOCCHI ROMAN STYLE

Gnocchi di Semolino alla Romana

SERVES 6

1 quart milk (1 l)

1¼ cups semolina (250 g)

Salt

2 egg yolks

6 tablespoons unsalted butter (90 g)

1¼ cups freshly grated Parmesan cheese (125 g)

These can be prepared a day ahead. They also freeze perfectly and are very, very good — highly recommended for children. These gnocchi are one of Rome's best-known dishes and are even prepared in the local restaurants, in small ovenproof dishes suitable for a single portion. At home, one large gratin dish is much easier to assemble.

1 Bring the milk to a boil in a large pot. Gradually sprinkle in the semolina "like rain," as the Romans say, stirring with a wooden spoon. Cook, stirring constantly, for about 6 minutes, until thickened. The semolina should be difficult to stir.

2 Remove from the heat and season the semolina with salt to taste. Mix in the egg yolks, 3 tablespoons of the butter, and half of the Parmesan cheese. Dampen a work surface (preferably marble but Formica will do) with cold water and turn out the semolina onto it. Quickly smooth with a dampened spatula or the blade of a large knife to a thickness of ½ inch. Let stand until completely cooled.

3 Using a 2-inch-round cookie cutter, cut as many rounds as possible from the semolina. Arrange them, overlapping slightly, in a buttered 16-by-18-inch (40-by-46-cm) gratin dish. Sprinkle the remaining Parmesan cheese evenly over the top and dot with the remaining butter. (The dish can be prepared up to this point 2 days ahead of time and refrigerated covered; or it can be frozen. Let return to room temperature before baking.)

4 When ready to cook the gnocchi, preheat the oven to 375°F (190°C). Bake the gnocchi for 30 minutes, or until they are piping hot and light brown on top.

VEGETABLE TIMBALE BETTOJA STYLE

Timballo con Verdura Bettoja

SERVES 8

Rich Pastry for Timballo
(recipe on page 84)

Cheese Sauce (recipe on
page 85)

3 tablespoons extra virgin
olive oil

¼ pound trimmed pancetta,
cut in fine julienne strips (110 g)

1 small onion, finely chopped

1 dried peperoncino, or hot red
pepper flakes to taste

2½ cups sliced fresh or frozen
artichoke hearts (350 g)

2 cups fresh or frozen fava beans
(360 g)

2 cups fresh or frozen peas
(250 g)

Salt and freshly ground
black pepper

For my mother-in-law's hundredth birthday we had a big family celebration cum family reunion with relatives from America, France, and Italy. We prepared it with great care, because they are all great cooks and very food conscious. It wasn't easy, but it was highly successful and nice to remember. This family recipe was one of the centerpieces of the meal.

Timballo is one of the great southern Italian assemblages: a rich dough encasing pasta, thick sauce (cream or tomato), and one of any number of fillings; it is baked in a springform pan and then unmolded to present a golden brown torte at table. This vegetable timballo is from my husband's family, and it is prepared in the spring when the famous Roman vegetables are at their best.

All versions of this dish are somewhat elaborate, but keep in mind that all the elements can be prepared in advance, and the timballo assembled and baked just before serving. It is, in fact, a spectacular dish for entertaining.

1 Make the pastry as directed on page 84. Allow to rest, according to the manner prepared.

2 Make the cheese sauce: If prepared in advance, cover the surface of the béchamel with plastic wrap to prevent a skin from forming. Let the béchamel cool to tepid, then refrigerate it. (The sauce can be made up to 2 days in advance.) Let return to room temperature before proceeding.

3 To make the filling: In a large flameproof casserole, combine the olive oil and pancetta and cook over moderate heat, stirring, until the pancetta is lightly colored, about 5 minutes. Add the onion and peperoncino and cook, stirring, until the onion is soft and translucent, 3 to 4

1½ tablespoons finely chopped
fresh mint

10 ounces small penne rigate
or sedanini (300 g)

¼ cup freshly grated Parmesan
cheese (25 g)

¼ cup freshly grated pecorino
Romano cheese (25 g)

1 egg yolk beaten with
1 tablespoon cold water

minutes. Put in the artichoke hearts along with 2 tablespoons hot water and stir for about 2 minutes. Add the fava beans with 1 tablespoon hot water and cook for 3 minutes. Add the peas with another tablespoon hot water and continue cooking for about 10 minutes, stirring now and then, until the vegetables are just tender. Discard the peperoncino and season the vegetables generously with salt and black pepper. Stir in the mint. Remove from the heat and let cool.

4 Bring a pot of salted water to a boil for the pasta. Cook the pasta until it is al dente and drain. Spread the pasta out on a marble surface or a large platter to cool. When cold, mix the pasta with the béchamel.

5 When you are ready to finish the *timballo*, preheat the oven to 375°F (190°C). Butter and flour a 10-inch (26-cm) springform pan.

6 Lightly flour a work surface, preferably of marble, where you will roll out the crust. Cut the pastry into 2 pieces, one larger for the bottom crust. Roll out the bottom crust about ⅛ inch thick. Detach the pastry from the work surface with a long metal spatula and drape it over the rolling pin. Unroll it onto the prepared springform pan and cut away the excess pastry.

7 Put half of the pasta with béchamel sauce into the pastry-lined springform pan. Over this put the cooled vegetable filling. Sprinkle with the remaining cheeses. Spread the rest of the pasta over the filling. Roll out the top crust and unfold it on top of the pasta. Fold any extra crust under the edges and crimp. Paint the crust with the egg yolk beaten with cold water.

8 Bake the *timballo* for 40 to 45 minutes, until the top is colored. Allow to rest for 15 minutes. Gently remove the sides of the pan and with the help of a large spatula, slide the *timballo* onto a serving platter. Cut into wedges to serve.

RICH PASTRY FOR TIMBALLO

Pasta Frolla

MAKES ENOUGH FOR A 10-INCH TIMBALE

3⅓ cups flour (400 g)

———

2 sticks (8 ounces) cold unsalted butter, cut into bits (200 g)

———

4 large egg yolks, at room temperature

———

½ cup superfine sugar (140 g)

———

Grated zest of 1 large lemon

———

This recipe contains more butter and egg yolks and a lot less sugar than the standard *pasta frolla* (page 256). It is our family's favorite version, and I give our traditional hand method. To make this same dough using a food processor or electric mixer, see page 257.

1 Sift the flour into a large bowl or directly onto an appropriate work surface, preferably marble.

2 Using your fingertips, quickly rub the butter and flour together, working it until the mixture is crumbly.

3 Beat the egg yolks with the sugar and lemon zest until blended. Make a well in the center of the flour mixture and pour in the yolks. Stir with your fingers or a wooden spoon until the dough is evenly moistened.

4 Press the dough into a ball, flatten into a disc, and wrap in waxed paper. Set aside in a cool place or refrigerate for at least 30 minutes before rolling out.

CHEESE SAUCE

MAKES ABOUT 2½ CUPS

2 tablespoons butter (30 g)

1 cup milk (250 ml)

¼ cup flour (30 g)

1 cup heavy cream (250 ml)

¼ cup freshly grated Parmesan
cheese (25 g)

¼ cup freshly grated pecorino
Romano cheese (25 g)

Salt and freshly ground
black pepper

1 Melt the butter in a heavy medium saucepan. Put the milk and flour in a blender and blend for a minute. Pour into the saucepan with the butter and add the cream.

2 Bring to a simmer, stirring constantly. Simmer, stirring often, for 5 minutes. Off the heat, stir in the Parmesan and pecorino Romano cheeses. Season with salt and pepper to taste.

St. Angelo's Bridge

TIMBALE OF THE LAZZARONI FAMILY

Timballo di Casa Lazzaroni

SERVES 8 TO 10

Rich Pastry for Timballo, recipe on page 84

White Sauce (recipe on page 88)

1 ounce dried porcini mushrooms (30 g)

1 small onion, coarsely chopped

1 small carrot, coarsely chopped

½ small celery rib, coarsely chopped

5 ounces pancetta, trimmed and coarsely chopped (140 g)

6 tablespoons olive oil

10 ounces moderately spicy sausages, casings removed, thinly sliced (280 g)

½ pound chicken livers, cut into small pieces (225 g)

Salt and freshly ground black pepper

When you are entertaining for a holiday or very special occasion, this is a *timballo* to consider. The recipe comes from my friend who entertains in the grandest fashion almost nightly. She uses quail eggs, which are charming for this recipe, but you can eliminate them — it's certainly rich enough already — or use quartered small hen's eggs. In Rome, *timballi* are often served warm, almost at room temperature, and so they are perfect for a buffet.

1 Make the pastry and allow it to rest, according to the manner prepared.

2 Make the White Sauce.

3 To make the filling: Soak the porcini in warm water to cover. When ready to use them, rinse thoroughly to remove any grit and chop them coarsely.

4 Make the *battuto*: Put the onion, carrot, celery, and pancetta on a cutting board and finely chop all together.

5 Heat 3 tablespoons of the olive oil in a very large deep skillet or flameproof casserole. Add the *battuto*, sausages, and chicken livers. Cook over moderate heat, stirring often, for about 10 minutes, or until the vegetables are soft. Add the chopped porcini mushrooms to the filling and simmer for 5 minutes. Season with salt and pepper to taste and set aside.

6 Mix the ground veal with the cream, rosemary, 2 tablespoons of the Parmesan cheese, and salt and pepper.

½ pound ground veal (225 g)

3 or 4 tablespoons heavy cream

1½ tablespoons finely chopped
fresh rosemary

⅓ cup grated Parmesan cheese
(45 g)

⅔ pound small penne rigate
or sedanini (300 g)

3½ tablespoons butter (50 g)

3½ tablespoons grated pecorino
Romano cheese

8 hard-cooked quail eggs

1 egg yolk, beaten with
1 tablespoon water

7 Make small meatballs, about 35, rolling them in the palm of your hand. Heat the remaining 3 tablespoons oil in a medium skillet and cook the little meatballs over moderate heat, turning, until they are golden brown.

8 In a large pot of boiling salted water, cook the pasta until it is al dente. Drain and toss with the butter, the remaining Parmesan cheese, and the pecorino Romano cheese. Spread out the pasta and let it cool completely.

9 When ready to bake the *timballo*, heat the oven to 375°F (190°C). Butter and flour a 10-inch (26-cm) springform pan.

10 Lightly flour a work surface, preferably marble, where you will roll out the crust. Cut the pastry into 2 pieces, one larger for the bottom crust. Roll out the bottom crust about ⅛ inch thick. Detach the pastry from the work surface with a long metal spatula and drape it over the rolling pin. Unroll it onto the prepared springform pan and cut away the excess pastry.

11 Mix together the cold pasta and the béchamel and spread half the pasta in the pastry-lined springform pan. Mix together the meatballs and the loose filling and distribute the mixture evenly over the pasta. Arrange the quail eggs evenly over the fillings. Cover with the rest of the pasta. Roll out the top crust and unfold it on top of the pasta. Fold any extra crust under the edges and crimp. Paint the crust with the yolk beaten with cold water.

12 Bake the *timballo* for 40 to 45 minutes, or until the top is golden brown. Let rest for 15 minutes on a rack. Gently remove the sides of the pan and with the help of a large spatula, slide the *timballo* onto a serving platter. Let stand for at least 15 minutes before cutting into wedges to serve.

WHITE SAUCE

Salsa Bianca

MAKES ABOUT 2½ CUPS

2 tablespoons butter (30 g)

2½ cups milk (600 ml)

¼ cup flour (30 g)

Salt and freshly ground pepper

Grated nutmeg

This is not as rich as the béchamel used in the Vegetable Timbale Bettoja Style, because the meats themselves are so unctuous.

1 Melt the butter in a heavy medium saucepan. Put the milk and flour in a blender and blend for 1 minute. Pour into the saucepan with the butter.

2 Bring to a simmer, stirring constantly. Simmer, stirring often, for 5 minutes. Season with salt and pepper and nutmeg to taste.

RICE AND EGGPLANT

Riso e Melanzane

SERVES 4 TO 6

1¼ pounds eggplant, the long,
narrow kind if possible (570 g)

⅓ cup plus 1 tablespoon extra
virgin olive oil (95 ml)

1 clove of garlic, peeled and
crushed

1 dried peperoncino, or hot red
pepper flakes to taste

Coarse salt and freshly ground
black pepper

1 pound Arborio, Carnaroli,
or other risotto rice (450 g)

About 6 cups simmering
chicken broth (1½ l)

2 tablespoons chopped parsley

Rice dishes in Rome have the Roman stamp, like this one from the Ghetto. It comes from a painter friend who married into a well-known Jewish family. The number of peperoncini or amount of hot red pepper flakes is up to you, but bear in mind that the finished dish should be a little spicy.

1 Trim the eggplant and cut into approximately ¾-inch dice.

2 In a large heavy saucepan, heat the olive oil with the garlic and peperoncino. When the garlic is light brown, add the eggplant. Season with coarse salt and pepper. Cook over moderate heat, stirring often, for 30 minutes. Discard the garlic and peperoncino.

3 Add the rice to the eggplant and cook, stirring often, for about 7 minutes. The eggplant will be almost a puree. Begin adding the broth as for a risotto, 1 cup at a time, stirring until absorbed. The rice will be ready in 18 to 20 minutes, depending on the rice and on your taste. Season with more salt and black pepper to taste.

4 Serve the hot rice in a large platter and sprinkle the parsley over the top.

MOLDED RICE WITH MUSHROOMS

Pasticcio di Riso con Funghi

SERVES 6 TO 8

1½ ounces dried porcini mushrooms (40 g)

⅓ cup plus 1 tablespoon extra virgin olive oil (100 ml)

1½ pounds mushrooms, trimmed, washed, and sliced (675 g)

Salt and freshly ground black pepper

3½ tablespoons butter (50 g)

3 tablespoons finely chopped onion

2 cups frozen peas (280 g)

2 cups Arborio or other risotto rice (400 g)

Rich Béchamel (recipe follows)

7 thin slices of boiled ham

½ cup freshly grated Parmesan cheese (50 g)

Rice is often served in the evenings for parties, and this recipe is just that: a party dish. Most of the preparations can be done in advance, but the rice must be boiled at the last minute. This recipe comes from a Roman family known for their good food.

1 Soak the dried porcini in a bowl of tepid water until they are soft, about 20 minutes. Remove the porcini, squeezing excess liquid back into the bowl. Rinse the mushrooms, trim off any hard bits, and chop the mushrooms not too fine. Strain the soaking liquid through a coffee filter or a double thickness of cheesecloth and reserve it.

2 While the porcini are soaking, heat ¼ cup (60 ml) of the olive oil in a large skillet. Add the fresh mushrooms and cook over moderately high heat, stirring often, until they are tender. Season with salt and pepper. Remove from the heat and set aside.

3 In a large flameproof casserole, melt 1½ tablespoons of the butter in the remaining 1 tablespoon olive oil over moderately low heat. Add the onion and cook, stirring occasionally, until soft, 5 to 7 minutes. Add the frozen peas and cook, stirring often, for 15 minutes. Add the chopped porcini and cooked mushrooms to the peas along with some of the reserved mushroom soaking liquid if the pan is dry, and simmer for 2 minutes. (This can be done ahead as long as you don't overcook the peas.)

4 When you are almost ready to serve, boil the rice in a large saucepan of boiling salted water until it is al dente, about 18 minutes.

5 While the rice is cooking, set aside ½ cup of the béchamel. Add the remainder to the peas and mushrooms and fold to mix. Warm gently until heated through. Use the ham slices to line a buttered 2-quart (2-liter) ring mold.

6 Drain the rice and dress it with the remaining 2 tablespoons butter, the reserved ½ cup béchamel, and the Parmesan cheese. Spoon the rice into the mold, packing it with the back of a spoon, and give the mold two firm raps on the counter to settle it. Turn the molded rice out on a large platter, preferably one with a rim, and spoon the mushroom and pea filling into the center. Serve at once.

RICH BECHAMEL

Balsamella Ricca

MAKES ABOUT 3 CUPS

2 cups milk (500 ml)

½ cup plus 2 tablespoons flour (80 g)

Salt and freshly ground pepper

5 tablespoons butter (70 g)

1 cup heavy cream (250 ml)

Put the milk in a blender with the flour, salt, and pepper and blend for 1 minute. Melt the butter in a heavy saucepan and add the milk mixture and the cream. Bring slowly to a simmer, stirring constantly, for 5 minutes. Remove from the heat and if not using at once, cover the surface of the béchamel with plastic wrap to prevent a skin from forming.

RICE WITH SQUAB

Riso con Piccioni

SERVES 8

4 ready-to-cook young pigeons (squab), about 1 pound each (1.8 kg total)

¼ cup plus 2 tablespoons extra virgin olive oil (60 ml)

Salt and freshly ground black pepper

Sprig of fresh rosemary

1 bay leaf

1 cup dry Marsala (250 ml)

½ teaspoon anchovy paste

4½ cups chicken broth (1,100 ml)

4 tablespoons butter (60 g)

1 medium onion, very finely chopped

3 cups (1⅓ pounds) Arborio, Carnaroli, or other risotto rice (600 g)

1 cup freshly grated Parmesan cheese (100 g)

Fresh black truffles (optional)

This grand first course, served in Rome in winter, looks truly elegant on a silver platter. The recipe is from a friend of mine who cannot cook but who is accustomed to good food; it is her family's recipe, and I am sure that each of their cooks must have added or taken away something over the years. This is the way Janif, her present cook, prepares it, always following the traditional family recipe.

1 Rub the pigeons with 1 tablespoon of the olive oil and season them with salt and pepper inside and with salt outside. Tie the legs and wings close to the body with kitchen string.

2 Put ¼ cup of the olive oil with the rosemary and bay leaf in a large flameproof casserole and set it over high heat. When the oil is hot, add the pigeons and brown them, turning, about 3 minutes for each side.

3 Pour ½ cup of the Marsala over the birds and mix the anchovy paste into the liquid in the center of the casserole. Turn the pigeons breast down, cover the pan with a lid, and reduce the heat to low. Cook for ½ hour, turning after 15 minutes. Pour on the remaining Marsala, cover, and finish cooking the birds, about 10 minutes longer. Test with the tip of a small knife: the juices in the thickest part of the thigh should run clear. Remove from the heat and transfer the birds to a cutting board. Remove and discard the rosemary and bay leaf; reserve the sauce in the casserole.

4 When the pigeons are cool enough to handle, cut them in half with kitchen scissors and remove and discard the skin. Pull the meat from the bones (discard the bones or save them for stock) and tear it into strips with your hands. Return the birds to the sauce in the pan.

(The recipe can be prepared to this point up to a day in advance. Cover and refrigerate.)

5 When you're ready to finish the dish, preheat the oven to 375°F (190°C). In a small saucepan, bring the broth to a simmer. In another pan that can go into the oven, melt the butter in the remaining 1 tablespoon olive oil over moderate heat. Add the onion and cook until soft and translucent, 3 to 5 minutes. Add the rice and cook, stirring, for several minutes, until it turns white and opaque. Add all of the simmering broth, stir once, and transfer the pan to the oven. Bake uncovered for 18 minutes, or until the rice is tender and has absorbed the broth.

6 While the rice is baking, gently reheat the pigeons in their sauce.

7 Remove the rice from the oven when it is ready and stir in the Parmesan cheese. Spoon the rice into a buttered 2-quart (2-liter) ring mold; pack it down and smooth it with the back of a spoon. Return to the oven for 2 minutes.

8 Remove the mold from the oven and let the rice stand for 2 or 3 minutes, then invert to unmold onto a large rimmed platter. Fill the center with the squab and its sauce. If black truffles are available, slice them generously over the finished dish and serve at once.

NOTE: To make the dish richer, add, with the birds, ½ very finely chopped onion, ½ pound chicken livers that have been cleaned and cut into small pieces, ½ pound crumbled sausages, and 1 ounce dried porcini mushrooms, soaked, drained, and chopped. Continue the rest of the recipe as above, adding 1 or 2 tablespoons of water if necessary. Add 1 tablespoon of extra butter when the dish is finished. This makes a much more substantial dish, an excellent main course. Adjust the seasonings at the end of the cooking time.

RISOTTO WITH PORCINI MUSHROOMS

Risotto con i Funghi Porcini

SERVES 4 TO 6

6 tablespoons butter (90 g)

½ medium onion, finely chopped

1 pound Arborio, Carnaroli, or other risotto rice (450 g)

½ cup dry white wine (125 ml)

1 pound fresh porcini mushrooms, cleaned and cut into ⅜-inch dice (450 g)

About 6 cups simmering beef or chicken broth (1½ l)

Salt and freshly ground black pepper

6 tablespoons freshly grated Parmesan cheese

Although rice is not eaten as often as pasta in Rome, when porcini are in season, they call for rice as well as pasta. This same recipe for the rice, without the porcini, is perfect for truffles, too. Simply slice the cleaned truffles with a mandoline on top of the finished risotto, as generously as you can afford to. Note: In earlier times, about 1 ½ ounces of veal bone marrow was sautéed in the butter with the onion for added richness.

1 In a large saucepan, melt 4 tablespoons of the butter over moderately low heat. Add the onion and cook until it is soft and translucent, 3 to 5 minutes.

2 Add the rice and cook, stirring, until the grains are shiny. Toast the rice over the heat for 2 to 3 minutes. Raise the heat to moderately high and pour in the white wine. Cook, stirring, until the wine evaporates. Add the porcini mushrooms.

3 Begin adding the broth, ½ cup at a time, stirring constantly. Continue adding broth, allowing each ½ cup to be absorbed before adding another, but leaving the rice always moist. After 15 minutes (count from the time the wine was added), begin to test the rice; it should be al dente. Cook for another 2 or 3 minutes and remove the risotto from the heat still moist, or all'onda. Season with salt and pepper to taste.

4 Add the remaining 2 tablespoons butter and the Parmesan cheese, cover, and allow the rice to rest for 3 or 4 minutes. Turn out onto a heated platter and serve with a pepper mill and extra cheese on the side.

NOTE: If fresh porcini mushrooms are not available or are prohibitively expensive, cultivated mushrooms may be substituted. This makes a good risotto, although it is not the same thing. You will need 1 pound of mushrooms, sliced about ¼ inch thick, and 1 ounce of dried porcini. Soak the dried porcini in warm water for at least ½ hour. Drain, rinse thoroughly under warm water to remove all grit, and chop coarsely. Add the dried mushrooms together with the fresh ones.

LETTUCE RISOTTO

Risotto alla Lattuga

SERVES 4 TO 6

6 tablespoons butter (90 g)

½ medium onion, finely chopped

1 pound Arborio, Carnaroli, or other risotto rice (450 g)

⅔ cup dry white wine (160 ml)

1 medium head of romaine lettuce, washed and shredded

About 6 cups simmering chicken broth (1½ l)

⅓ cup heavy cream (80 ml)

1 cup freshly grated Parmesan cheese (100 g)

Salt and freshly ground pepper

Although risottos take about 40 minutes from start to finish and you must spend all this time in the kitchen, they are still perfect supper dishes. The ingredients can be measured out and prepared in advance — in this recipe, even the lettuce, which can be washed and stored in the refrigerator. This risotto is particularly creamy and elegant for a dinner. In Rome, it is served as a first course.

1 Melt 4 tablespoons of the butter in a large saucepan. Add the onion and cook over moderate heat until it is soft and translucent, 3 to 5 minutes. Add the rice and stir until the rice is shiny, about 2 minutes. Pour in the wine and allow to evaporate, stirring.

2 Put the lettuce in the saucepan with the rice and add the broth, ½ cup at a time, stirring constantly. Continue adding broth, allowing each ½ cup to be absorbed before you add another, but keeping the rice always moist.

3 When the rice is al dente, after about 18 minutes, remove it from the heat and stir in the remaining 2 tablespoons of butter, the cream, and the Parmesan cheese. Cover with a lid and let it rest for 3 minutes.

4 Stir the rice once and turn out onto a heated platter. Serve at once with a pepper mill and extra cheese on the side.

SOUPS

Sette cose fa la zuppa:
Leva la fame e la sete tutta,
Sciacqua er dente,
Empie er ventre,
Fa smartire,
Fa abbellire,
Fa le guance colorire.

Soup does seven things:

Takes away all hunger and thirst,

Cleans your teeth,

Fills your stomach,

Orders your insides,

Makes you handsomer,

Colors your cheeks.

Unlike in other parts of Italy — the *pasta e fagioli* of Naples or *ribollita* of Florence — soups have never been very popular in Rome. We would much rather enjoy an extra serving of pasta before a meal than fill up on a liquid. While chicken soup is sometimes served on holidays, the broth is most commonly used in making risottos or offered to nursing mothers — the broth is supposed to "make milk." If you do see soup on a Roman menu, however, it is likely to be one of the ones that follow.

CHICKEN BROTH WITH EGGS AND SEMOLINA

Stracciatella

SERVES 4 TO 6

9 cups cold chicken broth (2¼ l)

3 large eggs

3½ tablespoons semolina

⅓ cup freshly grated Parmesan cheese (35 g)

Stracciatelli means "rags" in Italian, and the little bits of egg in the hot broth do look like shredded cloth. This is the soup you are given when you feel out of sorts, or if you are a child. It is also one of Rome's best-loved ways of serving broth.

1 Reserve 1 cup of cold broth and bring the rest of the broth to a gentle boil.

2 Beat together the eggs, semolina, and Parmesan cheese. Gradually beat in the reserved cup of cold broth. Slowly pour this mixture into the simmering broth, stirring constantly with a wire whisk. Simmer gently for 2 to 3 minutes.

3 Ladle the *stracciatella* into soup bowls and serve at once with extra Parmesan on the side, if you like.

FAVA BEAN SOUP

Minestra di Fave

SERVES 4 TO 5

2 ounces pancetta, coarsely chopped (60 g)

⅓ cup coarsely chopped white onion

2 tablespoons coarsely chopped parsley

1 small celery rib, coarsely chopped

¼ cup extra virgin olive oil (60 ml)

1 medium-small ripe tomato (about 2 ounces), very thinly sliced (60 g)

1 small potato, peeled and very thinly sliced

2¼ pounds fresh fava beans, shelled (1 kg)

½ pound romaine lettuce, shredded (225 g)

2 bouillon cubes, crumbled

Salt and freshly ground black pepper

1 cup (4 ounces) small soup pasta, such as quadrucci, farfallini, or cannolicchi (120 g)

3 tablespoons grated pecorino Romano cheese, plus extra for the table

We Romans eat our fava beans any way we can, and in soup is no exception. This is a simple, delicate dish prepared only when fresh fava beans are in season; it is not made with frozen ones. While fava beans used to be uncommon in America, they are now found in many supermarket produce sections from early spring to late fall. The only problem with fava beans is shelling them. It is pleasant but tedious work, best done with a friend or while listening to some good music.

1 Make the *battuto:* Finely chop together the pancetta, onion, parsley, and celery, using a mezzaluna in a wooden bowl, if you have one, or a large knife or a food processor.

2 Heat the olive oil in a large saucepan. Add the *battuto* and the tomato and cook over moderate heat, stirring often, until it is lightly colored, about 8 minutes. Add the potato and fava beans and cook, stirring, for 3 or 4 minutes longer.

3 Pour in 4½ cups hot water and add the lettuce and bouillon cubes. Season lightly with salt (the bouillon cubes are salty) and with black pepper to taste. Bring the soup to a slow boil and cook for 10 minutes, stirring occasionally.

4 Add the pasta to the soup and cook until it is al dente. Remove the soup from the heat and stir in the 3 tablespoons pecorino Romano cheese. Serve the soup hot, with extra cheese on the side.

ROMAN CHICKPEA SOUP

Minestra di Ceci alla Romana

SERVES 4 TO 6

1 pound dried chickpeas
(450 g)

6 cloves of garlic, peeled
and crushed

1 sprig of fresh rosemary,
plus 2 tablespoons finely
chopped rosemary

Salt and freshly ground
black pepper

⅓ cup extra virgin olive oil
(80 ml)

1 tablespoon anchovy paste

1 cup drained Italian plum
tomatoes (about 7 tomatoes), or
1⅓ pounds fresh ripe tomatoes,
peeled, seeded, and diced
(600 g)

½ teaspoon hot red pepper
flakes (optional)

4 or 5 slices of Italian bread,
about ½ inch thick

In Rome, chickpeas are sold already soaked and ready to cook, just the way salt cod is. Chickpeas vary greatly in their cooking time and can take as long as 4 hours to cook. However, you do not have to hover over this soup, only stir it now and then after the heat has been set to a gentle simmer. If your chickpeas are not presoaked, there is a sure way to shorten the cooking time. For 1 pound of chickpeas, dissolve 2 tablespoons kosher salt in a little water in a large pot over low heat. Remove from the heat. Add the chickpeas and cover them generously with about 3 inches cold water. Soak the chickpeas for 48 hours, drain, and proceed as in the recipe below. It will take only about 1 hour and 15 minutes, and the chickpeas will be cooked perfectly, with no hard skins.

This is a delicious and healthy soup, especially welcome in cold weather. Two versions are given: this recipe is served over toasted garlic bread; a variation which follows substitutes pasta for the bread. In summertime a lighter version is prepared without any bread or pasta. It is pureed and served cold, with a bit of fresh rosemary sprinkled on top. Like so many soups, chickpea soup is better reheated the next day.

1 If your chickpeas are not presoaked, immerse them in a large pot of cold water for at least 12 hours. Drain the chickpeas and add fresh water to about 2 inches above the chickpeas. Add 2 of the garlic cloves and the rosemary sprig. Bring to a boil. Cover the pot, reduce the heat slightly, and boil gently until the chickpeas are tender. Season generously with salt and pepper. Discard the rosemary sprig.

2 In a medium skillet, brown 3 of the remaining crushed garlic cloves in the olive oil. Add the anchovy paste, tomatoes, hot red pepper flakes, if using, and the chopped rosemary. Simmer for 5 minutes. Season lightly with salt and pepper and add to the chickpeas. Simmer for 5 minutes.

3 Remove 1½ cups of chickpeas and reserve. Puree the remaining soup in a blender or food processor. Return the puree and the reserved chickpeas to the pot and add more water, if necessary.

4 Toast the bread lightly and rub the slices of bread gently with the remaining garlic clove. Place a piece of bread on the bottom of each soup bowl and ladle the hot soup over it. Pass a cruet of olive oil and a pepper mill at the table for each person to add to their taste.

VARIATION: If desired, 1 cup ditalini, avemarie, or cannolicchi pasta may be added to the soup instead of the bread. Add the desired pasta to the soup with extra water if necessary and cook until the pasta is al dente. Or cook the pasta separately and let guests add the amount they desire to the chickpea soup. If you do this, toss the pasta with a few drops of olive oil to prevent it from sticking together.

LENTIL SOUP WITH RICE

Minestrone di Riso e Lenticchie

SERVES 6 TO 8

2 cups brown lentils (400 g)

2 teaspoons salt

2 ounces pancetta, rind discarded, coarsely chopped (60 g)

2 small spicy sausages, casings discarded, cut in pieces

1 clove garlic, peeled and sliced

1 medium onion, very thinly sliced

1 celery rib, cut into small pieces

Small handful of parsley

Freshly ground black pepper or hot red pepper flakes

¼ cup plus 1 tablespoon extra virgin olive oil (75 ml)

1¼ cups rice (250 g)

Freshly grated pecorino Romano cheese

Although Romans are not regular soup eaters, this is one of their favorites. It is a filling and warming soup, especially good in the wintertime. It also happens to be good for you, because lentils are rich in iron and potassium. While this dish does contain rice, it is not a usual Roman ingredient; we tend to prefer pasta. Unlike many soups, this is best eaten as soon as it is made; it does not taste better the next day.

1 Pour out the lentils onto a cookie sheet and pick them over to be sure there are no stones or other grit. Put them into a large flameproof casserole with 2 quarts water and the salt. Cover with a lid and bring slowly to a simmer. Simmer, stirring occasionally, for about 50 minutes, until the lentils are very soft.

2 Make the *battuto*: Put the pancetta, sausage, garlic, onion, celery, and parsley on a wooden chopping board and chop the *battuto* thoroughly, turning the ingredients as you work to be sure they are all well mixed together. If you have a mezzaluna, use that; if not, a chef's knife with a sharp blade will do. Season with salt and black pepper or hot red pepper flakes.

3 Heat the ¼ cup of the olive oil in a large skillet, add the *battuto*, and cook over low heat for about 20 minutes, stirring often, until soft. When done, pour it into the pot with the cooked lentils.

4 Meanwhile, boil the rice in a saucepan of salted water until it is quite al dente (needing about 2 minutes longer of cooking); drain. Add the rice to the hot lentils and simmer 2 to 3 minutes, until the rice is cooked and the soup is dense. Stir the remaining 1 tablespoon olive oil into the soup and remove from the heat. Serve at once, with a bowl of pecorino Romano cheese passed separately.

SIMPLE FARRO SOUP

Minestra di Farro

SERVES 4

3 tablespoons extra virgin olive oil

1 small onion, thinly sliced

¼ pound sausages, casings removed and discarded, cut into ½-inch slices (110 g)

2 small potatoes, peeled and very thinly sliced

¾ cup broken farro, or spelt (115 g)*

1 beef or chicken bouillon cube

Salt

½ cup freshly grated pecorino Romano cheese (50 g)

*This recipe uses "broken farro," or spelt. If using a regular, unbroken grain, extend the cooking time in a partially covered pan according to the time suggested on the package. Sometimes overnight soaking is required.

Farro, a grain also known as spelt, is probably one of the oldest staple foods we know. It was consumed by the Roman Legions while they were fighting for the Roman Empire two thousand years ago, and traces of farro were found in predynastic Egyptian tombs. The grain is grown on poor land and is no longer cultivated in Italy as widely as it once was. Immensely satisfying, it blends well with beans or potatoes, with tomatoes, with prosciutto or pancetta, or with sausages. As is appropriate for such an ancient food, this soup is simple, hearty, and satisfying.

1 Heat 3 tablespoons of the olive oil, add the onion, and cook over low heat until the onion is soft and translucent. Add the sausage slices and cook for 2 or 3 minutes, stirring occasionally, until the meat is no longer pink. Put in the potatoes, mix, and add 1 quart hot water. Bring to a boil, stir in the farro and the bouillon cube, and boil gently for 30 to 35 minutes, stirring frequently. Season with salt to taste.

2 Serve the hot soup in bowls with the pecorino Romano cheese sprinkled over the top. Pass a cruet of olive oil to trickle over the top, plus a pepper mill and more cheese.

FARRO SOUP WITH PANCETTA AND TOMATOES

Farricello

SERVES 6

1¾ cups farro, or spelt (350 g)*

¼ pound pancetta (110 g)

1 clove of garlic, peeled

1 medium onion

⅓ cup extra virgin olive oil (80 ml)

½ pound tomatoes, finely chopped (225 g)

1 large handful of basil, finely chopped

1 large handful of parsley, finely chopped

Salt and freshly ground pepper

1 beef or chicken bouillon cube

½ cup freshly grated pecorino Romano cheese (50 g), plus more

*When you buy farro (spelt), check the cooking time on the package. Some brands must soak overnight or longer and be cooked gently for 1½ to 2 hours, stirring very often. If "broken" farro is available, the cooking time is approximately 30 minutes, which makes life much easier.

Farro is probably what Romulus and Remus ate, a grain found in all the archeological sites, as old "as the world." The first Romans, shepherds, consumed it with their cheese and milk. Today it is reborn in Rome, after having languished for years, and it is still prepared — as in this recipe — as Mother used to make it.

1 Soak the farro in a bowl of cold water for 30 minutes; drain.

2 Meanwhile, trim the rind from the pancetta and make the *battuto* by finely chopping together the pancetta, garlic, and onion, mixing as you chop.

3 Heat the olive oil in a large flameproof casserole and add the *battuto*. Cook over moderate heat, stirring often, until the *battuto* is lightly colored, 7 to 10 minutes. Add the tomatoes, basil, and parsley. Season with salt and pepper and cook for 5 to 8 minutes, until the excess tomato liquid evaporates.

4 Pour 7 cups water into the casserole and crumble in the bouillon cube. Bring to a boil. Add the farro to the pot a little at a time, stirring. Reduce the heat slightly and boil the soup gently for 25 to 35 minutes, or until the farro is tender. If the soup thickens too much, add a little boiling water.

5 When the soup is ready, remove from the heat and stir in the pecorino Romano cheese. Serve the soup hot with a pepper mill and extra cheese on the side. If there is soup left over, refrigerate it and reheat gently the next day.

"COOKED WATER" SOUP

Acquacotta

SERVES 4

1 large head of broccoli, about
1⅓ pounds (600 g)

3 tablespoons extra virgin
olive oil

1 or 2 cloves of garlic, peeled
and crushed

1 dried peperoncino, or hot red
pepper flakes

1 cup chopped peeled, seeded
tomatoes

1 bouillon cube, crumbled

Salt and freshly ground
black pepper

4 slices of Italian bread, toasted
and rubbed lightly with garlic

Freshly grated pecorino Romano
cheese

We spend every weekend in the Roman countryside, near Barbarano Romano, a beautiful walled village of Etruscan origin, where the food is rustic, povero ("poor"), and very healthy. The villagers eat soups a lot, and many of their recipes derive from the wild greens and herbs they forage on the hillsides. Signora Grossi, who helped us there, used to prepare salads made exclusively from wild herbs she gathered, each one with its special local name. Sometimes she added these herbs to the acquacotta. The soup is universal in that area and can be varied with cauliflower, broccoflower, dandelion greens, and the like. A very thinly sliced potato may be added to the green vegetables, and chopped pancetta or chopped prosciutto is sometimes included as well.

1 Cut the florets away from the central stalk of the broccoli and halve the larger ones so that they are all approximately the same size. Rinse carefully in cold water. Drain and reserve.

2 Heat the olive oil in a large flameproof casserole or soup pot. Add the garlic and peperoncino or hot pepper flakes, keeping in mind the soup should be moderately spicy. Cook over moderately low heat until the garlic browns; discard the garlic and the peperoncino.

3 Add the tomatoes, raise the heat, and simmer for 5 minutes. Then add the broccoli florets and mix them in with a wooden spoon. Pour in 1½ quarts hot water, add the bouillon cube, and cover the pot. Bring to a boil, reduce the heat slightly, cover, and simmer the soup until the broccoli is tender but al dente, 10 to 15 minutes. Season with salt and black pepper to taste.

4 To serve, put a slice of toasted bread lightly rubbed with garlic in each soup plate and divide the soup among the plates. Serve very hot and pass the cheese separately.

COUNTRY VEGETABLE SOUP

La Scafata

SERVES 6

2 ounces pancetta, rind
discarded, coarsely chopped
(60 g)

_____

1 clove of garlic, peeled

_____

1 small onion, sliced

_____

1 small dried peperoncino, or
hot red pepper flakes to taste

_____

2 tablespoons extra virgin
olive oil

_____

½ cup chopped Italian plum
tomatoes, canned or fresh (if
canned, do not drain) (120 ml)

_____

1 pound (3½ cups) shelled fava
beans (450 g), about 3½ pounds
in the shell, rinsed and drained
(1.575 kg)

_____

1 small head of romaine lettuce,
shredded

_____

1½ tablespoons chopped
fresh mint

_____

2 beef bouillon cubes

_____

Near Rome, in the town of Barbarano Romano, there is a trattoria run by a woman called La Pacchiona ("the laid back one"), who is a walking history of Roman food. She is not very generous with her recipes — after all, it is her livelihood — but I know her daughter-in-law, whose wonderful father was our gamekeeper for years. As a young boy he read Ariosto while caring for his sheep;* today he is a poet who competes in Lazio's extemporaneous poetry contests. (When my daughter married, he composed a long poem for her and for her husband.) His daughter now works in the trattoria with La Pacchiona, and she has given me their recipe for _scafata_, a Roman soup (whose name is untranslatable) almost lost but for La Pacchiona.

1 Make the _battuto:_ Chop together very finely the pancetta, garlic, onion, and peperoncino or hot pepper flakes. This is the basic seasoning for the soup.

2 Heat the olive oil in a large soup pot and cook the _battuto_ over moderate heat, stirring, until it is lightly colored, 2 to 3 minutes. Add the tomatoes and cook, stirring, for 2 to 3 minutes longer. Add the fava beans, lettuce, and mint and mix, stirring often, until the lettuce wilts.

3 Pour in 1½ quarts hot water and crumble the bouillon cubes into the soup. Bring to a boil, lower the heat, cover the pan, and simmer the soup until the fava beans are tender, about 25 minutes. Season with salt and black pepper to taste.

*Salt and freshly ground
black pepper*

*6 slices of crusty Italian bread,
toasted*

*Freshly grated pecorino
Romano cheese*

4 To serve, put a slice of toasted bread in each soup bowl and divide the soup among the bowls. Pass a bowl of pecorino Romano cheese.

NOTE: The toasted bread here can be lightly flavored with garlic. Peel a clove of garlic and rub it over the toasted bread — *lightly*, or you will have garlic soup. Also, sometimes an egg is poached on top of the hot soup.

*Ariosto, poet of the sixteenth century, was so loved by shepherds that they traditionally read his epic poem "Orlando Furioso" while caring for their flocks.

OUR ROMAN PYRAMID

THE CESTIUS PYRAMID is a fitting monument for Testaccio, an old part of Rome that has become a gourmet center. Legend says that Cestius built his pyramid as a tomb for himself and then proceeded to eat himself into bankruptcy, serving the most grandiose meals, with special fish and other delicacies brought to him from all over the Roman Empire. My son says it isn't true, but it's such a good story. Also, just behind the Pyramid is the Roman Protestant cemetery where Keats and Shelley are buried, a very evocative place.

While you are in the Testaccio area, try to visit the museum ACEA Montemartini, a fabulous collection of ancient Roman sculptures which languished for ages in storerooms. They are housed in Rome's first power plant, in itself fascinating industrial archeology.

FISH AND OTHER SEAFOOD

L'ospite è come il pesce,
dopo tre giorni puzza.

Guests are like fish,

After three days they smell.

While Romans have long enjoyed shellfish like clams, mussels, and shrimp, with the exception of sole, cuttlefish, sardines, and sea bass, most fish were out of favor with Romans until recently. Of the above, only sea bass would have been found on the tables of ancient Rome, and it remained a favorite throughout the Middle Ages and the Renaissance.

Fashions change, though, even in the Eternal City. Today, a great variety of fish — even salmon — are extremely popular. Rome's three important ancient ports, Anzio, Civitavecchia, and Ostia Antica, have very efficient fishing fleets, which provide the city with a constant supply of the freshest seafood. In this city that is the home of the Vatican, the Friday fast, which prohibits meat, continues to be observed, and fish is the preferred alternative.

Seafood is sold proudly in Rome, both in shops and in open-air markets, with the heads — even of large fish like swordfish — prominently displayed, bragging of their freshness. Preserved salt cod is sold already soaked and ready to cook in Roman *salsamenterias*, but the eel found in fish markets has to be skinned at home. When frying small fish, only olive oil is used. As with most Roman food, simplicity in preparation is the rule for all fish dishes.

SALT COD IN SWEET-AND-SOUR SAUCE THE ROMAN WAY

Baccalà in Agrodolce alla Romana

SERVES 4 TO 6

1 pound dried salt cod,
or baccalà (450 g)

5 tablespoons olive oil

1 small onion, thinly sliced

2 cups pureed tomatoes (500 g)

Salt and freshly ground
black pepper

½ pound pitted prunes, halved
(225 g)

⅓ cup raisins (60 g)

2 teaspoons sugar

Juice of 2 lemons

2 tablespoons chopped parsley

Here is another of Rome's classical recipes that are rarely tampered with. The sweetness here comes mostly from dried fruit — only a little sugar is added — and the tartness derives from fresh lemons. Fruit and fish may sound like an odd combination, but they complement each other beautifully.

Salt cod is popular in many countries because of its keeping properties. Once an inexpensive fish used for Friday meals, it is now fairly pricey, which, of course, makes it more desirable to some. Our baccalà comes from Norway and the cold waters of the northern seas; it is sold in Rome already soaked and ready to cook — a great boon. Salt cod from most fish markets in America, however, must be soaked at home. I recommend 24 hours in several changes of cold water in the refrigerator to remove all the excess salt and soften the fish, so do plan ahead when you want to serve this dish.

1 Soak the salt cod in a bowl of cold water for 24 hours in the refrigerator, changing the water 2 or 3 times. Drain and dry the cod and remove any skin, bones, and bits of cartilage. Cut into pieces about 3 by 1½ inches.

2 In a large deep skillet or flameproof casserole, heat the olive oil. Add the onion and cook over moderately low heat, stirring often, until golden, about 10 minutes. Pour in the tomatoes and bring to a simmer. Cook for 15 minutes, stirring often. Season the sauce with salt and pepper to taste.

3 Add the cod to the tomato sauce and simmer for 5 minutes. Add the prunes, raisins, sugar, and lemon juice and simmer for 10 minutes longer. Pour the baccalà into a serving dish and sprinkle the parsley on top.

ANCHOVY PIE

Torta d'Acciughe

SERVES 4

1⅔ pounds fresh anchovies
(750 g)

2 tablespoons salted capers

¼ cup plus 3 tablespoons extra
virgin olive oil (100 ml)

15 anchovy fillets packed in oil,
drained and chopped

1 large handful of flat-leaf
parsley

2 tablespoons lemon juice

2 bay leaves

1 dried peperoncino, broken
in half, or hot red pepper flakes
to taste

6 tablespoons dried bread
crumbs

Fresh anchovies are the tastiest and probably the least expensive fish in the Roman markets. If you've never tasted a fresh anchovy, you may be surprised at their distinctive but pleasing character. While these were once scarce in America, better fish markets carry them often, and if you try them, I think you'll find they are a real treat.

The fish are usually prepared by dredging them lightly in flour and frying them in hot oil, to be eaten immediately, with lemon wedges on the side. This recipe for oven-baked anchovies requires a little more work because the bones are removed before cooking, but that can be accomplished easily by asking your fishmonger to clean and fillet the fish for you. That done, the dish needs only assembling. In fact, the "pie" can even be prepared a few hours in advance and refrigerated so that you are free just before serving.

1 Heat the oven to 350°F (180°C). Clean and debone the anchovies as described at right, or ask your fishmonger to prepare them for you, reminding him to keep the two fillets attached. Rinse the fresh anchovies 3 times in cold water and drain them on paper towels.

2 Rinse the capers to remove the external salt. Soak them in a bowl of cold water for 20 minutes, then drain well.

3 Heat ¼ cup of the olive oil in a small skillet. Add the chopped canned anchovy fillets and cook over moderately low heat, mashing them with the back of a wooden spoon, until they dissolve in the oil. Let cool slightly.

4 Chop together the capers and parsley. Add to the tepid anchovies dissolved in oil and stir in the lemon juice. Set the sauce aside.

5 In an 11-by-7-inch (28-by-18-cm) glass baking dish, arrange one-third of the fresh anchovy fillets, skin side down, in a single layer. Put 1 bay leaf and a peperoncino half (or a light sprinkling of hot pepper flakes) on top and drizzle half of the reserved sauce over the fish. Cover with another layer of anchovy fillets, another bay leaf, and the other peperoncino half. Drizzle on the remaining sauce. Top with the rest of the anchovies, still skin side down, and drizzle the remaining 3 tablespoons olive oil over the fish. Sprinkle the bread crumbs on top.

6 Bake for 30 minutes. Serve hot or at room temperature.

HOW TO CLEAN FRESH ANCHOVIES

USING KITCHEN SCISSORS, cut off and discard the head of the anchovy. With the scissors or using your thumbnail, open the fish along the stomach and remove and discard the entrails. Open the fish like a book, without separating the two parts of the body, and remove and discard the central bones and fins. Rinse well under cold running water and drain on paper towels.

CUTTLEFISH WITH SWEET PEAS ROMAN STYLE

Seppie e Piselli alla Romana

SERVES 4 TO 6

2 pounds cuttlefish or squid, cleaned (900 g)

¼ cup plus 3 tablespoons extra virgin olive oil (100 ml)

1 clove of garlic, peeled and crushed

1½ teaspoons salt

½ teaspoon freshly ground black pepper

⅓ cup dry white wine (80 ml)

2 tablespoons chopped parsley

2 pounds fresh peas in the pod, about 2 heaping cups shelled (900 g)

1 small white onion, very thinly sliced

A seasonal Roman dish *da leccarsi i baffi*, a phrase that is impossible to translate literally but means "lip-smacking good." These days in the Roman markets fresh peas are sold both in the pod or shelled for you.

1 Rinse the cuttlefish thoroughly in cold water. Drain and cut into ⅜-inch (scant 1-cm) slices.

2 Heat ¼ cup of the the olive oil in a large skillet. Add the garlic and cook until it browns; discard the garlic. Add the cuttlefish to the oil in the skillet. Season with the salt and pepper and cook over moderate heat for about 2 minutes.

3 Pour the wine into the pan, cover, reduce the heat to moderately low, and simmer, stirring every now and then, until the cuttlefish are tender, about 25 minutes. If the pan becomes dry, add a little hot water so that the cuttlefish are still moist at the end of the cooking time. Sprinkle on the chopped parsley.

4 While the cuttlefish are cooking, shell the peas. In a medium saucepan, heat the remaining 3 tablespoons olive oil. Add the onion and cook over moderately low heat until golden, 7 to 10 minutes. Add the peas and 2 tablespoons hot water. Cover the saucepan and cook the peas over low heat, stirring occasionally, until they are tender, 15 to 20 minutes. Season lightly with additional salt.

5 When ready to serve, reheat the cuttlefish, if necessary. Stir in the peas and mix well. Season with salt and pepper to taste. Simmer for a minute or two, then serve immediately. This dish should be served hot, not at room temperature.

SAUTEED FISH FILLETS WITH PARMESAN CRUMBS

Pesce Mediterraneo

SERVES 2

1 fresh sea bream, about
2 pounds (900 g), filleted
and skinned, or 2 slices,
about 1 pound, striped bass
or red snapper (450 g)

1 egg, beaten

Salt

¼ cup freshly grated Parmesan
cheese (25 g)

2 tablespoons fine dry
bread crumbs

1 clove of garlic

Handful of flat-leaf parsley

¼ cup extra virgin olive oil
(60 ml)

Lemon wedges

This is a simple breaded fish, Mediterranean in a subtle way via its ingredients: Parmesan cheese, olive oil, garlic, and lemon. Choose the fish according to which is freshest in the market that day and eat it as soon as it is cooked.

1 Wipe off the fish and pat it dry. Beat the egg with a pinch of salt in a shallow dish. Put the fish pieces in the egg and turn to coat. Let stand for 30 minutes, turning them every now and then.

2 Toss together the Parmesan cheese and bread crumbs. Chop together the garlic and parsley very finely. Mix with the Parmesan crumbs.

3 Turn the fish again and drain from the egg briefly. Dredge each fillet or slice of fish in the crumb mixture, pressing lightly to help the coating adhere.

4 Heat the olive oil in a large skillet, preferably nonstick, until it is very hot. Add the fish and fry over moderately high heat until the bottom is nicely browned, 3 to 5 minutes. Reduce the heat slightly. Using a large flat spoon with holes and a fork, turn the fish gently and cook for about 3 minutes longer on the other side. Remove the fish to a warm platter and season with a little salt. Serve hot, with lemon wedges.

OVEN-BAKED GROUPER WITH POTATOES

Cernia al Forno con Patate

SERVES 4

1¼ to 1½ pounds boiling
potatoes (650 g)

—

Salt and freshly ground
black pepper

—

4 tablespoons butter,
cut into bits (60 g)

—

½ teaspoon dried fennel flowers*

—

Flour for dusting the fish

—

1¾ to 2 pounds grouper fillets
(900 g)

—

1 tablespoon extra virgin
olive oil

—

2 tablespoons freshly grated
Parmesan cheese

—

*For this fish we use dried wild fennel
flowers gathered by the family. The
flowers are also sold in some markets in
Italy. If you cannot find them, toast regular fennel seeds in a small dry skillet,
stirring, until they are fragrant and lightly toasted. Grind them in a spice grinder
or crush with a mortar and pestle.

Until recently when Americans began serving
mashed potatoes with their fish, they were much
more likely to turn to rice as an accompaniment. In
the Mediterranean, we have known for a long time
how good fish and potatoes taste together. The
grouper used for this dish is of the kind found
along the northern Mediterranean; it is of excellent quality and
is considered a superior fish in Italy.

Grouper has firm flesh and usually is no larger than 10 pounds.
Either buy 2 pounds of grouper fillets, or purchase a whole fish
that weighs 8 to 10 pounds and have it filleted. Cut one fillet
into 4 pieces for this recipe, and freeze the other one; that's what
I usually do. Note the light dusting of flour on the fish; it helps
absorb the juices.

1 Preheat the oven to 375°F (190°C). Butter an oval gratin dish
about 9 by 15 inches (23 by 38 cm).

2 Peel the potatoes and cut them into very thin slices, on a mandoline if you have one. Soak them in a bowl of cold water until you are
ready to cook the dish.

3 Dry the potato slices. Layer enough of them over the bottom of
the buttered gratin dish, overlapping the slices to cover completely.
Season with salt and pepper. Distribute half of the cut-up butter
over the potatoes. Season with half the fennel flowers.

4 Sift a dusting of flour over one side of the fish fillets. Put the fish on top of the potatoes, floured side down. Sift a dusting of flour over the top of the fish. Dot with the remaining butter. Season with salt and pepper and sprinkle the remaining fennel flowers on top. With a sharp knife, divide the fish into 4 portions.

5 Cover the fish with the remaining potato slices; you may not need all of them. Season with salt and pepper and drizzle the olive oil over the potatotes. Sprinkle the Parmesan cheese evenly over the top.

6 Bake for 25 to 30 minutes, until the potatoes are tender and the grouper is cooked through but still moist.

BAKED MARINATED SALMON

Salmone al Forno

SERVES 8

Juice of 3 lemons

1 teaspoon white wine vinegar

½ teaspoon Tabasco sauce, or to taste

1 tablespoon extra virgin olive oil

Salt and freshly ground black pepper

1 large side of salmon (4-pound fillet), skin removed (1.8 kg)

3 or 4 ripe tomatoes, sliced ¼ inch thick

3 medium white onions, very thinly sliced

2 tablespoons extra virgin olive oil

Some of the vanishing professional Roman cooks have been replaced with African cooks (notably those from Senegal and Burkina Faso), who have become adept at Italian cooking. They have unerring taste with spices and are masters with peperoncino. They put lemon on everything. The Senegalese are particularly good with fish. Often they'll leave a job as a private chef in a home to open a restaurant, and some of them have met with great success. I've known several of these African cooks here in Rome, and many of their recipes are circulating among my friends. This Senegalese-Roman salmon is one of them.

Salmon is relatively new to Rome, but, as in America, it is available everywhere now. Because this recipe lends itself to being made in advance and because it feeds 8, it is an excellent dish for entertaining. Only a simple first course and a good salad are needed to complement the meal. A ripe pineapple to follow would be the perfect dessert.

1 I like to marinate the fish in the dish it will be cooked in and, perhaps, served in. I use a 15-inch shallow oval glass baking dish; ceramic or enameled cast iron would also be good choices.

2 Put the lemon juice, vinegar, Tabasco sauce, and olive oil in the dish. Season generously with salt and pepper. Put the salmon in the dish and turn to coat with the marinade. Cover with plastic wrap and refrigerate for a minimum of 30 minutes and up to 8 hours. It is not necessary to turn the fish again in the marinade.

3 When ready to prepare the fish, preheat the oven to 450°F (230°C). It must be very hot. Carefully remove the fillet to a large platter, reserving the marinade in the dish. Completely cover the bottom of the dish holding the marinade with half the tomato slices. Then add a layer of the finely sliced onions. Now place the salmon over the onions. Add another layer of onions and cover with the remaining tomatoes. Drizzle the olive oil and 1/4 cup water over all; season with salt and pepper.

4 Bake for 20 to 25 minutes, or until the fish is just opaque throughout and the juices released by the fish are no longer white. Let rest for 10 minutes before serving.

SQUID
A LA
ROMANA

*Calamari
alla Romana*

SERVES 4

2 pounds cleaned squid (900 g)

½ cup extra virgin olive oil
(120 ml)

3 cloves of garlic, peeled
and crushed

1 small dried peperoncino
(optional)

½ cup dry white wine (120 ml)

8 anchovy fillets packed in oil
or 1½ teaspoons anchovy paste

Salt and freshly ground
black pepper

3 tablespoons finely chopped
parsley

Fish is usually eaten twice a week, on Tuesday and Friday, when the fishmongers traditionally have the freshest, largest variety of fish. Although the Church no longer requires that the faithful abstain from meat on Friday, Romans continue to observe these days, just for the love of seafood. The squid is traditionally cooked and presented in a terra-cotta casserole; use one if you have it, with a Flame Tamer underneath. Serve with good Italian bread for the sauce.

1 Check that all the squid have been cleaned properly, rinse them under cold running water, and drain in a colander. Cut the squid into slices ⅜ inch thick. Separate the tentacles and cut them into pieces about the same size.

2 Reserve 1 tablespoon of the olive oil in a small saucer. Heat the rest of the oil in a large flameproof casserole with the garlic and the peperoncino, if you're using it. Cook over moderately low heat until the garlic is lightly browned, then discard it along with the peperoncino.

3 Raise the heat to moderately high and add the squid. Cook, stirring often, until the squid release their juices and the liquid is almost all evaporated, 10 to 15 minutes. Add the wine and the anchovy fillets mashed to a puree in the reserved 1 tablespoon oil. Cook until the wine has almost evaporated, about 5 minutes. Reduce the heat to moderately low, season with salt and pepper, and pour in ¼ cup hot water. Simmer for 15 to 20 minutes longer, stirring often and adding more hot water if necessary, until the squid are tender. Sprinkle the parsley over the squid and serve at once.

SWORDFISH BRAISED WITH GREEN PEPPER AND TOMATO

Pescespada a Pezzi

SERVES 2

¾ to 1 pound swordfish steak, cut ½ to ¾ inch thick, skin removed (450 g)

¼ cup extra virgin olive oil (60 ml)

1 clove of garlic, peeled and crushed

¼ teaspoon hot red pepper flakes, or to taste

1 small green bell pepper, cut into thin julienne strips

1 medium tomato, peeled, seeded, and cut into thin julienne strips

Pinch of dried oregano

3 tablespoons dry white wine

Salt and freshly ground black pepper

Swordfish, called *pescespada* in Italian, is a particularly popular fish in Rome, and this is a quick and easy way to prepare it. Since many Roman women work these days and are always in a hurry to fix supper, the men often help cook, which is a novelty in Italy. I was given this recipe by one of these new male home cooks. I have eaten fish cooked this same way all over Italy, with only slight adjustment. It is a good method, because the seasonings do not alter the fish's fine flavor.

1 Cut the swordfish into strips about ½ inch wide and 1½ inches long.

2 Heat the olive oil in a large nonstick frying pan. Add the garlic and brown lightly. Add the hot pepper flakes and the green pepper strips and cook slowly over moderately low heat until the pepper strips are softened, about 5 minutes. Add the tomato and cook for 2 minutes longer.

3 Raise the heat to moderate and add the fish. Cook on one side until about half done, 4 to 5 minutes. With a wide spatula, turn the pieces carefully. Add the oregano and wine. Raise the heat to moderately high and cook until the fish is just opaque throughout but still moist, 4 to 5 minutes longer. Season with salt and pepper and serve at once.

PAN-ROASTED SWORDFISH WITH PLUM TOMATOES

Pescespada in Padella

SERVES 4

⅓ cup extra virgin olive oil (80 ml)

2 cloves of garlic, peeled and crushed

3 salt-packed anchovies, rinsed in cold water, dried, and finely chopped

3 San Marzano tomatoes, or other large plum tomatoes, about 9 ounces, peeled, seeded, and cut into julienne strips 1½ inches long (250 g)

2 tablespoons finely chopped parsley

½ cup dry white wine (120 ml)

4 slices of swordfish, 5 to 6 ounces each, skin removed (750 g total)

Salt

2 dashes of Tabasco sauce (optional but good)

1 tablespoon lemon juice

This swordfish dish can be on the table in half an hour or less. Slices of fresh tuna may be prepared in the same way.

1 Heat the olive oil with the garlic in a large skillet. Cook slowly until the garlic is light brown; discard the garlic.

2 Add the anchovies to the hot oil, mashing them with a wooden spoon to dissolve them. Add the tomatoes and half the parsley. Pour in the wine. Cook slowly, stirring occasionally, until almost all the wine has evaporated.

3 Put the fish in the pan, season lightly with salt, and cook over moderately low heat for 8 minutes. Turn the fish over gently and salt again lightly. Raise the heat to moderately high and cook until the fish is just opaque throughout but still moist, 5 to 7 minutes.

4 Remove the fish to a warm serving platter. Stir the Tabasco, if using it, and the lemon juice into the sauce in the pan. Pour the sauce over the fish. Sprinkle the remaining parsley on top and serve at once.

BAKED TUNA LOAF

Polpettone di Tonno I

SERVES 4

12 ounces tuna packed in oil,
preferably olive oil, drained
(340 g)

2 tablespoons grated Parmesan
cheese

2 tablespoons fine dry bread
crumbs

1 tablespoon anchovy paste

2 eggs

2 tablespoons lemon juice

Peel of ½ lemon (yellow
zest only)

Caper Mayonnaise
(recipe on page 124)

Canned tuna is so easy, even we Romans use it many ways, particularly in the hot summer when we want to keep cooking to a minimum. This tuna loaf is baked in advance, then refrigerated to firm up. It is served as a cold supper dish, with some tiny tomatoes, sliced cucumbers, radishes, and olives. I like to offer a Caper Mayonnaise with it.

1 Put the tuna, Parmesan cheese, bread crumbs, and anchovy paste in a food processor and puree finely. Add the eggs and puree again until smooth.

2 Lay a sheet of foil on a flat work surface. Turn the tuna puree out onto the foil and form it into a sausage shape about 3 inches in diameter. Roll up and twist the ends of the foil tightly to seal. Prick the roll all over with a kitchen needle.

3 Fill a casserole with enough water to cover the tuna roll. Add the lemon juice and peel. Bring the water to a boil, add the loaf, and simmer for 30 minutes. Let the wrapped loaf cool in its poaching liquid for 1 hour. Then remove the loaf and let cool until tepid. Refrigerate for at least 6 hours or overnight to allow it to chill and set up.

4 Unwrap the tuna loaf and cut into slices about ½ inch thick. Serve with a bowl of Caper Mayonnaise on the side.

CAPER MAYONNAISE

Maionese con Capperi

MAKES ABOUT 1½ CUPS

1 egg, at cool room temperature

1 teaspoon dry mustard

½ teaspoon salt

A few grinds of black pepper

2 tablespoons fresh lemon juice

About 1 cup corn oil or light olive oil (250 ml)

3 tablespoons capers, rinsed and dried*

* If packed in salt, soak the capers for at least 20 minutes in a bowl of cold water, then drain and dry.

1 Put the egg, mustard, salt, pepper, and 1 tablespoon of the lemon juice in a blender or food processor and whirl for 30 seconds. With the machine on, gradually add the oil in a slow stream until the mayonnaise emulsifies and thickens. It may not take all the oil.

2 Add the remaining 1 tablespoon lemon juice and blend briefly to mix. Remove the mayonnaise to a small bowl and stir in the capers. Cover and refrigerate the mayonnaise until serving time.

3 If desired, a large handful of clean, dry watercress or parsley may be substituted for the capers. Add after the second tablespoon of lemon juice, stopping to scrape down the sides of the blender.

TUNA FISH PATE

Polpettone di Tonno II

SERVES 4 TO 6

2 cans (6 ounces each) tuna packed in oil, preferably olive oil, drained (340 g)

2 tablespoons anchovy paste

10 tablespoons unsalted butter, at room temperature (150 g)

⅓ cup dry Marsala (80 ml)

The recipe for this dish, which is not baked and is more of a cold tuna pâté, was given to me by Signora Ascarelli, who is a pillar of the Jewish community. It is more appropriate served in small amounts as a first course and is excellent spread on *crostone*.

1 Line a 3-cup loaf pan with plastic wrap.

2 Put all the ingredients in a food processor and puree until smooth. Spoon into the loaf pan and rap the pan sharply once or twice on a hard surface to remove any air pockets. Cover and refrigerate until firm.

3 To serve, cut into thick slices.

A ROMAN FLEA MARKET

WE HAVE A Sunday outdoor market in Rome called Porta Portese, which sells everything imaginable: antiques, books (valuable and not), furniture, dishes, glasses, clothes, linens, artwork, pots and pans, church candlesticks, wildly disparate piles of objects of all kinds. When the Russians first started fleeing their country years ago, their first stop was Rome, and Porta Portese was where they sold their beautiful enameled pins, among other treasures. Thieves supply it with what they have available. When my son Maurizio was renovating the Bettoja hotels, he bought old prints there for the rooms. He knows his way around well. In fact, he furnished his entire apartment at Porta Portese — everything, furniture and sofas included. I doubt you would want to take a sofa home, but you might find linens or dishes or something interesting. Go with an open mind, and remember to be very careful of your pocketbook and your pocket.

CHICKEN, BEEF, VEAL, LAMB, PORK, AND GAME

There isn't a single Italian proverb I know of that pokes fun at meat eaters. There's a good reason for this: meat couldn't be taken more seriously than it is in Italy — and especially in Rome. A really serious meal must include a generous amount of meat, simply prepared and of good quality.

Chicken dishes such as *pollo alla romana* — with pancetta, fresh tomatoes, and a healthy dose of rosemary, and *pollo con i peperoni*, with tomatoes and peppers, rank high among the more famous Roman specialities. In fact, we enjoy these traditional recipes so much and eat so much chicken that the bird, once so highly regarded that it reigned as *the* Sunday meat, has lost its charm as festive fare. Now we eat it every day of the week.

The Romans are not big beef eaters, though there are a few dishes, such as *il garofolato*, pot roast strongly seasoned with cloves and nutmeg, which are ancient and still enjoyed from time to time. Veal, on the other hand, can be found both in restaurant and home kitchens in a bewildering variety of guises, including scallopine, involtini, saltimbocca, and piccatine.

A Roman's preference is more likely, however, to turn to lamb — probably our favorite meat. Lamb is a particular Roman passion, especially *abbacchio*, the thirty-day-old spring lamb, which has milk white meat and is so tender you don't even need a knife. It is prepared *alla cacciatora*, stewed with tomatoes and peppers, *al forno con patate*, roasted with potatoes, even *brodettato*, in egg and lemon sauce. Baby lamb is also an essential part of the Roman Easter menu.

Pork ranks as the most versatile of Roman meats. We roast it, cure it, brine it, and grind it, producing sausages, prosciuttos, and all the grand variety of *salumeria* that are Roman favorites, too. But *porchetta alla romana*, roast suckling pig with fennel, is without question the most famous pork dish. It is still sold in certain shops in Rome and off vans in the street, already roasted and ready to take home and eat.

While beef has never been particularly popular with the Romans, we are very fond of offal and other odd parts, like oxtails and marrow bones. We also eat turkey, which we adopted from America, and in season, rabbit and game, especially wild boar, are relished.

CHICKEN ROMAN STYLE

Pollo alla Romana

Serves 4

¼ cup extra virgin olive oil
(60 ml)

1 clove of garlic, peeled
and crushed

2 ounces thickly sliced lean
pancetta or fatty prosciutto,
cut into thin strips (60 g)

1 chicken, 3 to 3½ pounds,
cut into 10 pieces (1.35 to
1.575 kg)

1 tablespoon chopped fresh
marjoram, or 1 teaspoon dried

Salt and freshly ground
black pepper

⅓ cup dry white wine (80 ml)

1 pound ripe tomatoes, peeled,
seeded, and cut into thin strips
(450 g)

½ teaspoon anchovy paste

This is a D.O.C. Roman recipe, not found anywhere else in Italy. Restaurants, trattorias, and families make this chicken almost exactly the same way. Only one adjustment is considered appropriate: sometimes two roasted peppers — one red and one yellow — peeled, seeded, and cut into strips, are added to the finished chicken for color, and are simmered for just a minute or two before serving.

1 Heat the olive oil in a skillet large enough to hold all the chicken. Add the garlic and cook slowly until brown; discard the garlic. Add the pancetta or prosciutto and the chicken pieces and brown over moderately high heat, turning the chicken as necessary. Season with the marjoram and salt and pepper to taste.

2 When the chicken is golden, pour in the white wine and simmer until it is reduced by half, turning the chicken once or twice. Add the tomatoes and the anchovy paste, mixing the paste into the liquid in the center of the pan. Cover and continue to simmer, turning the chicken every now and then, for 20 to 25 minutes. If necessary, add a few tablespoons water; there should be some sauce, but it should not be too liquid.

BAKED STUFFED CHICKEN BREASTS

Petti di Pollo al Sandwich

SERVES 4

4 small chicken breasts, about 1⅓ pounds, skinned and boned (600 g)

Salt and freshly ground black pepper

1 large clove of garlic, peeled and coarsely chopped

⅓ cup fresh sage leaves

1½ ounces pancetta, coarsely chopped, plus 4 slices (70 g)

3 tablespoons cold butter (45 g)

1 scant cup good-quality fresh bread crumbs

Olive oil for the baking dish

Italian taxi drivers are politically to the right and very verbal about it. They are mostly Roman and when questioned (I can never keep my mouth shut), are a fascinating group of people. They are tolerant and philosophical about their work, two strong Roman traits, and realize that they work in the most beautiful city in the world, in spite of the "mess the politicians have made of the traffic . . ."

More to the point, a surprising number of them cook. The recipe below is from a driver who held me in his cab for ten minutes, telling me how his grandmother taught him this chicken dish, as well as tomatoes and eggplant, which you'll happen upon later.

1 Preheat the oven to 400°F (200°C). With a sharp knife, slit each chicken breast in half horizontally and fold open like a book; do not sever the halves completely. Season with salt and pepper.

2 In a food processor or by hand, chop together the garlic, sage leaves, 1½ ounces pancetta, butter, and bread crumbs. Lay the chicken breasts open on a work surface and divide the filling among them. Fold over the other side to close and press gently to seal.

3 Oil a small baking or gratin dish and arrange the stuffed chicken breasts in the dish in a single layer. Season with salt and pepper and lay a slice of pancetta over each one.

4 Bake for 30 minutes. Raise the oven temperature to 425°F (220°C) and bake for 10 minutes. Transfer to a preheated broiler and grill about 6 inches from the heat until lightly browned, 10 more minutes.

CHICKEN WITH OLIVES AND FENNEL SEEDS

Pollo con Olive e Semi di Finocchio

SERVES 4 TO 6

1 tablespoon fennel seeds

1 chicken, 3 to 3½ pounds, preferably free range (1.35 to 1.575 kg)

Salt and freshly ground black pepper

½ cup extra virgin olive oil (120 ml)

2 cloves of garlic, peeled

1 peperoncino, or hot red pepper flakes to taste

1 cup dry white wine (250 ml)

½ teaspoon anchovy paste

1 cup oil-cured black olives, pitted (200 g)

We are fortunate in the Roman countryside to find wild fennel growing everywhere, and the seeds are incredibly pungent. We gather the flowers heavy with seeds at just the right moment and dry them, hanging them upside down in bunches. If you're not harvesting your own fennel, as most people are not, I recommend toasting the seeds you probably have in your spice rack already, before grinding them. You'll find this does wonders for them. If this easy dish is prepared a day ahead, the flavors improve markedly; reheat slowly, covered, so the dish remains moist.

1 Toast the fennel seeds in a small dry frying pan over moderate heat, stirring, until they are fragrant and light brown, 2 to 3 minutes. Let cool, then grind in a spice or coffee grinder or crush with a meat pounder or a heavy pan.

2 Rinse the chicken and cut it into 10 pieces. Dry on paper towels and season well with salt and pepper.

3 Heat the olive oil in a very large skillet and add the garlic and peperoncino. Cook slowly until the garlic is brown and then discard both garlic and peperoncino.

4 Raise the heat to moderately high, add the chicken, and brown about 5 minutes on each side, shaking the pan often. Pour in the wine and boil until it is reduced by about half. Sprinkle the fennel seeds over the chicken, stir in the anchovy paste, and reduce the heat to low. Cover the pan with a lid and cook for 20 to 25 minutes, turning the pieces twice. Remove the lid, add the olives, and simmer for 10 minutes longer.

RABBIT WITH OLIVES AND FENNEL SEEDS

Coniglio con Olive e Semi di Finocchio

Prepare the recipe as described above, but substitute 1 rabbit (3 to 3½ pounds; 1.35 to 1.575 kg) for the chicken.

CHICKEN COOKED AS A GAME BIRD

Pollo Uso Caccia

SERVES 4 TO 6

3 large skinless, boneless chicken breast halves, about 1½ pounds, or 6 large skinless, boneless chicken thighs (1.6 kg)

Salt and freshly ground black pepper

5 tablespoons extra virgin olive oil

2 medium-small onions, very thinly sliced

3½ tablespoons chopped fresh rosemary

½ cup plus 2 or 3 tablespoons dry white wine (165 ml)

12 ounces oil-cured black olives, pitted (335 g)

1 teaspoon anchovy paste

The architect Donatello Cecchini calls this *pollo uso caccia* ("chicken as game"), because he finds it has a gamey taste, which I attribute to the large amount of rosemary. He also says either boiled potatoes or a simple rice pilaf should be served with it and a salad afterwards — all with good bread, of course.

1 Cut the chicken breasts into 2-inch pieces. Leave the thighs whole. Season with salt and pepper.

2 Heat the olive oil in a large flameproof casserole. Add the chicken pieces and brown them over moderately high heat, turning as necessary. When the chicken is golden, add the onions, rosemary, and ½ cup of the white wine. Reduce the heat to low, cover the casserole, and simmer the chicken for 10 minutes, turning the pieces once or twice.

3 Add the olives and a pinch of salt to the chicken. Put the anchovy paste in the center of the pan and dissolve it into the sauce. Season with a very generous grinding of pepper. Cover again and simmer for 10 to 15 minutes, stirring occasionally and adding a few tablespoons more wine if the sauce is too dry.

4 Remove the chicken pieces to a warm serving dish. Pour the sauce with the olives into a food processor and chop very finely. Pour the sauce over the chicken and serve at once.

CHICKEN WITH TOMATOES AND PEPPERS

Pollo con i Peperoni

SERVES 4

¼ cup plus 2 tablespoons extra virgin olive oil (90 ml)

1 chicken, about 3½ pounds, cut into 10 pieces (1.575 kg)

Salt and freshly ground black pepper

2 ounces pancetta in 2 slices, cut crosswise into thin strips (60 g)

2 cloves of garlic, peeled and crushed

¼ teaspoon hot red pepper flakes, or more to taste

½ cup dry white wine (125 ml)

2¼ pounds ripe tomatoes,* peeled; seeded gently, leaving a little liquid; and cut into slices (1 kg)

1½ tablespoons chopped fresh marjoram, or 1 teaspoon dried marjoram or oregano

*If for any reason the tomatoes are not flavorful, add 2 teaspoons tomato paste when you add the tomatoes.

Pollo con i peperoni, which is what many Americans think of as chicken cacciatore (which is really a very different dish; see page 178), is traditionally eaten on Ferragosto, the "feast-days of Augustus." There's nothing Romans like better than a feast day, and Ferragosto comes right in the middle of August (during the ides of August), when a day off from the summer heat is most appreciated. Everyone goes off to the seashore, only a short distance from Rome, to places all along the coast or to Ostia Antica, Rome's port in the days of the Empire. Returning home at sundown, Romans sit down to enjoy the chicken they prepared the day before.

1 Heat ¼ cup of the olive oil in a large skillet over moderately high heat. Add the chicken pieces and cook, turning, until they are brown, 8 to 10 minutes. Season well with salt and pepper.

2 Reduce the heat to moderate and add the pancetta, garlic, and hot red pepper flakes to the pan. Cook, stirring often, until the pancetta is light brown. Pour in the wine and boil until it is reduced by half. Add the tomatoes and the marjoram. Reduce the heat to moderately low and simmer uncovered for 15 minutes, or until the sauce is thickened.

3 Meanwhile, in a separate skillet, heat the remaining 2 tablespoons oil and sauté the onion over moderate heat, stirring often, until it is golden, 5 to 7 minutes. Add the bell peppers, raise the heat slightly, cover, and cook for 5 minutes, shaking the pan occasionally. Remove the lid and cook, stirring, until the peppers are tender but still firm, 4 or 5 minutes. (The onion will be very brown.)

1 small onion, very thinly sliced

1½ pounds green bell peppers, seeded and sliced in thick strips about 1 inch wide (675 g)

4 Add the peppers and onion to the chicken and tomatoes and simmer, with the lid ajar, for 15 to 20 minutes. Taste for salt and pepper. Serve the chicken hot. This dish is one of those that are better the next day.

THE ROMAN WAY WITH HERBS

FRESH MARJORAM is the preferred herb in Rome, but flat-leaf parsley is used even more often. They say in Rome "Maria or Giovanna or Angelo is like parsley, seen everywhere." Other favorite herbs are mint, rosemary, and sage. When you shop in the outdoor markets, if you are a regular customer, you are given *gli odori* as a gift for the *battuto*, which means a carrot, parsley, and a stalk of celery. Parsley is called *erbetta*, or little herb; celery is called *sellero*, a Roman word. Celery was introduced to Rome in the 1500s by Cardinal Cornaro, who cultivated it in his garden at the Trevi Fountain. He would frequently offer two plants to the Pope and one plant to each Cardinal as exceptional gifts. Marjoram is called *persa*, which means lost. You can be sure they have given you a nickname too, but you may never come to know it.

BAKED CHICKEN CUTLETS WITH PARMESAN AND LEMON

Petti di Pollo Mina

SERVES 6 TO 8

2 pounds skinned and boned chicken breasts or chicken cutlets (about 900 g)

3 tablespoons fresh lemon juice

1⅓ cups fine dry bread crumbs (200 g)

3 tablespoons freshly grated Parmesan cheese

2 eggs

1 teaspoon salt

Freshly ground black pepper

1 stick of butter, cut into small pieces (120 g)

Thin slices of lemon, anchovies, and capers, for garnish

Parsley sprigs

Mina is a friend of mine who grew tired of cooking every day. She had figured out every short-cut in the book and became a specialist in preparing dishes in the morning that could be finished in the evening, so that she could just sit down with the family or enjoy her guests. I have eaten these chicken cutlets prepared by her so often that I consider them a part of my Roman life. A summer or winter dish, it takes just enough time in the oven to allow for an apéritif. She always accompanies them with a salad, often of fresh fennel with orange sections.

1 Either buy thinner sliced chicken cutlets or ask your butcher to divide each breast in half horizontally so that from each half breast you end up with 2 slices of chicken. Place each slice between sheets of waxed paper and pound the chicken until fairly thin, being careful not to tear the meat.

2 Put the chicken in a shallow dish and drizzle the lemon juice over it. Turn the pieces to be sure they all get some juice. Marinate at room temperature for 30 minutes. Pat dry.

3 Mix the bread crumbs with the Parmesan cheese in a shallow soup bowl. Beat the eggs in another soup bowl; season with the salt and pepper. Dip the chicken first in the eggs and then in the bread crumbs, pressing so that the crumbs adhere. Lay the slices flat on a tray. At this point they may be refrigerated, covered with plastic wrap, for up to 8 hours.

4 When ready to cook the chicken cutlets, heat the oven to 350°F (175°C).

5 Generously butter the bottom of a large glass baking dish or a roasting pan with one-third of the butter. Arrange the breaded chicken in the dish in a single layer. Dot with the remaining butter.

6 Bake for 25 minutes. Raise the oven temperature to 400°F (200°C) and bake for about 10 minutes longer, or until the coating is light brown.

7 While the chicken is cooking, prepare the garnish. In the center of each lemon slice place a drained anchovy, curled with a caper in the center. Put the chicken breasts on a heated platter and place a prepared lemon slice on each one. Decorate the edges of the platter with parsley sprigs and serve at once.

CHICKEN BREASTS ON TOAST WITH ANCHOVY BUTTER

Crostini di Pollo con Salsa d'Alici

SERVES 4

1 pound skinned and boned chicken breasts (450 g)

5 ounces thickly sliced prosciutto, about 3 slices (140 g)

2 slices of Italian bread, cut 1 inch thick, or more as needed

Freshly ground black pepper

Bay leaves, preferably fresh

6 tablespoons butter (90 g)

8 anchovy fillets

It's interesting that these crostini were once antipasti; now they are more often found as a main course. The bread, of course, is an important part of this dish. It should be good Italian bread, a day or two old and still with its Italian character.

Chicken breasts have a "fillet," which detaches easily from each breast half. If the rest of the breast is halved and then cut into 2 strips for each half, you will end up with 5 pieces of chicken for each half breast. Here are two ways to prepare these crostini, but the possible combinations are almost infinite, with or without the anchovy butter.

1 Preheat the oven to 400°F (200°C).

2 Place the chicken breasts on a cutting board and, pressing flat with one hand, slice in half parallel to the board. Pound the halves between sheets of waxed paper until they are very thin. Cut each half into strips about 2 inches wide.

3 Cut the prosciutto into 1¼-inch squares. Cut the bread into 1½-inch squares.

4 Place a piece of prosciutto at the center of each strip of breast, dip your fingers in the pepper, spread it on the meat, and roll up that strip. Thread the bread and chicken onto 4 thin metal skewers, alternating with bay leaves and the remaining prosciutto, in this order: bread, bay leaf, chicken roll, prosciutto, bay leaf, bread, and so on.

5 Put the skewers in a roasting pan. Melt 3 tablespoons of the butter and use it to baste the skewers. Roast in the oven for 20 to 25 minutes, turning once, until the bread is toasted and the chicken is cooked through.

6 Heat the remaining 3 tablespoons butter and dissolve the anchovies in it, mashing them with a wooden spoon. Pour the anchovy butter over the crostini and serve at once — they must be hot. The dish can be garnished with bay leaves.

CHICKEN BREASTS FOR THE PRINCESS

Sovrane di Pollo Principessa

SERVES 4 TO 6

6 skinned and boned chicken breast halves, about 1⅓ pounds (1.2 kg)

⅓ cup flour (45 g)

½ teaspoon salt

⅛ teaspoon freshly ground white pepper

6 tablespoons butter (90 g)

1 tablespoon olive oil

¼ cup dry Marsala (60 ml)

1 cup heavy cream (250 ml)

2 tablespoons lemon juice

Julienne of black truffles, if available or minced parsley or chives

Signor Ettore Nibbi, once the chef in one of my husband's hotels, started his kitchen life as a scullery boy in a princely Roman palace owned by a very aristocratic Roman family. He was taught his craft with kicks and slaps, he said; no mistakes were allowed. But his teacher was an exceptional cook, and in those few years of apprenticeship, he learned almost everything he knew.

Signor Nibbi gave me lots of his recipes, which were often used in the grand houses. This is one of his simple ones, cut down to size, because he always had what he called a *brigata* ("brigade") helping him in the kitchen and most of us are helped only by our two hands. Who or what the princess was, I know not, but that is what he called this dish. Signor Nibbi suggests serving these with steamed asparagus tips, dressed with melted butter and a dusting of Parmesan cheese.

1 Pound the chicken breasts to flatten them somewhat. (If they are very thick, halve them horizontally.) Put the flour on a plate and season it with the salt and white pepper. Dredge the chicken in the seasoned flour; shake off any excess.

2 Melt 5 tablespoons of the butter in the olive oil in a very large skillet over moderately high heat. Add the chicken and cook, turning once, until cooked through and light brown, 5 to 7 minutes. Remove the chicken to a heated serving dish and cover to keep warm.

3 Pour the Marsala into the skillet and bring to a boil, scraping up the brown bits from the bottom of the pan. Add the cream and simmer, stirring, until it is slightly reduced, about 5 minutes. Add the lemon juice and the remaining 1 tablespoon butter, whisking to amalgamate the sauce. Taste for seasoning and pour the sauce over the chicken breasts.

4 Garnish with the black truffles, if you have them. If not, try a sprinkling of parsley or chives. Serve at once.

AROMATIC BEEF WITH CLOVES AND MARJORAM

Il Garofolato

SERVES 6 TO 8

⅓ cup fresh marjoram sprigs, or
2½ teaspoons dried marjoram

2 cloves of garlic, peeled

2½ ounces fatty prosciutto or
pancetta, in a single slice (75 g)

2¼ pounds beef bottom round,
trimmed (1 kg)

1 small onion, sliced

1 medium carrot, sliced

1 medium celery rib, sliced

2 tablespoons coarsely
chopped parsley

⅓ cup extra virgin olive oil
(80 ml)

Salt and freshly ground
black pepper

1 cup dry red wine (250 ml)

Il garofolato is a beef dish that is distinctly Roman, though today, this classic pot roast is probably prepared more in trattorias than in private homes. Its highly aromatic quality is attributable to a healthy dose of both cloves and fresh marjoram, Rome's favorite herb. The Roman name for marjoram is *persa*, which means "lost," which is a mystery to me since you can find the herb, almost a cross between thyme and oregano, all over the city. The open-air markets carry large bunches of fresh marjoram tied and hanging, smelling of a Mediterranean country breeze.

1 Finely chop the marjoram and 1 garlic clove together and put onto a small plate. Cut the prosciutto into strips about ½ inch wide and 2 inches long. Using a sharp, thin knife, make slits in the beef, spacing them evenly. Roll the prosciutto strips in the chopped garlic and marjoram and then use them to lard the meat all over, pushing the prosciutto pieces down into the meat. Tie the meat so that it keeps its shape.

2 Make the *battuto*: Finely chop together the remaining garlic cloves, the onion, carrot, celery, and parsley.

3 Heat the olive oil in a large flameproof casserole over moderate heat and stir in the *battuto*. As soon as the vegetables begin to sizzle, add the meat and cook, turning and seasoning it with salt and pepper, until it is light brown all over, about 20 minutes. Stir the vegetables often.

4 Add the wine, nutmeg, and cloves. When the wine has almost evaporated, add the tomatoes and enough water to almost cover the meat. Cover, reduce the heat to moderately low, and simmer until the meat is very tender, about 2 hours, turning the roast every now and then.

*½ teaspoon freshly grated
nutmeg*

4 whole cloves

*3 cups finely chopped peeled
tomatoes, seeded if fresh*

 Remove the meat to a carving board. If the sauce is too liquid, boil uncovered until it is slightly thickened. Cut the meat into fairly thick slices. Arrange on a platter and ladle some of the sauce over the meat. The remaining sauce is used on fettuccine — better if homemade — and sprinkled with pecorino Romano cheese and black pepper.

THE ARTISANS OF ROME

ROME STILL HAS an army of artisans, menders, restorers, and reproducers who can copy almost everything. This is very helpful when you break your grandmother's pitcher or lose your precious coral earring. In my house, our specialty is breaking silver objects, lids to antique sauce boats, candlesticks, and the like. Not to worry, Signor Rocchi and sons can mend almost anything, especially household treasures. You have to be willing to wait for a few months if the job is complicated, but he and his two sons are wizards. They are also very nice people.

Marcello Rocchi e Figli, Via Margutta 51A, 00187 Roma, telephone 06 320 7678

Via Margutta was once, and still is to some degree, the artists' street. There were artists' studios all up and down Via Margutta, which have been converted into chic apartments and pieds-à-terre. This is the street where Federico Fellini, famous as the director of *La Dolce Vita*, lived. It is only two steps from Piazza di Spagna and is also known for its antique shops.

The fountain on the right as you enter Via Margutta (coming from Piazza di Spagna) is interesting; it is by a Fascist sculptor and, as far as I know, is the only one of its kind in Rome.

BRAISED OXTAILS WITH CELERY

Coda alla Vaccinara

SERVES 6

4 pounds oxtails, cut into 1½-inch lengths (about 1.8 kg)

1 whole bunch of celery

¼ pound fatty pancetta (110 g)

1 small carrot, peeled

2 cloves of garlic, peeled

1 medium onion, sliced

2 or 3 sprigs of fresh marjoram, or 1¼ teaspoons dried

3 tablespoons extra virgin olive oil

Salt and freshly ground black pepper

1 cup dry white wine (250 ml)

2 tablespoons tomato paste

La coda alla vaccinara, another famous Roman dish, was particularly appreciated in the Regola, one of the Roman city zones. In this part of the city there were most all of the tanners and a great number of cow herders. This is a recipe of the 1800s but still eaten today with very few changes. It is considered a treat because oxtails are not so easy to find now and often have to be ordered. If desired, 2 tablespoons of golden raisins, 2 tablespoons of pine nuts, and 1 tablespoon of grated unsweetened chocolate may be added when the pan is removed from the heat at the end of the cooking time.

1 Rinse the oxtails in cold water and drain. Remove and reserve 1 medium celery rib. Set the remaining celery aside.

2 Make the battuto: Using a mezzaluna or a large chef's knife on a cutting board, chop together the 1 celery rib with the pancetta, carrot, garlic, onion, and marjoram. Turn the ingredients as you chop to be sure they are well mixed together.

3 Heat the olive oil in a large flameproof casserole. Add the battuto to the oil and cook over moderately low heat, stirring, for about 10 minutes, until the vegetables are soft and the onion is golden. Add the oxtails, season with salt and pepper on all sides, and raise the heat to moderate. Continue cooking and stirring until the oxtails are a deep brown, about 10 minutes longer.

4 Pour in the wine and bring to a boil. Put the tomato paste in the center of the pan and mix it into the wine. Reduce the heat to moderately low, cover the pan, and simmer for 10 minutes. Pour in

enough hot water to almost cover the oxtails. Bring to a simmer, cover again, and cook for about 2 hours, or until the meat is so tender it falls from the bones.

5 While the oxtails are cooking, prepare the celery. Trim and cut into 2-inch lengths. In a large saucepan of boiling salted water, cook the celery until it is al dente; drain.

6 When the oxtails are done, add the celery to the casserole and simmer for 5 minutes. Remove the meat and celery to a serving dish. If the sauce is too watery, boil to reduce. Season with additional salt and pepper to taste. Pour the sauce over the oxtails and serve.

"Le Regolante
So' ttutte magna code e sso' carine,
So ttute magna code e sso' galante."

The girls from Regola
Are all oxtail eaters and pretty,
Are all oxtail eaters and are graceful.

(Roman *stornello* from the 1880s — a song sung to a familiar tune, often off color and almost always ironic!)

MEATBALLS IN SAVORY TOMATO SAUCE

Polpette con Sugo Finto

SERVES 6 TO 8

Savory Tomato Sauce
(recipe opposite)

1⅓ pounds ground beef,
ground twice (600 g)

2 large slices of Italian bread

1 teaspoon salt

½ teaspoon freshly ground
black pepper

¼ teaspoon freshly grated nutmeg

1 ounce pancetta (30 g)

½ small peeled clove of garlic

Small handful of parsley

1 large sprig of fresh marjoram
leaves, or 1 teaspoon dried

2 eggs

¼ cup freshly grated Parmesan
cheese (25 g)

¼ cup raisins, plumped in
warm water and drained (30 g)

This is a fabulous meatball recipe, seasoned with Parmesan and herbs and studded with raisins and pine nuts. The meatballs are simmered in a sauce, which in Italian is called "fake sauce," probably because it does not contain any meat except for a bit of pancetta. Of course, with the meatballs cooked in it, no additional meat is needed. This dish is so ubiquitous and commonly eaten in Rome, you could almost think of it as our equivalent of a hamburger.

1 Prepare the sauce first. To make the meatballs, put the ground beef in a large bowl. Trim the crusts from the bread and tear the bread into pieces. Soak the bread in cold water. Drain and squeeze out the water. Using your hands, mix the softened bread into the beef. Season with the salt, pepper, and nutmeg.

2 Chop together the pancetta, garlic, parsley, and marjoram and add to the meat. Beat the eggs and stir them in along with the Parmesan cheese, raisins, and pine nuts. Mix all the ingredients together thoroughly with your hands. Form 10 large meatballs (polpette), about 3 inches in diameter, slightly flattened on top. Roll them in the dry bread crumbs until they are well coated.

3 Heat the olive oil to shimmering in a large skillet and fit the polpette into the pan. Sauté over moderately high heat, turning, until the meatballs are brown outside and cooked through, about 15 minutes.

4 Drain the meatballs on paper towels. Gently lower them into the Savory Tomato Sauce and simmer for 5 to 8 minutes.

⅓ cup pine nuts (35 g)

1 cup fine dry bread crumbs,
or more as needed (100 g)

½ cup olive oil (120 ml)

SAVORY TOMATO SAUCE

Sugo Finto

MAKES ENOUGH SAUCE FOR PASTA
FOR 6 PEOPLE

2 ounces pancetta (60 g)

Small handful of parsley

1 small celery rib, trimmed

1 small carrot, peeled

1 small clove of garlic, peeled

¼ cup extra virgin olive oil
(60 ml)

1 small onion, finely chopped

3 pounds ripe tomatoes, peeled,
seeded, and chopped (1.35 kg),
or 2 cans (28 ounces) Italian
peeled tomatoes with their
juices (1.6 kg)

Salt and freshly ground black
pepper

NOTE: Ground pork can also be used for the *polpette*, with 1 or 2 sausages, stripped of their casings and crumbled, mixed together with the ground meat.

1 Make the *battuto:* Chop together the pancetta, parsley, celery, carrot, and garlic, turning the ingredients with your knife and mixing as you chop.

2 Heat the olive oil in a large pot. Add the onion and cook over moderate heat, stirring often, until the onion is softened and golden, about 5 minutes. Add the *battuto* and continue cooking over moderately low heat until the vegetables are very soft and the onion is golden, 7 to 10 minutes, adding 1 or 2 tablespoons of water every now and then to allow the seasonings to cook without burning.

3 Add the fresh tomatoes, or the canned plum tomatoes with about three-quarters of their juice. Season with salt and pepper to taste and finish cooking the sauce for 15 minutes over moderate heat, mashing the tomatoes with the back of a wooden spoon and stirring often.

MINA'S MEAT LOAF

Polpettone di Mina

SERVES 8 TO 10

12 ounces ground beef or veal (340 g)

12 ounces ground pork (340 g)

6 ounces ground chicken (170 g)

¼ pound mortadella, very finely chopped in a food processor (110 g)

2 whole eggs

2 egg yolks

1 cup freshly grated Parmesan cheese (100 g)

⅔ cup finely chopped flat-leaf parsley (15 g)

1½ teaspoons salt

¾ teaspoon freshly ground black pepper, or to taste

¼ teaspoon freshly grated nutmeg

½ cup milk (120 ml)

1 to 1¼ cups fine dry bread crumbs (about 100 g)

My Roman friend Mina has many meat loaf recipes that practically cook themselves. This one is my favorite. It keeps easily in a turned-off oven for about 30 minutes, but should not be left too long, or it will dry out. In winter I serve this with a hearty mustard; in summer, with the green sauce that follows as well as a variety of fresh and marinated vegetables, including radishes, pickled onions, artichokes in oil, lettuce, and tomatoes.

1 If possible, have your butcher grind together the pork, beef or veal, chicken, and mortadella twice. Preheat the oven to 400°F (200°F).

2 With your hands, blend the ground meats and mortadella with the eggs, egg yolks, Parmesan cheese, parsley, salt, pepper, nutmeg, milk, and ½ to ¾ cup of the bread crumbs, just enough to make the loaf hold together.

3 Sprinkle the remaining bread crumbs on a flat work surface or large platter. Form the ground meat mixture into 2 loaves and roll each loaf in the crumbs to coat it. Coat the bottom of a baking dish that will hold both loaves with the remaining 2 tablespoons olive oil. Put the loaves in the dish, making sure they are not touching. Drizzle 1 tablespoon oil over each loaf.

¼ cup extra virgin olive oil (60 ml)

½ cup dry white wine (120 ml)

Italian Green Sauce (recipe follows) or hearty mustard

ITALIAN GREEN SAUCE

Salsa Verde all'Italiana

MAKES ABOUT 1½ CUPS

2 tablespoons finely chopped onion

2 tablespoons capers, rinsed and dried*

1 clove of garlic, chopped

¼ cup fresh bread crumbs (25 g)

3 tablespoons white wine vinegar

3 anchovy fillets, cut into pieces

2 large handfuls of parsley, washed and dried

Salt and freshly ground black pepper

2 sour gherkins, cut into pieces

About ¾ cup olive oil (180 ml)

* If you have capers packed in salt, soak them in a bowl of cold water for at least 20 minutes, then drain and dry on paper towels.

4 Bake for 40 minutes. Turn the loaves over and bake for another 20 minutes. Pour the wine over the meat loaves and bake for 5 more minutes. If serving the meat loaves hot, let them rest for 10 minutes before slicing. Otherwise, let them cool, then wrap and refrigerate. Let return to room temperature before serving. Accompany with Italian Green Sauce or mustard.

Salsa verde is one of the great Italian sauces. It is simple but unbelievably tasty. We Italians use it for everything from meats to seafood to chicken to vegetables. It is exceptional with cold meats. The sauce can be made a few hours ahead, but it is best at room temperature.

Put all the ingredients except the olive oil into a blender or food processor. Puree, scraping down the sides. With the machine on, gradually add the oil in a slow stream, until the sauce emulsifies and thickens to the consistency of a thick mayonnaise.

VEAL SCALOPPINE

ALTHOUGH THE following three veal scaloppine recipes are Roman, they are known all over Italy, if not throughout the entire world. They are simple and easy to prepare, even look quite elegant when presented with lemon slices or sage leaves surrounding the thin slices of meat. The important thing here is to find a good butcher with fresh, tender veal.

VEAL SCALOPPINE MONTE CENCI WITH BRAISED ARTICHOKES

Scaloppine Monte Cenci con Carciofi

SERVES 4 OR 5

Braised Artichokes (recipe opposite)

1 pound veal scaloppine, divided into 12 pieces and pounded until thin (450 g)

Salt and freshly ground black pepper

Flour, for dredging

3 tablespoons butter (45 g)

1 tablespoon extra virgin olive oil

½ cup dry white wine (120 ml)

These are called *scaloppine Monte Cenci* because the recipe comes from the Ghetto, where the Cenci Palace still stands.

1 Prepare the artichokes as directed at right. Cover to keep warm while you sauté the veal.

2 Heat a serving platter for the scaloppine in a warm oven.

3 Season the scaloppine with salt and pepper and dredge them lightly in flour, shaking off any excess. Melt the butter in the olive oil in a large skillet over moderately high heat. In batches, sauté the scaloppine rapidly, turning, until brown on both sides, 3 to 4 minutes. Set the scaloppine aside on a plate as they are cooked.

4 Pour in the wine and scrape up the brown bits from the bottom of the pan. Return all the meat to the skillet. Cook until the wine is reduced by about one-third. Transfer the scaloppine to the warm platter, scatter the artichoke slices over the meat, and pour the hot sauce over all.

BRAISED ARTICHOKES

SERVES 4 OR 5

6 medium artichokes, cleaned,
rubbed with lemon, and soaked
in cold acidulated water (see
page 211)

———

2½ tablespoons fresh lemon juice

———

¼ cup extra virgin olive oil
(60 ml)

———

3 cloves of garlic, peeled

———

Salt and freshly ground black
pepper

———

1 Drain the artichokes and cut each of them in half. Remove the choke with a small spoon and check to be sure that all the tough leaves have been eliminated. Put the lemon juice in a bowl. Cut the artichoke halves lengthwise into thin slices and toss the slices with the lemon juice in the bowl.

2 Heat the olive oil in a large skillet, preferably nonstick. Add the garlic and cook slowly over low heat until the garlic is light brown; then discard the garlic.

3 Add the artichoke slices to the skillet. Cook over low heat, stirring every now and then, for 20 to 25 minutes, or until they are tender but firm. Season with salt and pepper to taste.

SALTIMBOCCA ALLA ROMANA

SERVES 4

8 veal scaloppine, about 1 pound (450 g)

Salt and freshly ground black pepper

8 large fresh sage leaves

8 thin slices of prosciutto

4 tablespoons butter (60 g)

1 tablespoon olive oil

½ cup dry white wine (120 ml)

Flour, for dredging

I offer only one name here, since this dish is such a classic all over the world. By now, most people know that the name means "jumps into the mouth," because the dish is so good, but the Italian name also conjures up the distinctive combination of flavors: veal, sage, and prosciutto. Serve with fresh peas or a puree of potatoes.

1 Trim the scaloppine if necessary and gently pound them to flatten evenly. Dry them with paper towels. Season the meat with salt and pepper and place a sage leaf and a slice of prosciutto on each scaloppine. Secure the sage and prosciutto to the meat with a toothpick.

2 Dredge the scaloppine on both sides in flour, shaking them to remove any excess. They should be lightly floured.

3 Heat the butter and oil in a large skillet, preferably nonstick, over moderately high heat. Add the scaloppine, veal down, prosciutto up. Cook for about 3 minutes, or until golden brown on the bottom. Turn them over and cook for about 2 minutes. Carefully transfer the scaloppine to a warm platter. Remove and discard the toothpicks.

4 Pour the white wine into the skillet and scrape up the browned bits from the bottom of the pan. Cook until the wine is reduced by half. Pour it over the *saltimbocca* and serve at once.

VEAL SCALOPPINE WITH LEMON

Piccatine al Limone

SERVES 4 TO 6

1⅓ pounds veal scaloppine
(600 g)
———

Flour, for dredging
———

3 tablespoons extra virgin
olive oil
———

2 tablespoons butter (30 g)
———

Salt
———

3 tablespoons dry white wine
———

1 large egg yolk, at cool room
temperature
———

⅓ cup fresh lemon juice (80 ml)
———

2 tablespoons chopped parsley
———

Le piccatine, veal scaloppine pleasingly tart with fresh lemon juice, should be prepared just before serving and eaten right away, which is not difficult to do since it takes only about 5 minutes. The dish is easy to make, it is perfect summer or winter, and it does not require complicated ingredients. There are several variations of veal piccata. This particular manner of preparing it was given to me by a university professor friend who likes to cook — and eat — well.

1 Pound the scaloppine lightly with a meat pounder. Dredge the slices in flour and shake in a sifter to remove any excess.

2 Heat the oil and butter in a very large skillet over moderately high heat. Cook the scaloppine in 2 batches, salting after turning them. Remove the scaloppine to a warm platter and pour the white wine into the skillet, stirring to incorporate any brown bits from the bottom of the pan.

3 Whisk together the egg yolk and lemon juice until blended. Remove the skillet from the heat and pour the yolk mixture into the pan, whisking constantly. Pour the sauce over the veal, sprinkle the parsley on top, and serve at once.

VEAL CHOPS WITH A KISS

Cotolette di Vitello al Bacio

SERVES 2

2 veal loin or rib chops, about 12 ounces each (180 g total)

2 tablespoons flour

Salt and freshly ground white pepper

3 tablespoons unsalted butter (45 g)

1 teaspoon extra virgin olive oil

¼ cup dry Marsala (60 ml)

½ bouillon beef or chicken cube

Thin strips of fresh white truffle (optional)

Valentine's Day is not a holiday in Italy, but romance is perennial. Here's a perfect recipe for two — quick and delicious — luxurious with a "kiss" of white truffles at the end. If fresh truffles are not available, finish with a light drizzle of white truffle oil. Serve with roasted potatoes, mushrooms sautéed in butter, and sautéed artichoke slices or baby green beans.

1 Leaving the bone in, lightly pound the meat of the chops to thin them to cutlets.

2 Lightly flour the veal cutlets on both sides, shaking off any excess. Salt very lightly (the bouillon cube is salty) and season with white pepper to taste.

3 Melt 2 tablespoons of the butter with the olive oil in a large skillet. Brown the veal over moderate heat. Pour a generous quantity of Marsala over them and, add the ½ bouillon cube. Mix, then add a small piece of cold butter, whisking.

4 Put the cutlets in a warm platter. Pour the sauce over the veal. *Dulcis in fundo,* "the best part at the end" — top with julienned white truffles.

STUFFED VEAL SCALOPPINE, called *involtini*, are also very Roman. Here are three of my favorites.

STUFFED VEAL SCALOPPINE

Involtini di Scaloppine di Vitello

SERVES 6

1⅓ pounds veal scaloppine, trimmed (600 g)

Salt and freshly ground black pepper

¼ pound ground pork (110 g)

¼ pound ground veal (110 g)

¼ pound ground mortadella (110 g)

1 slice of bread, crust removed, soaked in water

2 small eggs

Grated zest of 1 lemon

½ cup freshly grated Parmesan cheese (50 g)

3 tablespoons butter (45 g)

3 tablespoons olive oil

½ cup plus 2 tablespoons dry white wine (150 ml)

1 The scaloppine should be more or less the same size. Divide the scaloppine into 12 small slices and flatten them gently with a meat pounder. Season lightly with salt and pepper.

2 Make the stuffing: Mix the pork, veal, and mortadella together in a small bowl. Squeeze the water from the bread and crumble the bread into the meat. Add the eggs, lemon zest, and Parmesan cheese and stir with a fork until all is combined and the eggs are absorbed. Season with salt and pepper.

3 Divide the stuffing among the scaloppine, placing a spoonful in the center of each. Roll one up, tucking in the ends, if possible. Fasten the roll with a toothpick. Continue until you have stuffed all the scaloppine.

4 Heat the butter and oil in a large skillet. Arrange the involtini in the pan in a single layer and sauté them over moderately high heat, turning, until brown all over, about 8 to 10 minutes total. Pour ½ cup of the wine over the meat and allow it to evaporate for about 30 seconds. Reduce the heat to moderately low, cover the pan, and cook for 30 minutes, turning the involtini every now and then.

5 When the involtini are ready, remove them to a heated platter. Use the remaining 2 tablespoons wine to scrape up the brown particles from the bottom of the skillet. Pour the pan juices over the involtini and serve.

VEAL SCALOPPINE STUFFED WITH MORTADELLA AND PARMESAN CHEESE

Involtini di Scaloppine di Vitello Rosanna

SERVES 4 TO 6

1⅓ pounds leg of veal, cut into small scaloppine (600 g)

—

5 ounces thinly sliced mortadella (140 g)

—

4½ ounces Parmesan cheese in a single chunk (125 g)

—

Salt and freshly ground black pepper

—

3 tablespoons butter (45 g)

—

3 tablespoons olive oil

—

⅓ cup plus 2 tablespoons dry white wine (110 ml)

1 Lay out the scaloppine on a work surface. Trim the mortadella slices so that they are the same size as the scaloppine. With a sharp knife, cut 4 or 5 slivers of Parmesan cheese and place the slivers over the mortadella on each of the scaloppine. Roll up the scaloppine carefully, and close the rolls with toothpicks, tucking in the ends. Season lightly with salt and pepper.

2 Heat the butter and oil together in a large skillet over moderate heat. Put the involtini into the skillet and cook, turning, until they are brown all over, about 8 to 10 minutes. Add ⅓ cup of the wine and continue cooking for 20 to 25 minutes turning the involtini now and then.

3 Remove the involtini to a warm plate. Pour the remaining 2 tablespoons wine into the skillet and scrape up the browned bits from the bottom of the pan. Pour the pan juices over the involtini and serve.

STUFFED VEAL SCALOPPINE WITH FENNEL, PANCETTA, AND CAPERS

Involtini di Scaloppine di Vitello Giovanna

SERVES 4 TO 6

2 tablespoons salt-packed capers*

1⅓ pounds small veal scaloppine, trimmed (600 g)

Salt and freshly ground black pepper

¼ pound pancetta, sliced (110 g)

4 tablespoons olive oil

1 clove of garlic, peeled and coarsely chopped

2 small fennel bulbs, trimmed and coarsely chopped

2 tablespoons coarsely chopped parlsey

2 tablespoons butter (30 g)

½ bouillon cube

⅓ cup white wine (80 ml)

* If you cannot find salt-packed capers, use brined capers, well rinsed and drained.

1 Rinse the capers and soak in a bowl of cold water for 20 minutes. Drain and dry on paper towels.

2 Meanwhile, lay out the scaloppine on a work surface and season lightly with salt and pepper.

3 In a small skillet, fry the pancetta in ½ tablespoon of the olive oil until it is brown but not too crisp. Remove the pancetta with a slotted spoon and chop coarsely. Reserve the oil in the skillet.

4 Finely chop together the pancetta, garlic, fennel, parsley, and capers. Season lightly with salt and pepper. Divide this mixture among the scaloppine, roll them up, and close the rolls with toothpicks.

5 Heat the butter, the remaining olive oil, and the reserved pancetta cooking oil in a large skillet. Place the involtini slowly into the pan and add the wine. Raise the heat to a simmer and cook for 15 to 20 minutes, turning the involtini occasionally.

SWEET-AND-SOUR VEAL TONGUE A LA ROMANA

Lingua in Agrodolce alla Romana

SERVES 6 TO 8

1 veal tongue, about 2 pounds
(900 g)

15 whole black peppercorns

4 whole cloves

1 medium onion, thickly sliced

1 bay leaf

2 strips of lemon peel, about
2 inches long (yellow zest only)

1 tablespoon coarse salt

10 pitted prunes

½ cup raisins (60 g)

3½ tablespoons sugar

3 tablespoons white wine vinegar

3 cloves of garlic, crushed

For this modern way of preparing sweet-and-sour tongue, my butcher sent me to Mario, a fruit and vegetable vendor at my open-air market, just two blocks from the Trevi fountain in the heart of Rome. Mario is very Roman, not at all shy, and he immediately reeled off all the ingredients needed for the dish. His customers waited patiently, and then all began talking at once and contributing their versions. I've been making mine this way ever since that day, and I *think* all the ingredients are Mario's.

1 Wash the tongue in cold water. Drain well.

2 In a casserole large enough to hold the tongue, put the tongue, peppercorns, cloves, onion, bay leaf, lemon peel, and salt. Add enough hot water to cover the meat and put a lid on the pan. Bring to a boil and skim, if necessary. Cover the pot again, reduce the heat to low, and simmer the tongue for about 2 hours, or until it is tender when pierced with a kitchen needle or the tip of a knife.

3 Transfer the tongue to a bowl of cold water and let stand for 1 to 2 minutes. Slit the skin underneath the tongue from the tip to the base and peel away and discard the skin and any small bones or gristle. Return the tongue to its broth in the casserole and let it cool in the liquid until tepid.

4 Soak the prunes and raisins separately in bowls of hot water to plump them. Drain both; quarter or halve the prunes.

6 tablespoons fresh lemon juice (90 ml)

———

1 peperoncino, or hot red pepper flakes to taste

———

3 tablespoons chopped parsley, plus parsley sprigs to decorate the dish

———

¼ cup pine nuts, lightly toasted (65 g)

———

5 In a small nonreactive saucepan, dissolve the sugar in the vinegar. Add the garlic, lemon juice, peperoncino or hot pepper flakes, and chopped parsley. Add the prunes and raisins to the sauce.

6 Thinly slice the cooled tongue and arrange in a serving dish. Pour the sauce over the tongue, taking care to cover all the meat. Sprinkle the pine nuts on top, cover, and let it marinate in the refrigerator overnight. Let return to room temperature for at least 2 hours. Decorate with parsley sprigs before serving.

SAUTEED CALF'S LIVER WITH BROWNED ONIONS

Fegato alla Macellara

SERVES 2 TO 4

1 pound thinly sliced calf's liver
(450 g)

¼ cup lard (75 g) or extra virgin
olive oil (60 ml)

½ pound sweet white onions,
sliced (225 g)

¼ cup dry white wine (in Rome
it would be Frascati) (60 ml)

Salt

Lemon wedges and chopped
parsley, for garnish

At the end of 1800, a modern abbatoire was built in
Testaccio on the site where the antique Romans disposed of
their broken pottery; even today, Romans call this place Monte
dei Cocci ("mountain of broken pottery"). The abbatoire was
the most modern in Europe, and hundreds of workers sought
work there. To pad their earnings, the men were paid in offal:
head, tongue, tail, spleen, heart, liver, tripe, etc. They would
take their share to the nearest osteria to be prepared for them.
From this was born a rich and varied Roman cucina that soon
became food favored by all the Romans, not just the inhabitants of Testaccio.

1 Clean the liver of fat and remove the membrane on the edges by simply pulling it away gently. Cut the liver slices into smaller pieces, about 3 inches square.

2 In a large skillet, heat the lard or olive oil over moderately high heat and sauté the liver slices rapidly on both sides until they are nicely browned outside but still rosy in the center. Remove them to a platter and keep warm.

3 Reduce the heat to moderate and add the onions to the pan. Cook, stirring and adding the wine a few tablespoons at the time, until the onions are soft and golden brown, about 15 minutes.

4 Return the liver to the pan and heat quickly. Transfer the slices to a warm platter and season with salt. Arrange the onions on top. Garnish the liver with wedges of lemon to squeeze over it. Top with chopped parsley and serve at once.

ROAST BABY LAMB WITH POTATOES

Abbacchio al Forno con Patate

SERVES 4

3 pounds baby lamb, ribs and shoulder boned (1.35 kg)

———

4 cloves of garlic, peeled and crushed

———

3 ounces pancetta or pork fat, sliced (85 g)

———

3 tablespoons chopped fresh rosemary, plus sprigs for garnish

———

Salt and freshly ground black pepper

———

¼ cup plus 1 tablespoon extra virgin olive oil (75 ml)

———

1½ pounds potatoes, peeled and sliced (675 g)

———

When you mention baby lamb to a Roman, he behaves as he does at the mention of *porchetta*, roast suck-ling pig — his eyes glaze over with pleasure. As they should. The baby lamb sold in Rome is the very best: ten-der and very tasty. The sheep graze all over Lazio, and each season they are moved to another pasture for the sweet grasses and herbs, which flavor the meat. The sheep give birth two times a year, insuring the region baby lamb, as well as lamb, ricotta, and pecorino. Without these products Roman cooking would be another thing altogether.

Baby lamb is a must at Easter, but it is also eaten during the year, whenever it is available. Usually the roast is accompanied by potatoes, as it is here, and a lovely salad called *misticanza*. Misticanza is composed of many salad greens, much like the American mesclun, which are *di taglio*, which means the salad is cut, not uprooted, and therefore grows again, to be cut and eaten again, much like your mesclun, which in America started in California, but originally came from the Mediterranean.

1 Preheat the oven to 400°F (200°C).

2 Lay out the lamb, boned side up, on a very lightly oiled baking sheet. Rub half the lamb with 1 of the garlic cloves and leave them on the roast; put 2 slices of pancetta on top. Season with 1 table-spoon of the rosemary and salt and pepper to taste. Fold the other half of the lamb over the seasoned half. Arrange the remaining pancetta on top and tuck 2 garlic cloves underneath the slices. Drizzle ¼ cup of olive oil over the lamb. Season lightly with salt and pepper, and sprinkle on another tablespoon of rosemary.

3 Drain and dry the potatoes and put them into a bowl with the remaining garlic clove, 1 tablespoon chopped rosemary, and the remaining tablespoon of oil. Season the potatoes with salt and toss to mix thoroughly. Scatter the potatoes around the meat and roast the lamb and potatoes for 30 minutes, turning and mixing the potatoes twice, after 15 minutes and again after 30 minutes.

4 Raise the oven temperature to 475°F (245°C). Roast the lamb and potatoes for another 15 minutes.

5 Remove the lamb to a cutting board and let it rest for 10 minutes. Cover the potatoes to keep them warm. Cut the lamb into serving pieces and arrange on a warm platter with the potatoes. Drizzle any pan juices over the meat. Garnish with sprigs of rosemary and serve.

BRAISED BABY LAMB WITH EGG AND LEMON SAUCE

Abbacchio Brodettato

SERVES 6 TO 8

3-pound boned leg of young lamb, bone reserved (1.35 kg)

2 ounces prosciutto, fat and lean, coarsely chopped (60 g)

1 small onion, coarsely chopped

2 tablespoons lard or olive oil

1 tablespoon olive oil

Salt and freshly ground black pepper

½ cup dry white wine (125 ml)

1 tablespoon flour

1 clove of garlic, finely chopped

1½ tablespoons finely chopped parsley

3 egg yolks

2 tablespoons freshly grated Parmesan cheese

2½ tablespoons fresh lemon juice

Abbacchio brodettato is usually served simply with a salad of mixed greens, dressed with oil and lemon, often with an anchovy mashed into the dressing. Sweet Peas with Prosciutto (page 228) or artichokes could also accompany this *romanissimo* dish.

1 Have the butcher cut the bone into pieces so it will fit into the pot. Trim most of the fat from the lamb and remove any tendons. Cut the meat into 1-ounce pieces (you may want to ask your butcher to do this for you).

2 Finely chop together the prosciutto and onion to make a *battuto*. Heat the lard and olive oil (or just olive oil) in a large flameproof casserole. Add the meat, *battuto*, and bones for extra flavor. Season with salt and pepper and cook over moderate heat, stirring often, until the meat is light brown. Pour in the wine and cook, stirring, until almost all of it evaporates. Sift the flour over the meat and cook, stirring, 1 to 2 minutes. Add enough water to almost but not quite cover the meat. Cover with a lid and continue to cook over moderate heat, stirring every now and then, for 45 to 60 minutes, or until the lamb is tender.

3 Discard the bones and stir in the chopped garlic and parsley. Simmer 10 minutes longer, uncovered if the sauce seems too thin.

4 In a medium bowl, beat the egg yolks with the Parmesan cheese and lemon juice. Gradually whisk in ½ cup of the hot sauce from the casserole to warm the yolks. Stir this yolk mixture into the sauce remaining in the casserole. Simmer over the lowest heat for 3 to 5 minutes, stirring, until the sauce turns creamy, but do not allow it to boil. Transfer the lamb and sauce to a warm dish and serve at once.

BRAISED BABY GOAT WITH EGG AND LEMON SAUCE

Capretto Brodettato

Prepare as above but substitute kid, baby goat, for the lamb. Allow longer cooking time for the goat, up to 3 hours.

ROMAN ROAST SUCKLING PIG

Porchetta alla Romana

SERVES ABOUT 20

1 suckling pig, about 25 pounds (11 k)

———

12 large cloves of garlic, in their skins

———

2½ ounces wild fennel,* tender stalks and leaves (70 g)

———

Coarse salt and freshly ground black pepper

———

2 tablespoons dried fennel flowers, or 2 tablespoons fennel seeds

———

Extra virgin olive oil

———

* If wild fennel is not available, use the feathery green fronds of a fennel bulb — not the same, but a good substitute.

Porchetta is still sold on the streets in Rome; there are even shops that sell only *porchetta* to go and trattorias that specialize in it. The rich meat makes a big show at an outdoor buffet, where it is traditionally presented whole on a bed of laurel, with a lemon in its mouth. It is perfect accompanied by fruit chutney. In Rome it is always served at room temperature or even cold, with big thick slices of crusty Italian bread and what is called (in Roman dialect) a *foietta* — ¼ liter — of wine from the Castelli Romani.

This white wine is the pride of the Romans. They are particularly pleased that it doesn't travel, which makes it exclusively Roman. It is called *frascati*, is a pale yellow color, and goes down deceptively easily. It is still brought into Rome in big barrels, though less commonly than before, and on trucks instead of horse-drawn carts with huge one-sided umbrellas. It is delicious, and should be served cool but not icy.

(continued)

1 The pig must be boned, and it is such a long, tedious job that you should cajole your butcher into doing this for you. Ask him to leave the trotters intact and to save you the liver, heart, and tongue. These should be cut into 1-inch pieces, so if you want, you can ask him to do that, too. Also, ask him to weigh the meat after boning. For every 2½ pounds of pork, you will need 1 ounce salt; this may sound like a lot, but it's necessary.

2 Put the garlic and wild fennel in hot water and bring to a boil. Boil for 2 minutes and drain. Remove the skins from the garlic. Chop the wild fennel coarsely.

3 Lay the pig on its back on a work surface, cut side up. Salt the interior of the pig generously, particularly in the hams and the meatier parts. Rub the pig with the garlic, crushing the cloves with your hands. Sprinkle the chopped wild fennel over the pig. In a bowl, season the cut-up liver, heart, and tongue with salt and pepper and distribute the pieces down the middle of the pig. Sprinkle the fennel flowers or dried fennel seeds on top.

4 Close up the pig, securing the skin with short metal skewers every 2 inches and cross-tying with twine. (You'll need help for this; it takes at least four hands.) Then, to give a shape to the pig, tie up the whole body with twine every 3 inches, tightening only slightly to leave room for expansion. Refrigerate the seasoned pig for at least 8 hours, or overnight, turning it every now and then from one side or the other.

5 When ready to cook the *porchetta*, preheat the oven to 450°F (230°C). Cover the ears, snout, and tail with foil. Put the pig on its stomach on a large baking sheet and, dipping your hands in olive oil, rub it generously all over the pig.

6 Bake the pig in the hot oven for 40 minutes. (Check after 30 minutes to be sure it does not brown too rapidly.) Reduce the oven temperature to 375°F (190°C) and cook for about 2½ hours, or until the juices run clear. It is impossible to give a specific time, because ovens and pigs vary. Let the *porchetta* cool completely before slicing and keep it in a cool place until ready to serve. Do not refrigerate.

7 When ready to serve the *porchetta* cut into 1-inch-thick slices, beginning at the hind feet: With a sharp knife, score the slices. Use a sharp kitchen scissors to cut the crusty skin first, then slice the meat. *Porchetta* will keep at least 5 days in the refrigerator and is almost always better for it. Let the meat come to cool room temperature before serving.

NOTE: This *porchetta* is to be made at home. The *porchettari*, vendors who sell roast suckling pig in their shops, debone pigs weighing up to 200 pounds or more. They use exactly the same condiments, in proportion to the size of the animal. Ariccia, in the Castelli Romani, is famous for their *porchetta*, which is considered the best in Lazio.

PORK ROAST WITH FRUIT

Arista di Maiale con Frutta

SERVES 8

1 boneless pork rib roast,
about 5 pounds (2.3 kg)

2 tablespoons brown sugar

1½ teaspoons coarse salt

½ teaspoon freshly ground
black pepper

3 tablespoons butter (45 g)

¼ cup extra virgin olive oil (60 ml)

2 medium onions, very thinly sliced

1 cup dry white wine (250 ml)

2 bouillon cubes

2 large lemons, sectioned*

1¼ pounds seedless green grapes,
or the sections from 3 ripe oranges
(575 g)

2 tablespoons Cointreau (optional)

---

* To make lemon or orange sections, cut away a
slice from the top and bottom of the fruit. Set
one end of the fruit on a cutting board and,
using a sharp knife, cut away pith and peel
together all around the fruit. Remove the sections, with the sharp knife, taking care to
remove all the pith, as it can be very bitter.

Sweet-and-sour dishes have been Roman favorites
since antiquity, and, as in Chinese cuisine, pork lends
itself particularly well to that curious and enormously
appealing combination of flavors. All around Rome,
small farmers, even weekend gentlemen farmers, raise
hogs for themselves, feeding them mainly table scraps. After
butchering, the meat is used in a great variety of ways —
eaten as roasts; cured and dried to make hams, sausages,
and salamis; and so on. Commercially raised pork is also
very good in Rome and is often prepared in the sweet-and-
sour way, with fruit or with chocolate, sugar and vinegar, as
in Pork in Sweet-and-Sour Sauce (page 170) or Wild Boar
in Sweet-and-Sour Sauce à la Romana (page 182).

Although the pork roast here is modern in technique, its
soul is definitely antique.

1 Have the butcher leave just a thin layer of fat on the roast for
flavor. Tie the roast with kitchen string so it will hold its shape.

2 On a plate or a sheet of waxed paper, mix together the
brown sugar, salt, and pepper. Roll the roast in the seasonings
to coat evenly.

3 In a large flameproof casserole, preferably oval so the roast
will fit nicely, melt the butter in the olive oil over moderately
high heat. Put the roast into the pan and brown it all over,
turning as necessary with two wooden spatulas so you don't
pierce the meat. This will take 10 to 15 minutes.

4 Reduce the heat to moderate. Add the onions and cook, stirring, until they are soft and golden, about 10 minutes. Pour in the wine and bring it to a boil, scraping up any browned bits from the bottom of the casserole. Crumble the bouillon cubes into the casserole and add the lemon sections and grapes or orange sections. Cover, lower the heat to a simmer, and cook the roast, turning every 15 or 20 minutes, until the meat is tender, 1½ to 2 hours.

5 Transfer the roast to a cutting board and let it rest for at least 10 minutes before slicing. Skim any excess fat off the top of the sauce and stir in the Cointreau, if using. Slice the pork and serve with its sauce, hot or at room temperature. (This is even better the next day.)

NOTE: If it is necessary to thin the sauce, add a little water. If the sauce is too thin, uncover the pan, raise the heat, and boil until the sauce is slightly thickened.

Er mejo legume è la carne de porco. . . .

The best legume is pork. . . .

PORK IN SWEET-AND-SOUR SAUCE

Maiale in Agrodolce

SERVES 3 OR 4

3 tablespoons extra virgin olive oil

2 ounces pancetta, cut into thin julienne strips* (60 g)

1 pound boneless pork tenderloin, cut into thick medallions (450 g)

Salt and freshly ground black pepper

⅓ cup dry white wine (80 ml)

1 tablespoon sugar

1 tablespoon grated semisweet chocolate

2 tablespoons white wine vinegar

4 pitted prunes, plumped in warm water and cut into pieces

2 tablespoons sultana raisins, plumped in warm water

2 tablespoons pine nuts

1 tablespoon candied orange peel, in very thin slivers (optional)

*Two ounces (60 g) julienned prosciutto may be used instead of the pancetta, but it should be added after the pork is brown, when the other ingredients are added in step 2.

Here is a simple and quick way to prepare pork, in the sweet-and-sour sauce loved by the Romans.

1 Heat the olive oil to hot but not smoking in a large skillet. Add the pancetta and the pork slices, season with salt and pepper, and cook the slices, turning, until the slices are brown on both sides.

2 Pour the wine into the skillet and scrape up any browned bits from the bottom of the pan. Simmer until the wine is reduced by half. Add the sugar, chocolate, and vinegar, stirring to dissolve the sugar. Mix in the prunes, raisins, and pine nuts, and the optional orange peel, if using. Allow the flavors to blend for a minute or two and serve the pork hot. If the sauce is too thick, stir in a few tablespoons of water.

SPARERIBS AND SAUSAGES WITH POLENTA

Costerelle di Maiale e Salsicce con Polenta

SERVES 6

3½ pounds spareribs, halved into 3- to 4-inch lengths (ask your butcher to do this) (1.575 kg)

6 large sausages, about 1 pound (450 g)

1 small carrot, peeled and coarsely chopped

1 small celery rib, coarsely chopped

1 small onion, coarsely chopped

1 tablespoon fresh marjoram leaves, or 1½ teaspoons dried marjoram

2 tablespoons extra virgin olive oil

1 cup dry white wine (250 ml)

2 pounds (4 cups) Italian plum tomatoes, coarsely chopped (900 g)

Salt and freshly ground black pepper

Polenta for the spareribs (recipe on page 172)

½ cup freshly grated pecorino Romano cheese or a mixture of pecorino and Parmesan (50 g)

Romans prepare and eat their polenta *alla maniera antica,* "the ancient way." Polenta is a winter family dish, at one time eaten with everyone seated around the table, helping themselves directly from the polenta poured onto a wooden board in the middle of the table. The sauce was served over it and pecorino grated on top. It was and is usually prepared with a sparerib sauce, or with pork sausages, or both, as below. It is a convivial dish.

1 Trim away and discard most of the excess fat from the ribs but leave a little for flavor. Prick the sausages all over with a kitchen needle.

2 Finely chop the carrot, celery, onion, and marjoram by hand or in a food processor.

3 Heat the olive oil in a large, deep sauté pan or a flameproof casserole over moderately high heat. Add the ribs and cook, turning, until they are browned, about 7 minutes. Add the whole sausages, chopped vegetables, and marjoram and cook, stirring often, until the sausages brown lightly, 10 to 15 minutes.

4 Pour in the wine and let it evaporate almost completely. Add the tomatoes and season with salt and pepper to taste. Reduce the heat to moderately low, cover, and simmer for 40 to 45 minutes, or until the meat on the ribs starts to fall off the bone and the sauce has thickened.

5 Serve the hot spareribs and sausages over the hot polenta, generously sprinkled with cheese. Pass extra cheese at the table.

(continued)

POLENTA FOR THE SPARERIBS

Polenta per le Spuntature

SERVES 6

5½ cups water, plus 1 cup cold water (1.55 l total)

1½ teaspoons salt

1 pound good-quality polenta or finely ground cornmeal (450 g)

The inhabitants of Borgo, the part of Rome nearest to Saint Peter's, are called *magna pulenta* (great polenta eaters) because of their love for polenta. Although nowadays we think of polenta as made solely of cornmeal, remember that maize was brought over from America only in the sixteenth century. Before that, Romans ate grain porridge made with ground toasted farro, or spelt, and other cereals.

This somewhat unusual — and foolproof — way of making polenta was given to me by a truly wonderful cook whom I don't dare to name . . . he swore me to secrecy but surely cannot object to faraway foreigners learning his trick. He is someone very handsome, very nice, and very, very knowledgeable about food.

1 In a large saucepan, heat 5½ cups water with the salt until barely simmering. Remove from the heat and gradually whisk in the polenta, first a little, then the rest in 3 or 4 additions, continually whisking to avoid lumps. Return the pan to moderate heat and cook, stirring, until the polenta has thickened.

2 With a wooden spoon or spatula, make a hole in the center of the polenta all the way down to the metal of the pan. Pour in 1 cup cold water, cover the pan tightly, and turn the heat down as low as possible. (The polenta must go *plop, plop.*) The polenta will be ready in 45 minutes.

NOTE: Should there be any leftover cold polenta, cut it into thick slices about 2 or 2½ inches long and dredge the slices lightly in flour. Fry them in hot oil and drain on paper towels. Or cook them under the broiler in the oven until light brown. Serve with roast meats or with a sauce.

PRESSURE COOKER POLENTA

SERVES 4

3 cups plus 1¼ cups boiling salted water (750 ml)

⅔ pound of polenta (300 g)

My daughter has given me her method, which uses a pressure cooker — completely unconventional in Italy, but certainly quick. If you want the polenta softer, add a little more water. If you want it a little stiffer, use a little less water. This can be doubled for 8.

 1 Bring 3 cups of salted water to a gentle boil in the pressure cooker, pull it away from the heat, and gradually whisk in the polenta, adding it "like rain." Stir for 5 minutes over low heat.

2 Add 1¼ cups boiling salted water, mix, and close the pressure cooker. Count 20 minutes from the whistle, and your polenta is ready.

INSTANT POLENTA

IN ADDITION TO polenta made the traditional way or in a pressure cooker, there is also precooked polenta meal, which usually takes about 8 minutes. (Follow the instructions on the package.) It is best used in dishes to be cooked or grilled in the oven. For example, after cooking the contents of a package of instant polenta, mix in 2 tablespoons of butter and turn the polenta out on a dampened surface to cool slightly. Then either take up the polenta in spoonfuls or cut as for Semolina Gnocchi Roman Style (page 81) with a cookie cutter and put the gnocchi in a buttered gratin dish. Cut up 3 more tablespoons butter and sprinkle the pieces on top, together with ½ cup freshly grated Parmesan cheese and ⅓ pound *gorgonzola dolce latte* cut into small pieces. Drizzle ⅓ cup cream on top and sprinkle with another ¼ cup Parmesan cheese. Put into a preheated 400°F (200°C) oven for 10 to 15 minutes, or until the cheese has melted.

These cheeses may be changed or added to, but Parmesan or Parmesan and pecorino Romano are almost always used. If gorgonzola is too strong a taste, fontina or other bland cheeses may be used, along with more cream, if desired.

SPARERIBS AND SAUSAGES WITHOUT TOMATOES

Costerelle di Maiale e Salsicce in Bianco

SERVES 4 OR 5

2 tablespoons extra virgin olive oil

5 ounces thickly sliced pancetta, cut crosswise into thin strips (150 g)

1⅓ pounds spareribs (600 g)

¾ cup dry white wine (180 ml)

8 small sausages, pricked all over with a fork, about 1 pound 2 ounces (500 g)

Salt and freshly ground pepper

Here's another version of spareribs and sausages. *In bianco,* which means "white," indicates a dish without tomatoes. Serve with polenta (see page 172) sprinkled with pecorino Romano cheese.

1 In a large, deep sauté pan or flameproof casseole, heat the olive oil. Add the pancetta and spareribs and cook over moderate heat, turning once or twice, until the spareribs are light brown, about 10 minutes.

2 Pour in the wine and raise the heat to moderately high. Add the sausages, stir, and after 2 or 3 minutes, cover the pan and lower the heat again.

3 Cook for about 25 minutes, turning the pieces occasionally. If necessary, add a little water or extra wine. At the end of the cooking time, leave the lid off so the liquid can evaporate.

SIMPLE SAUSAGES AND SEASONED BREAD

Salsicce e Pan'unto

Pancetta, sliced ½ inch thick and cut into 2-inch pieces

———

Bay leaves

———

Sausages, pricked all over with a kitchen needle

———

Crusty Italian bread

———

When in our country house in northern Lazio, in the Etruscan countryside called Tuscia, we often roast on a spit in front of the fireplace. This is quite common in Barbarano Romano, the village near us, which has remained very unspoiled. The villagers cook in front of the fire on spits and roast potatoes or other vegetables in the ashes. Hogs are killed when it turns cold in the wintertime, and every part of the animal is eaten, as in rural communities almost all over the world. Sausages are among the first meats prepared from the pig, and they are roasted on the spits with large slices of crusty bread below them to catch the fat. This bread is called *pan' unto* (seasoned bread), and must be a custom as old as the village itself.

Skewer a 2-inch piece of pancetta, a bay leaf, a sausage, and so on — as many as you like. Place the spit in front of the fire with the bread set below to catch the drippings, and grill, turning until the pancetta is crisp and the sausages are done. Serve at once, with the bread serving as a plate.

NOTE: The sausages and pancetta may also be laid on the bread and cooked in a hot oven. Watch carefully that the bread does not brown too rapidly. You will have to turn the meat at least once during cooking.

SAUSAGES AND BEANS

Salsicce e Fagioli

SERVES 6 TO 8

16 ounces dried borlotti or
cranberry beans or cannellini
beans (450 g)

---

6 fresh sage leaves

---

2 pounds Italian pork sausages,
pricked all over (900 g)

---

2 ounces pancetta, coarsely
chopped (60 g)

---

1 small onion, coarsely chopped

---

1 small clove of garlic, peeled

½ medium celery rib,
coarsely chopped

---

3 tablespoons extra virgin
olive oil

⅓ cup dry white wine (80 ml)

---

1 can (28 ounces) Italian peeled
plum tomatoes, juices reserved
(800 g)

Salt and freshly ground
black pepper

In the countryside around Rome, farmers still raise hogs, chickens, and rabbits for themselves and make their own hams, pancetta, salamis, and sausages. The sausages, like the Italians, are very individualistic, and they vary widely in taste. Try to find flavorful Italian sausages — mild or spicy, according to your preference. This savory and hearty dish is perfect for the middle of winter, especially if you've just come down off the slopes.

1 Rinse the beans and pick them over to remove any grit. Soak the beans overnight in a large pot in enough cold water to cover by at least 2 inches.

2 Drain the beans and add enough fresh water to cover by about 1½ inches. Add the sage leaves, bring to a boil, cover, and reduce the heat to low. Cook, testing after 45 minutes, until the beans are tender but not soft; they may take up to 2 hours. (Remember, they will cook for another 15 minutes with the tomatoes and sausages.)

3 Prick the sausages all over with a kitchen needle or the tip of a small knife.

4 Make the *battuto*: Finely chop together the pancetta, onion, garlic, and celery, turning the ingredients with your knife blade to mix as you chop.

5 In a very large, deep skillet or flameproof casserole, heat the olive oil. Add the sausages and cook over moderate heat, turning, until they are brown, about 10 minutes. Pour in the wine and cook until it is almost completely evaporated, then remove the sausages to a plate.

6 Add the *battuto* to the skillet and cook over moderately low heat, stirring, and adding a tablespoon of water every now and then if necessary to prevent burning, until golden, about 10 minutes. Add the tomatoes with their juices. Season with salt and a generous amount of black pepper. Boil gently for 15 minutes, stirring often and breaking up the tomatoes with a wooden spoon.

7 Add the sausages and tomatoes to the hot beans and simmer everything together for 15 minutes, stirring often. The finished dish should not be too soupy; the beans and sauce should be level. If there is too much liquid (different beans absorb liquid differently), remove the excess with a ladle before adding the sausages. Check the seasoning again before serving.

RABBIT BRAISED WITH VINEGAR, GARLIC, AND ROSEMARY

Coniglio alla Cacciatora

SERVES 4 TO 6

3 salt-cured anchovies, boned
and rinsed under cold water, or
6 anchovy fillets packed in oil,
drained and patted dry

3 cloves of garlic, peeled

2 tablespoons finely chopped
fresh rosemary

⅓ cup white wine vinegar
(80 ml)

1 rabbit,* about 3 pounds,
dressed and cut into 10 or 12
pieces (have your butcher do
this or see the following recipe)
(1.35 kg)

Salt and freshly ground
black pepper

⅓ cup olive oil (80 ml)

Pinch of flour

*Unless you are buying fresh rabbit from a butcher,
as is far preferable, most rabbit sold in America is
offered frozen and is labeled "rabbit meat."

Mild-flavored rabbit is a favorite Roman meat, and *coniglio alla cacciatora* is a classic way to prepare it. In Rome, *cacciatora* suggests vinegar, garlic, and rosemary. Elsewhere in Italy, as in America, it can mean a completely different dish — sometimes even one prepared with mushrooms, onions, white wine, peppers, parsley, and tomatoes. But in the Eternal City, it is simple and savory. Of course, this same dish can be prepared with chicken or even baby lamb, as can any of the rabbit recipes that follow.

1 Either by hand or with a small food processor, finely chop the anchovies, garlic, and rosemary together. Put into a small bowl and pour in the vinegar. Set this infusion aside until it is needed. Season the rabbit on both sides with salt and pepper.

2 Heat the oil in a large skillet, preferably nonstick, over moderately high heat. Add the rabbit pieces and sauté, turning, until brown all over, about 4 minutes on each side. Scrape the anchovy/vinegar infusion into the pan. Cover, reduce the heat to low, and cook for 40 minutes, or until the rabbit is tender, turning the pieces 3 or 4 times.

3 Sprinkle the flour over the rabbit pieces. Raise the heat to moderate and cook, stirring, for 1 to 2 minutes, then serve.

RABBIT WITH GRAPES

Coniglio all'Uva

SERVES 4 TO 6

1 rabbit, about 2½ pounds
(1.15 kg)

5 tablespoons extra virgin
olive oil

½ cup dry red wine (120 ml)

1 medium onion, thinly sliced

1 clove of garlic, peeled
and crushed

1 pound seedless red grapes,
plus extra for garnish (450 g)

Grated zest of 1 small lemon

Salt and freshly ground
black pepper

2 tablespoons fresh lemon juice

Serve with this easy dish polenta and a salad.

1 Cut the rabbit in half lengthwise. Cut away the front legs. Cut off the back legs and cut them into 2 pieces each. Cut each half rabbit into 3 pieces. You will have 12 pieces of rabbit. Rinse them under cold water and drain. When ready to cook the rabbit, dry the pieces on paper towels.

2 In a large sauté pan, preferably nonstick, or flameproof casserole, heat 3 tablespoons of the olive oil over moderately high heat. Add the rabbit pieces and cook, turning, until they are nicely browned, about 10 minutes. With tongs, transfer the rabbit pieces to a bowl.

3 Add 2 tablespoons of the wine to the pan and scrape up the browned bits from the bottom of the pan. Add the rest of the oil, the onion, and the garlic. Cover, reduce the heat to low, and cook, stirring every now and then, until the onion is soft, about 5 minutes.

4 Return the rabbit to the pan along with any juices that have collected in the bowl. Pour in the rest of the wine. When almost all of the wine has evaporated, add the grapes, lemon zest, salt, and pepper. Cover the pan and cook for 30 minutes, turning the pieces every now and then.

5 Remove the lid and, if the sauce is too thin, reduce it over higher heat for a minute or 2. Stir in the lemon juice, check the seasoning, and serve the rabbit hot, garnished with more grapes.

BRAISED RABBIT WITH WHITE WINE AND DRIED PORCINI

Coniglio in Padella in Bianco

SERVES 4

1 rabbit, about 3 pounds
(1.3 kg)

Salt and freshly ground
black pepper

1 ounce dried porcini
mushrooms (30 g)

2 white bunching onions or 1
medium white onion, chopped

1 medium carrot, chopped

½ small celery rib, chopped

1 sprig of rosemary, chopped

1 small sprig of sage, chopped

1 small peperoncino, or hot red
pepper flakes to taste

½ cup extra virgin olive oil
(120 ml)

Assunta Grossi, who helps us in the country near Barbarano Romano, makes this rabbit in the local fashion. It is their basic way of preparing any white meat: rabbit, chicken, or even veal. It's very easy, and you might like to try the dish with the Marsala, which has a distinctive nutty flavor, almost like sherry.

Assunta fries half slices of Italian bread to place around the dish. Toasted Bruschetta (page 13) can be served the same way, with a little extra virgin olive oil drizzled over the top, and salted.

1 Divide the rabbit into about 20 small pieces: Cut the rib cage in half and cut each half into 3 pieces; cut the thighs into 2 pieces each (cut along the bone); and, as much as possible, cut all of the other pieces roughly the same size. Season the rabbit with salt and pepper and set aside.

2 Soak the dried porcini in a bowl of warm water for at least 1 hour. Rinse well and chop coarsely.

3 Make the *battuto*: Chop together the onions, carrot, celery, rosemary, sage, and peperoncino, turning the ingredients to mix them well as you chop. Do not make a paste but chop medium-fine.

4 Heat the olive oil in a large skillet, preferably nonstick, or flameproof casserole over high heat. Add the rabbit and cook, stirring and turning the pieces often, until they are a deep golden color.

5 Add the pancetta and cook, stirring, for about 2 minutes, then add the *battuto* and the bay leaf. Cook, stirring, for about 2 minutes longer. Pour in the wine and turn the heat down to "an energetic simmer," as Assunta puts it. Cover with a lid and cook for 40 minutes.

2 ounces pancetta, chopped (60 g)

1 whole bay leaf

2 cups white wine or dry Marsala (500 ml)

6 Add the chopped porcini to the rabbit and continue to cook, covered, for 15 to 20 minutes more. Season the sauce with salt and pepper to taste. Discard the bay leaf before serving.

ROMAN LACE

L'occhio vuole la sua parte is another one of Rome's sayings. It means "The eye wants its part," referring to the way dishes are presented and how the table looks. This does not necessarily mean an elaborate display of flowers and silver, although that is expected on certain occasions, but enough to show your guests you are glad to have them. Tablecloths are used for *le feste comandate*, "the feast days ordered [by the church]," and if you have a lace one, you bring it out for these occasions. I collect antique laces and bring these out for Christmas and Easter, planning the menu around the tablecloth (that means no red wine). I buy laces from a small shop just off the antique dealers' street, Via dei Coronari. The shop is kept by two very intelligent women. They have just organized a magnificent exhibition of laces at the Convent of Cassino, whose monks are famous for their lace collection, which covers six centuries. The shop is in a small square, near Palazzo Lancellotti (the palace is not open to the public), and is filled with laces. The women also mend important pieces and work for all the grand families of Rome.

If you go to see the laces, you'll find many antique shops along the way, and just before Via dei Coronari there is a famous Caravaggio painting in Sant'Agostino church . . . and three others in San Luigi dei Francesi church. And everything is near Piazza Navona!

Il Telaio, Piazza Lancellotti 2, Roma 00186, telephone 06 686 5141

WILD BOAR IN SWEET-AND-SOUR SAUCE A LA ROMANA

Cinghiale in Agrodolce alla Romana

SERVES 8 TO 10

4 pounds wild boar, cut into
1½-inch cubes (1.8 kg)

2 medium onions, coarsely
chopped

2 small carrots, peeled and
coarsely chopped

3 bay leaves

20 peppercorns

2 tablespoons fresh thyme leaves,
or 1 tablespoon dried thyme

1 small celery rib, coarsely
chopped

4 juniper berries

½ cup plus ⅓ cup red wine
vinegar (200 ml)

2 cups good red wine (500 ml)

Wild boar is greatly prized in Italy, where many people do their own hunting, and I understand it is gaining
popularity in the United States as more people develop
a taste for game. This fabulous recipe, a distinctively
Roman preparation of the rich, dark meat, appropriate for
the best of dinner parties, comes from our former cook,
Signor Nibbi. The use of chocolate, dried fruits, and nuts
in this sauce is particularly Roman.

Not too long ago in Rome, near the Trevi Fountain, there was a
butcher who sold only game and hung entire wild boars at his
shop's entrance. Unfortunately, the owner decided to give up
his shop for his art, and he became a painter. But wild boar can
still be found in Rome, and boar hunts (cacciarelle) are organized all over Lazio.

Cacciarelle are traditional wild boar hunting parties organized
in upper Lazio and Maremma (also all over Europe), but the
ones in Lazio have a special and complicated ceremony. And no
one else prepares wild boar as they do in Lazio, although there
are many recipes for it in Europe. As a courtesy, my husband
and I are given quantities of meat by the hunters, usually from
the local hunters club, when they hunt on our land. These boar
hunts are permitted because of the damage the boars do to
crops, and especially to grapevines.

Serve this stew with polenta (see page 172) or hot boiled potatoes.

Flour, for dredging

9 tablespoons olive oil

Salt

1½ bouillon cubes

2½ tablespoons sugar

½ cup raisins (80 g)

30 pitted prunes

⅓ cup pine nuts (80 g)

1½ ounces semisweet chocolate (40 g)

2 tablespoons Cognac

1 Put the meat into a large bowl. Add the onions, carrots, bay leaves, peppercorns, thyme, celery, juniper berries, ½ cup of the vinegar, and the wine. Stir to mix well. Cover and refrigerate for 48 hours, stirring occasionally.

2 When ready to finish the dish, remove the meat cubes from the marinade and dry on paper towels. Strain the marinade, reserving both the vegetables and herbs and the liquid separately.

3 Dredge the meat cubes in flour and shake them in a sieve to remove excess flour. Heat 3½ tablespoons of the olive oil in a large skillet. Add half the meat, salt well, and sauté over moderately high heat, stirring and turning the cubes often, until they are brown, about 10 minutes. Transfer to a large flameproof casserole and repeat with another 3½ tablespoons oil and the remaining meat.

4 In the same skillet, heat the remaining 2 tablespoons oil. Add the reserved vegetables from the marinade, cover, and cook over moderately high heat, stirring often, for about 10 minutes, until the vegetables have softened and are beginning to brown. Add the vegetables to the casserole with the meat, pour in the liquid from the marinade, and add the bouillon cubes. Cover and simmer over low heat for about 2 hours, stirring occasionally.

5 When the meat is tender (test with a kitchen needle), remove as much of the vegetables and seasonings as you can. The onions will have disintegrated, but the carrots, peppercorns, and juniper berries can be removed and discarded. Stir in the remaining ⅓ cup vinegar and the sugar, a little at a time. Add the raisins, prunes, and pine nuts. Simmer for 1 or 2 minutes. Add the chocolate gradually, tasting as you go. The sauce should be sweet but slightly acidic.

6 Just before serving, heat the Cognac in a ladle, flame it, and pour it over the *cinghiale*. Stir it into the sauce and serve.

ROME'S MIXED FRIES: *FRITTO MISTO*

ROME'S *FRITTO MISTO,* or "mixed fry," deserves a page all to itself; so I've given it its own chapter. Although fried foods are popular all over Italy, the *fritto misto romano* is special — "a royal dish of the Roman kitchen, unsurpassed in all the world," as one Roman cookbook declares. Flowery language, but true. In former times, *fritto misto* was an economical dish, because the fats for frying — lard or olive oil — were very inexpensive, and the *fritto* was composed principally of vegetables and offal, organ meats. Today, good olive oil alone makes it fairly expensive. Lard, once used together with oil for frying mushrooms, polenta, and so on, today is used by itself only for a dish called *pandorato* (see page 18).

Fritto misto is usually offered as an antipasto or as a first course. It is a Roman tradition to serve *fritti* on Christmas Eve. At weddings and receptions of all kinds, there is usually a very crowded part of the buffet, always a separate table, where a *fritti* specialist is cooking up tempting mouthfuls of good things to whet the appetite, much like a chef at a tempura bar. Guests line up or crowd in with plates in hand, or with cornucopias of butcher paper, ready for the tempting crisp morsels. It is always the most crowded place at the party.

Rome's *fritto misto romano, fritto vegetale,* and *fritto di mare* are all done with bite-size pieces of vegetables, meats, fish, even ricotta. Each piece to be fried is prepared with its own particular coating. Sometimes the pieces are dipped into a flour and yeast mixture, or maybe egg and flour, or only flour, or maybe egg and bread crumbs.

My friend Anna Maria Cornetto is a *romana di Roma:* a Roman whose family has lived in Rome for at least five generations. Her great-grandfather was a sculptor who loved company and invited friends every Sunday to eat his wife's famous *fritto vegetale.* Her Aunt Nannina remembers that there were always too many artists for the *fritto,* and her mother used to say to the guests, "Do help yourselves, my daughter and I aren't hungry." Poor Nannina would run crying into the kitchen, asking why it was she who was not hungry, when she had four siblings.

COATING THE INGREDIENTS

The most complicated part of a *fritto misto* is the coating for the ingredients. Polenta and potatoes are usually not coated with anything. Artichokes are floured and rolled in beaten, salted eggs (and should be fried at a lower temperature, in oil that is hot but not smoking). All of the other ingredients can be coated in this way too, with flour and seasoned beaten eggs. There is also *pastella*, a batter that can be used for pumpkin, apple, broccoli, broccoflower, cauliflower, zucchini flowers, and salt cod. Sometimes brains, lamb's testicles, tiny lamb chops, and sweetbreads are floured lightly and rolled in beaten salted egg, and then in very fine dry bread crumbs.

FRITTO MISTO BATTERS, OR PASTELLE

Following are two batters. The second takes more time, because it contains yeast and must rise for 2 hours. The first can be used immediately.

BATTER I

1 cup flour, sifted (140 g)

Pinch of salt

1 egg, separated

1 tablespoon olive oil

1 tablespoon dry white wine
or grappa

This batter can be used as soon as it is made. For convenience, you can prepare the egg yolk batter up to an hour ahead and then fold in the beaten egg whites just before you begin frying.

1 Put the flour and salt in a small bowl. Work in the egg yolk, olive oil, and wine or grappa. If necessary, add 1 or 2 tablespoons of water to produce a batter that is not thick but not too liquid, either. With a little practice, you will get it exactly right — not too thick and not too thin.

2 When ready to use, beat the egg white until it is stiff but not dry. Fold the beaten egg white into the batter.

BATTER II

1 whole egg

1 egg yolk

1⅔ cups flour, sifted (200 g)

Pinch of salt

2 tablespoons olive oil

½ ounce compressed fresh yeast, dissolved in a little white wine (14 g)

Beat together the whole egg and egg yolk until blended. Slowly mix in the flour, salt, olive oil, and dissolved fresh yeast. If the mixture is too thick, work in 1 or 2 tablespoons of water, so that it is neither too liquid nor too thick. Set it aside to rise in a warm place for 2 hours.

SIMPLE EGG COATING

The most common way to coat the ingredients for *fritto misto* today is simply to dredge the pieces in flour, shake them in a sifter to remove excess flour, and then roll the pieces in beaten eggs that have been lightly salted.

FRYING THE INGREDIENTS

The frying pan should be large and deep, of seasoned iron, washed once in soapy water when bought, and afterwards only wiped out thoroughly with paper towels and put away in a paper bag until it is needed again. (Of course, a deep-fat fryer would work very well.) The olive oil should be abundant and "smoking" — that is, at 375°F (190°C) — when you put in the pieces to be fried.

CHOOSING THE INGREDIENTS FOR A FRITTO MISTO

Following are several different sets of ingredients for mixed fries. While I realize organ meats are not as popular in America as they are in Italy, I include these options, so at least you can read about what is authentic.

ROMAN MIXED FRY

Fritto Misto Romano

One unusual ingredient in an authentic Roman *fritto misto* is lamb's testicles. Luckily, they are not easy to find today, and so are not included here. These are the usual ingredients offered at a Roman *fritti*. Choose whichever you like, but make sure to create an assortment of tastes and textures. The number of people any mixed fry will feed depends upon the quantity of ingredients. Generally, count on 8 pieces of food per person; this is a generous amount.

Yellow pumpkin in bite-size pieces

Broccoli, separated into bite-size florets, boiled briefly until it is al dente, drained and cooled

Apple, peeled, cored, and cut into ½-inch rounds

Cauliflower, separated into bite-size florets, boiled briefly until it is al dente, drained and cooled

Zucchini, if no more than 6 inches, cut lengthwise into 6 pieces; if larger, cut diagonally into ¾-inch slices

Zucchini flowers, the pistil removed and discarded, washed, dried, and halved lengthwise through the center of the blossom

Polenta (see page 172), prepared the day before so that it is dry and compact, cut into 1-by-2-inch rectangles

Cold boiled potatoes, peeled and cut into bite-size pieces or as for thick French fries

Artichokes, cleaned, trimmed to the hearts, choke removed, rubbed with lemon and cut into wedges

Salt cod fillets, soaked and cleaned as described on page 111, divided vertically into 2 parts about 4 inches long, dried

MIXED FRY WITH MEAT

Fritto Misto di Carne

Lamb's testicles, boiled for a few minutes in lightly salted water, cut in half vertically, the skin removed and discarded; cut into bite-size pieces and dried

———

Calf's liver, cut into 2-inch-square pieces about ½ inch thick (often substituted for the lamb's testicles)

———

Lamb or veal brains, cleaned, covered with cold water and brought to a boil, removed at once, the membrane removed; cut into 4 pieces (or small pieces if using the veal brains) and marinated for an hour in lemon juice, parsley, and 1 tablespoon extra virgin olive oil

———

Baby lamb chops, trimmed of excess fat

———

Zucchini, if no more than 6 inches, cut lengthwise into 6 pieces; if larger, cut diagonally into ¾-inch slices

———

Artichokes, cleaned, trimmed to their hearts, choke removed; rubbed with lemon and cut into wedges

———

Apples, peeled, cored, and cut into ½-inch rounds

———

VEGETABLE FRY

Fritto Vegetale

This popular fry is made up of any assortment of vegetables with squares of polenta sometimes added.

MIXED FISH FRY

Fritto di Mare

Sole, red mullet, and fresh codfish no more than 6 inches long, better if 4 inches, fried without coating of any kind

———

Salt, minced garlic, and parsley; for garnish

———

Sprinkle the seafood with salt, garlic, and parsley chopped together very fine after frying.

CHOICE FRIED PIECES

Fritto Scelto

Brains, prepared on page 191

———

Artichokes, prepared on page 191

———

1 Boil the brains for 1 or 2 minutes and then cool them.

2 Marinate them in lemon juice with olive oil, chopped parsley, and salt and pepper. Dry the brains and the artichokes, dredge them in flour, and roll them in lightly salted beaten egg before frying. Serve with *pandorato* (see Golden Bread, page 18).

EGGS

L'amore è come l'ova,
E bbono quann'è fresco.

Love is like eggs, good when fresh.

Eggs are taken seriously by the food-loving Romans, all of whom seem to have their own special vendor who supplies the freshest country eggs. Not all that long ago, during the second World War, hens were kept in garages and courtyards and on peoples' terraces so they could provide the family with eggs, not chicken. Hard-cooked eggs are frequently served with antipasto, and simple fried eggs very often comprise a light, wholesome supper meal when it's just the family around. Italians also have their soufflés. But of all egg preparations, it is the frittata that is a specialty of Rome.

A frittata is a thick egg cake, or omelet. Unlike the French omelet, which is cooked quickly over high heat and often served on the runny side, the Italian frittata is cooked slowly over low heat until it is firm throughout. Any number of vegetables, aromatics, and cheeses can be combined with eggs in a frittata, and for some reason, the whole always seems larger than the sum of its parts — in terms of taste, at least.

One of the things I like best about the frittata is that it is so versatile. And it is good hot, warm, or at room temperature, which makes it appropriate for any number of meals and occasions, not least of which might be a picnic in the Lazian countryside.

ASPARAGUS WITH POACHED EGGS

Uova e Asparagi

SERVES 6

2 pounds fresh asparagus
(900 g)

Salt

½ cup distilled white or
white wine vinegar (125 ml)

6 large eggs

4 tablespoons butter, melted
(60 g)

Freshly ground black pepper

½ cup freshly grated Parmesan
cheese (50 g)

Free-range eggs, if available, are best for this simple dish, because the true taste of the eggs takes center stage. This is a supper dish in Rome, but it also makes a good starter.

1 Preheat the oven to 350°F (180°C).

2 Wash and clean the asparagus, discarding the tough ends. Steam the cleaned asparagus until tender but firm, 12 to 15 minutes for medium spears. Keep the asparagus warm while preparing the eggs.

3 Put 1½ quarts water in a stainless steel frying pan; add a large pinch of salt and the vinegar. Bring to a simmer and slide the eggs in one after the other, using a large spoon or a saucer, whatever is easiest for you. Poach until the whites are set but the yolks are still runny, 3 to 4 minutes. Carefully remove the eggs with a slotted spoon and drain them on paper towels.

4 Arrange the asparagus on a warm serving platter that can go into the oven briefly, with the thick end of the stalks toward the center and the tips pointed outward. Pour half the melted butter over the asparagus and arrange the eggs on top. Drizzle the rest of the butter over the eggs. Sprinkle a little salt and pepper over them. Dust generously with the Parmesan cheese and set the platter in the oven for just 1 or 2 minutes. Serve at once.

ASPARAGUS WITH FRIED EGGS

Prepare the dish as described above, but fry the eggs gently in half the butter and drizzle melted butter only over the asparagus.

ARTICHOKE PIE

Tortino di Carciofi

SERVES 6

6 large globe artichokes
or 9 small ones

½ lemon

Flour, for dredging

Salt and freshly ground
black pepper

¾ cup extra virgin olive oil
(180 ml)

9 eggs

⅔ cup freshly grated Parmesan
cheese (70 g)

½ cup heavy cream (120 ml)

When artichokes are in season in Rome, this is everybody's favorite supper dish. Italians delight in vegetables, eggs, and cheeses in the evening. They rarely eat meat at night unless they have guests. Roman artichokes are considered by the Romans to be the best in the world, but, naturally, anything Roman is superlative. This is good hot, warm, or at room temperature, which also makes it very appropriate as a picnic dish or a starter.

1 Preheat the oven to 350°F (180°C). Butter a baking dish about 11 by 7 inches (28 by 18 cm).

2 Trim the artichokes down to the bottoms as described on page 211. Soak the cleaned artichoke hearts in cold water with the juice of the ½ lemon until needed.

3 When ready to prepare the *tortino*, drain and dry the cleaned artichokes. Cut them in half and remove the choke with a demitasse spoon. Cut each half in ⅜-inch wedges. Season the flour with salt and pepper and dredge the artichokes in the flour. Toss in a sieve to remove excess flour.

4 In a large skillet, heat the olive oil over moderately high heat. Add the artichokes in batches without crowding and fry until light brown. Line a colander with paper towels and drain the artichoke slices on the paper towels. (This can be done several hours in advance; leave the artichokes in the colander until needed. The excess oil will drain off.)

5 Beat the eggs thoroughly with a whisk and season to taste with salt and pepper. Mix in the Parmesan cheese and then the cream.

6 To assemble the *tortino*, scatter the artichokes over the bottom of the prepared baking dish and pour the egg mixture on top, covering the artichokes almost completely.

7 Bake for 30 minutes, or until the eggs are set and slightly browned on top.

MY BAKERY

RIGHT IN FRONT of the Trevi Fountain there is a bakery called Riposati, which means "rested". It is a very inappropriate name because they practically never close and certainly are not rested because they tear around constantly. An entire family works there, and their helpers have been there forever. They sell a little bit of everything, but they have kept their ovens and still make their bread, only once a day now, but still of fine quality. During Carnival they make the traditional sweets, *frappe* and *castagnole*, which are particularly good, and small simple pastries all year long. They have small and large rolls of all kinds, Terni loaves, bread with and without salt, squares of "white" pizza painted with olive oil and sprinkled with kosher salt, "red" pizza with tomato sauce on top, rough white country bread, Arab bread, brown coarse loaves, and so on. You can also buy fresh baker's yeast from them and order bread in advance. The nicest thing about the shop, which is always full, is that they are nice, in spite of the heavy Trevi Fountain traffic in and out. There are other bakeries in Rome that are certainly grander, on Via Veneto and in Piazza Campo dei Fiori, but this is my bakery.

Needless to say, you have Trevi Fountain in front of you, and the sculpture certainly makes you look at it. The pharmacy in the piazza was established in the sixteenth century and has beautiful medicine boxes and jars. There is also a very interesting church kitty-corner to the Fountain, and two blocks away in small Piazza Scanderbeg is the Pasta Museum, informative and instructive.

Riposati, Via delle Muratte 8 (Piazza Fontana di Trevi), Roma 00187, telephone 06 678 0099

EGGPLANT SOUFFLE MAFALDA

Soufflé di Melanzane Mafalda

SERVES 8 TO 10

Olive oil

Fine dry bread crumbs

3 large eggplants, about 3 pounds (1.35 kg)

6 large eggs

3 tablespoons flour

1 cup milk (250 ml)

½ teaspoon salt

¼ teaspoon freshly ground black pepper

⅔ pound Italian fontina or scamorza cheese, finely diced (300 g)

½ pound mozzarella cheese, finely diced (225 g)

⅓ cup freshly grated Parmesan cheese (35 g)

This is a recipe from an architect friend, who is an excellent cook and very *simpatico*, as we say in Rome. Since the egg whites are not whipped, it is really more of a baked frittata than a soufflé, but whatever you call it, it's a very good supper dish. This substantial "soufflé" can be served, hot, warm, or even at room temperature. A light tomato sauce is often trickled over the top of the finished dish.

1 Preheat the oven to 375°F (190°C). Lightly oil a 10½ by 14 inch (26 by 36 cm) baking dish, or whatever you have that is comparable. Dust with bread crumbs and give the dish a rap upside down to eliminate excess crumbs.

2 Trim the eggplants and peel away about half the skin in strips, so the vegetables look striped. Cut the eggplants into ½ to ¾ inch dice. In a large pan of boiling salted water, cook the eggplant until just tender. Drain in a colander until needed.

3 In a large bowl, beat the eggs with the flour, milk, salt, and pepper until smooth. Stir in the fontina and mozzarella cheeses, and mix well. Add the eggplant and the Parmesan cheese. Pour into the prepared dish and bake for 45 minutes.

OVEN-BAKED FRITTATA WITH ZUCCHINI AND PEAS

Frittata al Forno

SERVES 8

2½ tablespoons butter (40 g)

1 tablespoon extra virgin
olive oil

2 medium white onions,
thinly sliced

2¼ pounds fresh small zucchini,
halved and sliced ¼ inch thick
(1 kg)

3 cups (14 ounces) frozen peas
(400 g)

Salt and freshly ground
black pepper

8 eggs

⅓ cup freshly grated Parmesan
cheese (35 g)

¼ cup milk (60 ml)

2 tablespoons chopped fresh
basil or mint (optional)

While no true frittata is baked, this simple, light supper dish, studded with zucchini and peas, passes for one. Just be sure not to overcook it. This dish can be halved to serve 4, but be sure to use a smaller baking dish.

1 Heat the butter and olive oil in a large, deep sauté pan or flameproof casserole. Add the onions and cook over moderate heat, stirring occasionally, until they are soft, 5 to 7 minutes.

2 Add the zucchini and the peas, still frozen, cover, and continue to cook over moderate heat, stirring every now and then, for 15 minutes. Uncover the pan, raise the heat, and cook for about 5 more minutes, until all the liquid has evaporated. Season with 1 teaspoon salt and pepper to taste and turn into a lightly buttered 10-by-15-inch (25-by-38-cm) baking dish. Let cool to room temperature.

3 Preheat the oven to 400°F (200°C). Beat the eggs in a bowl with the Parmesan cheese and milk. Season with salt and pepper to taste. If using basil or mint, scatter it over the vegetables in the baking dish. Beat the eggs again and pour them over the vegetables evenly.

4 Bake the "frittata" for 15 to 18 minutes; the eggs should still be soft. Serve at once.

ZUCCHINI FRITTATA

Frittata con le Zucchine

SERVES 4 TO 6

5 tablespoons extra virgin olive oil

3 tablespoons finely chopped onion

1½ pounds fresh zucchini,* washed, dried, and thinly sliced (675 g)

1½ teaspoons salt

Freshly ground black pepper

8 large fresh eggs

* If you find zucchini with their flowers attached, wash the blossoms, dry them, and slice them lengthwise. Cook the flowers with the zucchini.

La frittata is made with eggs and zucchini or potatoes or green beans or almost any vegetable you choose. Flavored with onion, maybe garlic, and seasoned with oregano or basil or marjoram or parsley or your favorite herb, it is a perfect supper dish, and an absolute necessity for a picnic in Rome. It is usually served hot or warm, but it can wait and be just as tasty — if not more so — at room temperature. Although the dish is eaten throughout Italy, the Roman *frittate* are special.

1 In a heavy 10-inch (25-cm) nonstick skillet, heat the olive oil. Add the onion and cook over moderate heat, stirring constantly, for about 1 minute, until softened.

2 Add the zucchini (the pan will be full) and season with 1 teaspoon of the salt and a generous grinding of pepper. Cover and cook for 5 minutes, shaking the pan occasionally and stirring once. Remove the lid and cook the zucchini, stirring frequently with a wooden spatula, until the slices are tender but not falling apart, 10 to 15 minutes. This may be done in advance.

3 When ready to make the frittata, beat the eggs thoroughly in a bowl. Season with the remaining ½ teaspoon of salt and more pepper to taste. Reheat the zucchini over moderate heat, if necessary. Pour the eggs over the zucchini and stir with a wooden spatula so that the eggs penetrate and coagulate. Spread the zucchini evenly in the pan and leave for 3 minutes. When you hear a frying noise, invert the skillet to unmold the frittata onto a plate. Slide the frittata back into the skillet with the the uncooked side down. Leave for 1½ to 2 minutes, then turn out onto a round platter. Serve hot or at room temperature.

FRITTATA WITH ARUGULA AND ONIONS

Prepare the Zucchini Frittata as described above, but in place of the zucchini, cook 1½ pounds (675 g) white onions, sliced extremely thin, in the olive oil slowly until soft and translucent. Add ¼ pound (110 g) washed, dried, chopped arugula; cook, stirring for a couple of minutes, until it wilts. Then add the eggs and proceed with the recipe.

BROWNED ONION FRITTATA

Prepare the Zucchini Frittata as described above, but in place of the zucchini, cook 1½ pounds (675 g) white onions, sliced extremely thin, in the olive oil slowly, stirring often, until meltingly soft and golden brown. Be patient; coloring the onions can take 15 to 20 minutes. Then add the eggs and proceed with the recipe.

SPINACH FLAN WITH DRIED PORCINI RAGOUT

Flan di Spinaci con Ragù di Funghi

Serves 4 to 6

1¼ pounds fresh spinach (570 g)

1 cup milk (250 ml)

3 tablespoons flour

1 teaspoon salt

½ teaspoon freshly ground black pepper

1½ tablespoons butter (20 g)

6 large eggs, at room temperature, separated

1 cup freshly grated Parmesan cheese (100 g)

Mushroom Ragout (recipe opposite)

A simple but savory mushroom sauce dresses up this easy version of spinach flan from my cooking school. A thick béchamel forms the base for the flan, and it can be made ahead of time, if you wish. The savory mushroom sauce, laced with chicken and ham, can also be prepared in advance. Serve this as a supper dish all by itself, or offer it as a separate course, after the meat, as part of a more elaborate meal.

1 Rinse the spinach well. Cook it in a large saucepan in the water clinging to the leaves, adding it in batches and stirring and turning the leaves as they wilt. Cook, stirring, for about 3 minutes, until the spinach is tender and still bright green; drain and rinse. When cool, squeeze as much moisture from the spinach as you can with your hands.

2 In a blender or food processor, combine the milk, flour, salt, and pepper in a blender. Process for 30 seconds. Melt the butter in a medium saucepan. Whisk in the milk mixture and bring to a simmer, stirring constantly. Simmer for 5 minutes, whisking often. Let cool, then cover and refrigerate; the béchamel should be cold when used.

3 When ready to finish the flan, preheat the oven to 400°F (200°C). Butter a 6-cup nonstick ring mold. Place a shallow pan of hot water large enough to contain the mold in the oven.

4 In a blender or food processor, combine the spinach with the cold béchamel. Puree until smooth and well blended. Pour into a bowl and add the egg yolks and Parmesan cheese; mix well. In a clean bowl or an electric mixer, beat the egg whites until they are stiff but not dry. Fold them into the spinach base. Turn into the prepared ring mold and smooth the top.

5 Put the filled mold into the water bath and bake the flan for 1 hour. While it bakes, make the mushroom ragout.

6 When the flan is done, let it stand for 5 minutes, then unmold onto a large platter. Reheat the mushroom ragout briefly, if necessary. Fill the center of the flan with the ragout and serve at once.

MUSHROOM RAGOUT

Ragù di Funghi

MAKES ABOUT 2 CUPS

1 ounce dried porcini mushrooms (30 g)

3 tablespoons butter (45 g)

⅔ pound breast of chicken, cut into thin julienne strips (300 g)

1 tablespoon flour

¼ cup dry Marsala (60 ml)

⅓ pound boiled ham, cut into thin julienne strips (150 g)

¼ cup plus 2 tablespoons heavy cream (90 ml)

Salt and freshly ground black pepper

1 Soak the porcini in a bowl of tepid water until they are soft, 20 to 30 minutes. Remove the mushrooms from the soaking liquid and rinse them to remove any grit. Chop them coarsely.

2 Melt the butter in a medium skillet over moderate heat. Add the chopped mushrooms and cook for 2 minutes. Add the chicken and cook, stirring, until it is lightly colored, 3 to 4 minutes. Sift the flour over the chicken and cook, tossing, for 1 more minute.

3 Pour the Marsala into the skillet and bring to a boil. Add the ham and cream, reduce the heat slightly, and simmer for a few minutes, until thickened to a nice sauce consistency. Season with salt and pepper to taste.

THE BARONESSA'S SPINACH AND RICOTTA FLAN FILLED WITH MUSHROOMS

Sformato di Spinaci e Ricotta della Baronessa

SERVES 6

3 pounds fresh spinach
(1.35 kg)

———

4 tablespoons butter, plus butter
for the mold (60 g)

———

Salt and freshly ground
black pepper

———

¾ teaspoon grated nutmeg

———

Fine dry bread crumbs, for
the mold

———

1 pound fresh ricotta, drained
(450 g)

———

5 eggs

———

¾ cup freshly grated Parmesan
cheese (75 g)

———

Sautéed Mushrooms for the
Sformato (recipe follows)

———

Spinach flan can be a first course, a one-dish meal for supper, or a third course, served after the main course. It is most often presented with *funghi porcini trifolati* (sautéed porcini mushrooms), but plain cultivated mushrooms, to which a few dried porcini have been added, may be substituted. This is a recipe from a friend who cannot herself cook but who has good cooks and knows her food.

While much more complicated than the previous recipe, this dish is rich and elegant, perfect for a special dinner party. *Sformati*, when served as a third course, are served usually at an "important" dinner, as a separate vegetable course after the main course of meat. The meat is usually preceded by a light pasta dish or a cream soup.

1 Wash and trim the spinach and cook it in the water clinging to its leaves; drain. When cool, squeeze the spinach to remove as much water as possible. Melt 4 tablespoons butter in a skillet and sauté the spinach, stirring for about 5 minutes, or until dry. Season the spinach with salt, pepper, and nutmeg; let cool.

2 Preheat the oven to 375°F (190°C).

3 Butter a 2-quart (2-liter) ring mold and coat it with the bread crumbs, turning so that all of the interior is covered.

4 In a food processor, puree the spinach together with the ricotta, eggs, and Parmesan cheese. Taste for seasoning and spoon the mixture into the prepared mold. Give the mold a rap to eliminate air.

5 Put a pan in the oven with enough hot water to reach about 2 inches up the sides of the mold. Put the mold in the water bath and cook the flan for 45 minutes; after about 25 minutes put a loose sheet of aluminum foil on top of the mold if the top is browning too rapidly.

6 Turn out the flan onto a round platter and serve with the mushrooms. The mushrooms can be served in the center of the *sformato*, or around the base, or offer separately as an accompaniment.

SAUTEED MUSHROOMS FOR THE SFORMATO

1 ounce dried porcini mushrooms (optional) (30 g)

---

5 tablespoons extra virgin olive oil (75 ml)

---

1 clove of garlic, peeled and crushed

---

3 pounds mushrooms of your choice, cleaned and sliced about ½ inch thick (1.35 kg)

Salt and freshly ground black pepper

---

1 If using dried porcini, soak them in warm water for about 1 hour. Rinse them to eliminate any grit, chop them finely, and add them to the skillet when you add the fresh mushrooms.

2 Heat the olive oil in a skillet large enough to contain the mushrooms. Add the garlic and sauté slowly until lightly colored, then discard the garlic. Add the fresh mushrooms and the chopped porcini. Sauté them slowly for about 20 minutes (depending on the mushrooms), or until the fresh mushrooms release their liquid and then reabsorb it. Season with salt and pepper. Sauté a few minutes longer and then serve with the *sformato*.

VEGETABLES
AND SALADS

Piu erba se magna,
piu bestia se diventa.

The more greens you eat,

the more beastlike you become.

On the previous page is one of Rome's proverbs, but not to be believed, at least today. It is true that Romans once considered only a meal with meat and pasta completely satisfying, but times and tastes have changed. Today greens of all kinds are an important part of the Roman table.

A Roman is pleased to have only a good vegetable and perhaps eggs or cheese for his or her supper, and, again contrary to the proverb, cannot really appreciate a meal without greens of some kind, particularly in the evening.

Salads are usually noonday dishes, to accompany a main course or to start a meal. Artichokes, broccoflower, fresh peas, broccoli, fava beans, fennel, and the many varied fresh salads, such as *puntarelle* and *misticanza*, are considered by the Romans to be their property — best prepared only by a Roman.

ARTICHOKES, FAVA BEANS, AND PEAS

La Vignarola

SERVES 4 TO 5

5 artichokes, trimmed
as on page 211

½ lemon

3 tablespoons extra virgin
olive oil

These vegetables mean spring really has arrived. My recipe comes from the woman at my market who sells me these perfect artichokes, fava beans, and fresh peas. In Rome, this mixture of vegetables is called *la vignarola*, "vineyard worker," because in days gone by it was taken to the people working in the vineyards as a one-dish meal, to be eaten on the spot.

This dish can be served hot or at room temperature. It is better the day after it is prepared. If possible, leave in a cool place without refrigerating. If not, refrigerate it and either bring it to room temperature or heat gently before serving.

2 ounces finely chopped
pancetta (60 g)

1 medium onion, thinly sliced

2¼ pounds fava beans,
shelled (1 kg)

2¼ pounds garden-fresh peas,
shelled (1 kg)

Salt and freshly ground pepper

1 Cut the artichokes in half and remove the choke with a small spoon. Place the artichokes cut side down on a cutting board and slice into wedges about ½ inch thick. Place in a bowl of cold water with the juice of the lemon half and the lemon itself until ready to use.

2 Heat the olive oil in a large, wide saucepan or flameproof casserole and add the pancetta. Cook over moderate heat, stirring, until the pancetta is lightly colored, about 5 minutes. Add the onion and cook, stirring occasionally, until soft and translucent, 3 to 5 minutes.

3 Add the artichokes and ¼ cup hot water and cook over moderate heat, stirring, for about 3 minutes. Next add the fava beans and another ¼ cup hot water and cook for 2 or 3 minutes. Now add the peas, stir, cover the pan, and reduce the heat to low. Cook, stirring occasionally and shaking the pan, until the vegetables are tender but still have plenty of flavor, 15 to 20 minutes. Season with salt and pepper to taste before serving.

LA VIGNAROLA

ALSO CALLED la vignarola is a sort of bruschetta, which was carried to the women working by day in the vineyards. Originally during their midday break, they probably ate bread and grapes. Slowly other foods were brought — leftover greens, sausages, and perhaps a little wine. This evolved into sausages removed from their casings and cooked with garlic, oil, and peperoncino in a little tomato sauce. The greens, usually wild chicory in the country, were then mixed with the sausage sauce and piled on top of lightly toasted slices of bread.

FRIED ARTICHOKES THE JEWISH WAY

Carciofi alla Giudia

SERVES 8

8 large, tender artichokes, chokes removed

½ large lemon

1½ generous quarts olive oil (1½ liters)

Salt

The Roman artichokes used for *carciofi alla giudia* are also called *cimaroli* — the top artichoke and the biggest of the plant. These artichokes are grown in the countryside near Rome and are considered the best in Europe, and not only by the Romans. They are so tender they can be eaten raw, sliced thin, and dressed with salt, oil, and lemon. They are one of the vegetable marvels of the Easter season, prepared in any way. *Carciofi alla giudia* means "artichokes the Jewish way"; it is one of the best known of the ancient Jewish recipes. The large quantity of olive oil is necessary, but the oil can be strained and reused several times; another oil really cannot be substituted. The total cooking time for *carciofi alla giudia* depends upon the tenderness of the artichokes, but they usually take about 40 minutes from start to finish, including a rest time in between the two fryings.

1 Clean the artichokes as explained at right, rubbing each one with the lemon half to prevent discoloration. As soon as they are ready, put them into a bowl of cold water, together with the lemon half.

2 When ready to cook the artichokes, heat the olive oil in a large wide saucepan or flameproof casserole over moderately high heat.

3 While the oil is heating, prepare the artichokes: Remove them from the cold water and, holding them by the stem, press them down on a hard surface to open up the leaves. Salt them inside and outside and put them, stem side up, on paper towels.

4 When the oil is hot, after about 6 minutes (you can test by flicking a drop of water into the pan; it will make a frying noise), put the artichokes into the hot oil and fry them, turning them gently every now and then, using 2 forks, for about 15 minutes. They will begin to brown. Test them with the fork at the base of the stem to see that they are tender but still al dente. Remove the artichokes from the oil and put them, stems up, on a platter. Let them cool for about 20 minutes, or until you are ready to serve them. Leave the oil in the pan.

5 Turn up the heat under the oil. Using a fork inserted at the stem's base to hold each artichoke upright, put the artichokes one at a time into the hot oil and fry for 3 or 4 minutes. The leaves will open up like flowers and will brown in the hot oil. Drain on paper towels and serve at once.

HOW TO CLEAN ARTICHOKES

PREPARE A LARGE BOWL of cold water and several washed, halved lemons, according to the number of artichokes to be cleaned. Remove the outer leaves of the artichokes until you reach the light yellow and green inner leaves. Place your thumb at the tender base of the outer leaves and, one at a time, break off the tips until you arrive at the very tender leaves. Cut 1 inch off the top of the artichoke and rub the artichoke all over with half a lemon. With a small spoon, remove the "beard" (choke) and the small prickly leaves and discard them. Cut off the stem about 3 inches from the base and peel away the stringy outside. Rub again with lemon (this prevents discoloration). Put the artichokes in the cold water with the lemons and their juice until you are ready to use them.

ROMAN-STYLE ARTICHOKES STUFFED WITH MINT

Carciofi alla Romana

SERVES 8

1½ lemons

16 fresh medium artichokes, cleaned as on page 211

2 or 2¾ packed cups fresh parsley (see below), washed and dried

2 packed cups fresh wild mint or 1¼ packed cup fresh mint (see below), washed and dried

5 cloves of garlic, peeled and cut in pieces

Salt and freshly ground black pepper

1¼ cups extra virgin olive oil (300 ml)

Carciofi alla romana is one of Rome's more famous dishes, particularly so because of the special Roman artichoke. *Mentuccia*, a wild mint with tiny leaves, which grows rather close to the ground, is an essential part of the preparation, but I doubt it can be found easily outside of Italy. In Rome, it can be found in all the open-air markets. Mint and marjoram are Rome's special herbs. Romans being Romans, they always have slight variations for everything; this recipe adds herbs and a little liquid at the end. I have allowed for substituting cultivated mint for the wild mint and have calculated 2 artichokes per person.

1 Squeeze the juice of 1 lemon into a bowl of cold water large enough to contain the cleaned artichokes and add the artichokes.

2 If the wild mint is available, use 2 packed cups of parsley and 2 packed cups of wild mint. If it is not available, use 2¾ cups of parsley and 1¼ cups of cultivated mint. Chop the herbs together with the garlic, either by hand or in a food processor. If using a food processor, pulse to chop, do not puree. Put the herbs and garlic in a small bowl, season with salt and pepper, and pour ⅓ cup of the olive oil over them.

3 Remove the artichokes from the water and rub them all over with the remaining ½ lemon.

4 With your finger, make a hole in the center of each artichoke and fill it with the chopped herbs, reserving about 4 tablespoons. Put the artichokes in 1 or 2 pans, with the stems up. Pour the remaining olive oil evenly over the artichokes and sprinkle them with salt and pepper. Cover the pan(s) with a lid and cook the artichokes on very low heat for 40 to 45 minutes. Test at the base with a kitchen needle or the tip of a small knife for doneness.

5 Add the lemon juice from the remaining lemon half and a scant 1 cup water to the reserved herbs and oil. When the artichokes test done, turn up the heat and pour the water and herbs over them. Bring to a strong boil, uncovered, lower the heat to medium, and cook for about 10 minutes in all, or until the water has evaporated.

6 Serve the artichokes hot or at room temperature. They are better the next day.

Che l'acqua ti vada per l'orto.

May water run through your vegetable garden.

WHITE BEAN AND TUNA SALAD

Fagioli in Insalata

SERVES 4 AS AN ANTIPASTO
OR 2 AS A MAIN COURSE

⅔ pound cannellini beans,
picked over and soaked
overnight (300 g)

2 cloves of garlic, peeled
and crushed

¼ cup extra virgin olive oil
(60 ml)

1 tablespoon white wine vinegar

Salt and freshly ground
black pepper

2 tablespoons finely
chopped parsley

⅔ cup thinly sliced scallions

1 or 2 cans (6 ounces each)
tuna fish, preferably packed in
olive oil, drained (170 or 340 g)

The white beans that the Italians eat today, the cannellini of *pasta e fagioli* fame, actually came from America and are a fairly recent addition to the list of legumes eaten in Italy. They were adopted enthusiastically and are still cultivated all over Lazio, becoming Roman and, therefore the best in Italy, according to the Romans.

Use more or less tuna depending upon whether you are serving the salad as an antipasto, an accompaniment, or a main course. This recipe can be doubled easily.

1 Drain the beans, put them in a large pot with enough fresh cold, lightly salted water to cover by 2 inches. Add 1 of the garlic cloves and cover the pot. Simmer the beans until they are tender but not falling apart, 45 minutes to 1½ hours, depending upon the beans. Drain, transfer to a large bowl, and let cool.

2 Whisk together the oil, vinegar, remaining garlic clove, and salt and pepper to taste in a small bowl. With a fork, mix in the parsley last. Pour this *salsa* over the drained beans and add the scallions. Toss to mix well.

3 Put the salad on a platter and arrange the tuna in chunks around the beans. Serve at room temperature, with a pepper mill on the side.

GREEN BEANS SAUTEED WITH TOMATOES AND BASIL

Fagiolini in Padella

SERVES 4

2 pounds fresh green beans
(900 g)

⅓ cup extra virgin olive oil
(80 ml)

1 clove of garlic, peeled
and crushed

1 small onion, very thinly sliced

1 pound ripe tomatoes, peeled,
seeded, and cut into strips

Salt and freshly ground
black pepper

1½ tablespoons chopped basil
or flat-leaf parsley

The green bean preparation here is truly Mediterranean; I have eaten almost the same dish in Turkey and in Greece as well as all over Italy. Because of the simplicity of the recipe, I highly recommend you make this only when garden-fresh young beans and sweet sun-ripe tomatoes are in the market. As with many of the recipes in this chapter, it makes a fine buffet or picnic dish, and it is delicious hot, warm, or at room temperature.

1 Rinse the beans well. Snap off the ends of the beans and discard. If the beans are long, break them in half.

2 Bring a pan of lightly salted water to a boil and add the beans. Cook uncovered until barely tender and bright green, 3 to 5 minutes. (They will finish cooking with the tomatoes.) Drain and set aside.

3 In a large skillet, heat the oil and garlic over moderately low heat. Cook until the garlic is light brown; then discard it. Add the onion to the oil and cook, stirring, until lightly colored, 5 to 7 minutes. Add the tomatoes and simmer, stirring occasionally, for 15 minutes.

4 Add the beans to the tomatoes and season with salt and pepper. If using parsley, add it now; basil goes in later. Cover with the lid ajar. Raise the heat to moderate and continue to cook for 15 to 20 minutes, until most of the tomato juices are evaporated. If using basil, stir it in at the end.

ROMAN BROCCOFLOWER WITH WHITE WINE

Broccolo alla Romana

SERVES 3 OR 4

2½ pounds broccoflower
or cauliflower (1.125 kg)

⅓ cup extra virgin olive oil
(80 ml)

2 cloves of garlic, peeled

Salt and freshly ground
black pepper

1 cup dry white wine (250 ml)

Pale green broccoflower, called both *broccolo romano* and *broccolo romanesco* in Rome, is not only delicious but also mathematically correct. Green and pointed, its florets are perfectly and equally numbered; it is a beautiful and versatile vegetable. Cauliflower, called *cavolfiore*, is also prepared this same way with white wine, and it is called *broccolo ubriaco*, or "drunken cauliflower." Substitute cauliflower for the broccoflower when the latter is not available.

1 Break up the broccoflower into florets; cut any large ones in half. Reserve any tender leaves. Wash thoroughly in cold water and drain.

2 Heat the olive oil in a large skillet and brown the garlic lightly. Add the broccoflower florets, and the leaves if there are any, and sauté the vegetable for about 8 to 10 minutes over moderate heat, stirring. Season with salt and pepper.

3 Add the white wine, cover the skillet, and simmer for about 20 minutes, or until the broccoflower is tender but firm, stirring every now and then. Season with additional salt and pepper to taste and serve hot.

BROCCOFLOWER WITH PROSCIUTTO AND HOT PEPPER

Cook and drain the broccoflower as described above. Lightly brown 2 cloves of garlic in the olive oil and at the same time slowly cook ¼ pound (110 g) thickly sliced prosciutto, cut into thin strips, and 1 peperoncino, or crushed hot red pepper flakes to taste. Add the broccoflower, season with salt and freshly ground black pepper, and stew it in the oil, covered, for about 15 minutes, stirring occasionally.

EGGPLANT IN THE JEWISH WAY

Melanzane alla Giudia

SERVES 4

2 pounds eggplant, the long kind if possible (900 g)

Kosher salt

¾ cup extra virgin olive oil (180 ml)

2 tablespoons chopped parsley

This recipe was given to me by an American painter who married into a Roman Jewish family. The same dish is also called *melanzane al funghetto*, or "eggplant as mushrooms," because the pieces look like small mushrooms when cooked. An excellent way of preparing eggplant, it is sometimes used as a sauce for spaghetti, as in the variation below.

1 Wash and dry the eggplants. Quarter them lengthwise, then cut each wedge crosswise into 1-inch pieces. Rinse the eggplant again and layer the pieces in a colander, sprinkling each layer with kosher salt. Put a plate on top, weight it, and leave for at least 1 hour, better 2. When ready to use the eggplant, rinse it again, squeeze it as dry as possible, and drain on paper towels.

2 In a large deep skillet, heat the olive oil to very hot but not smoking. Add the eggplant and cover with a lid. Turn the heat to moderate. Shake the pan and stir the eggplant every now and then for 5 minutes, or until the eggplant is soft when pierced with a fork. Remove the lid and continue frying, stirring often, until the eggplant is lightly browned, about 15 minutes.

3 Drain the eggplant, transferring it with a slotted spoon onto paper towels and then onto a serving plate. Garnish with parsley and serve.

EGGPLANT SAUCE FOR SPAGHETTI

Sauté 2 crushed garlic cloves with a peperoncino in the oil before adding the eggplant. Add 2 or 3 peeled, seeded, julienned tomatoes after the first 5 minutes, and add chopped fresh oregano or basil instead of the parsley. Do not drain away all the oil; you'll need it to dress the pasta. Use 1 pound (450 g) dried pasta with this amount of eggplant.

FRIED EGGPLANT SALAD

Melanzane Fritte in Insalata

SERVES 4 TO 6

2 pounds eggplant, the round kind, if possible (900 g)

Coarse salt

¾ cup extra virgin olive oil (180 ml)

3 cloves of garlic, peeled and crushed

1 large white onion, very thinly sliced

Freshly ground black pepper

6 tablespoons lemon juice

Dried oregano, to taste

2 tablespoons finely chopped parsley

Lemon wedges or slices, for garnish

Back when eggplants were strictly seasonal, this was strictly a summer dish. Now it can be made year-round. Tart with lemon and spiked with garlic, this salad is wonderful with grilled meats, on a buffet table, as an antipasto, or as one of several dishes for a vegetarian meal. Its great advantage is that it should be prepared a day before serving. Feel free to add chopped pitted olives or hot pepper to the onion, if you so desire.

1 If the eggplant are not very fresh, peel them; eggplant skins can turn bitter as they age. Slice the eggplant crosswise into ¼-inch-thick rounds and put the slices into a colander, salting each layer. Put a weight on top and let stand for 1 hour. Rinse and pat dry.

2 Heat the olive oil in a large skillet, preferably nonstick, until very hot. Add the eggplant slices, in batches as necessary, and fry, turning once, until light brown. Drain in a colander lined with paper towels. Salt the eggplant while hot.

3 Measure 2 tablespoons of the eggplant cooking oil and put it in a clean skillet. Heat the oil and add the garlic. Cook the garlic until brown, then discard it. Add the onion and season with salt. Cook over moderate heat, stirring and adding a tablespoon of water now and then, until the onion is light brown.

4 Make a layer of one-third of the eggplant slices in a platter, season with a grinding of pepper, and layer on half of the browned onion. Sprinkle 2 tablespoons of the lemon juice and a large pinch of oregano over the eggplant. Repeat the layer, using half the remaining eggplant, the remaining onion, and another 2 tablespoons of the lemon juice, and end with the rest of the fried eggplant slices, seasoning them with the remaining 2 tablespoons of lemon juice and a pinch of oregano. Sprinkle the parsley on top when serving, and garnish with lemon wedges or slices.

5 This can be made a day in advance. If you do so, some of the oil will drain out of the salad and can be removed.

BAKED STUFFED EGGPLANT WITH FRESH TOMATO SAUCE

Melanzane Farcite

SERVES 4 TO 6

6 medium to small eggplant,
about 2 pounds (900 g)

¾ cup extra virgin olive oil
(180 ml)

Salt and freshly ground pepper

½ pound ground veal or beef,
ground twice (225 g)

1 clove of garlic, peeled
and crushed

1 small onion, minced

Small handful of fresh basil

3 ripe tomatoes, about 1 pound,
peeled and sliced (450 g)

In Italian cooking, stuffed vegetables often include meat, and this one is no exception, giving you a choice of veal or beef. This substantial vegetable is usually served as a first course or a main dish.

1 Preheat the oven to 350°F (180°C).

2 Cut the eggplants in half lengthwise. With a spoon, scoop out and reserve the pulp, leaving a shell about ⅜ inch thick. Rub about ½ teaspoon of the oil over the inside of each eggplant shell and season with salt and pepper. Use 1 tablespoon of the oil to grease a baking dish or roasting pan large enough to hold all the eggplant shells, arrange the shells on it in a single layer, and set aside.

3 Using a fork, mash the eggplant pulp; or pulse the pulp in a food processor to chop coarsely. Mix the eggplant with the ground meat and season well with salt and pepper.

4 In a large skillet, heat ¼ cup olive oil. Add the garlic and the onion and cook over moderately low heat, adding a tablespoon of water every now and then, until the onion is golden, 7 to 10 minutes. Add the meat and eggplant and raise the heat to moderately high. Cook, stirring, for 3 minutes; then reduce the heat to moderately low and cook, stirring often, until the meat is brown and the eggplant is tender, about 5 minutes.

5 Tear up half of the basil leaves and stir them into the eggplant. Remove from the heat and let cool for a few minutes.

6 Put the tomatoes in a medium skillet with 1 tablespoon of the olive oil. Cook over moderately high heat, mashing the tomatoes with the back of a wooden spoon, for 10 minutes, or until most of their juices evaporate and they form a sauce. Season with the rest of the basil, torn, and salt to taste.

7 Spoon the meat and eggplant pulp into the eggplant shells. Trickle about 1 teaspoon of olive oil over each filled shell and bake the eggplant for 45 minutes, until lightly colored . Remove from the oven and divide the tomato sauce among the filled shells, dolloping it over the filling; do not spread it evenly. Serve hot or at room temperature.

THE TAXI DRIVER'S EGGPLANT

Melanzane del Tassista

SERVES 4 TO 6

3 medium-large eggplant,
about 2 pounds (900 g)

Coarse salt

1 large or 2 small cloves
of garlic, peeled

1½ packed cups flat-leaf
parsley sprigs

1 cup coarse dry bread crumbs
(50 g)

Freshly ground black pepper

About 1 cup flour (120 g)

2 eggs

Olive oil, for frying

This is not some apocryphal taxi driver, it's mine — the same one who gave me the recipes for Baked Stuffed Chicken Breasts (page 131) and The Taxi Driver's Tomatoes (page 235). When he learned I was a cooking school teacher and cookbook writer, there was no stopping him. He explained these three but claimed he had a hundred up his sleeve. I hope we meet again.

Eggplant prepared this way can be served as part of an antipasto, as a side dish, or — with some cheese and maybe a little sauce — as the filling for a hearty sandwich.

1 Slice the eggplant slightly less than ½ inch (1 cm) thick. Layer the slices in a colander, salting each layer. Put a plate on top, add a weight, and leave the eggplant for at least 1 hour. When ready to prepare the eggplant, dry the pieces on paper towels.

2 In a food processor or by hand, chop the garlic very fine; add the parsley and chop it very fine with the garlic. Put into a large, flat dish with the bread crumbs and mix well, adding salt and pepper to taste.

3 Put the flour in a shallow soup bowl and beat the eggs with a pinch of salt in another. One by one, dredge the eggplant slices on both sides in the flour, shake off the excess, and then dip in the beaten eggs. Now coat the slices with the seasoned bread crumbs, pressing gently to help the crumbs adhere.

4 Heat about 1 inch (2½ cm) of olive oil in a large skillet, preferably nonstick, until it is very hot. Fry the eggplant slices on one side and then gently turn them to fry the other side. Test with a fork for tenderness. Drain on paper towels and keep warm in a turned-off oven until all the eggplant slices are ready. Serve hot.

EGGPLANT WITH UNCOOKED TOMATO SAUCE

Melanzane con Pomodori

SERVES 6

2⅔ pounds firm ripe tomatoes, peeled, seeded, and finely diced (1.2 kg)

1 clove of garlic, peeled

2 tablespoons chopped parsley

1½ tablespoons chopped fresh basil

½ cup salt-packed capers, rinsed and soaked in cold water for 20 minutes

¼ cup extra virgin olive oil, plus more for frying (60 ml)

Salt

4 pounds large oval eggplants, peeled (1.8 kg)

Ninetta Cecacci Mariani is the chef at Checchino dal 1887, a very well known Roman restaurant in Testaccio. All the members of her family work in their restaurant, each in his or her preferred area of specialty. Ninetta is often consulted on the authenticity of older Roman recipes. But this is a private family recipe, so appreciated by her grandchildren, that it has been added to the restaurant's menu. It can be offered as an antipasto or an accompaniment to grilled meats, or for a buffet table. You will note that for this dish she does not salt the eggplants before cooking. After frying, the eggplant is marinated with the uncooked tomatoes. This is best prepared in the morning for the evening.

1 Put the tomatoes into a small bowl. Either finely chop the garlic or cut it into slices and add to the tomatoes along with the parsley and basil. Drain the capers and pat dry on paper towels. Add the capers and the ¼ cup olive oil to the tomatoes. Salt lightly; the capers will have retained some salt.

2 Cut the peeled eggplants into slices a scant ½ inch thick. Pour ½ inch olive oil into a large skillet and heat over high heat until very hot but not smoking. Add the eggplant slices quickly, working in batches as necessary, and fry until they are light golden brown. (If the oil gets too hot, reduce the heat slightly.) Remove the slices with a strainer or slotted spoon and drain on paper towels. Repeat with the remaining eggplant.

3 Arrange the eggplant slices on a serving dish, covering each slice with spoonfuls of the uncooked tomato sauce and making as many layers as the eggplant and tomatoes permit. Cover the dish with aluminum foil and let stand at room temperature until serving time.

FAVA BEANS THE ROMAN WAY

Fave alla Romana

SERVES 3 OR 4

5½ pounds fava beans in the
pod (2½ kg)

¼ cup extra virgin olive oil
(60 ml)

1 medium onion, finely chopped

2 ounces pancetta, finely
chopped (60 g)

Salt and freshly ground
black pepper

Fava beans must have been with us since the Stone Age; traces of them have been found in Egyptian tombs and in Greek temples. They are one of Rome's favorite vegetables, especially in the spring, when they are in season. We don't even peel the tender, young beans. This is a simple and satisfying preparation.

1 Shell the fava beans; you will end up with about 1½ pounds shelled beans. Rinse the fava beans in cold water after shelling and drain them in a colander.

2 In a medium saucepan, heat the olive oil over moderately low heat. Add the onion and cook, stirring, until it is beginning to soften and almost translucent, about 3 minutes. Add the pancetta and continue to cook, stirring, until the pancetta is lightly colored, about 5 minutes longer.

3 Add the fava beans and ½ cup hot water and season with salt and pepper. Cover the pan with a lid and cook the beans, stirring occasionally, until they are tender, about 10 minutes. It is impossible to give a precise time as the quality of the fava beans varies. Serve hot, with a pepper mill on the table.

NOTE: If the fava beans are not in their prime, they should be peeled before cooking.

FRESH FENNEL BAKED IN MILK

Finocchi con Latte al Forno

SERVES 4 TO 6

6 fresh medium fennel bulbs, about 3½ pounds (1.575 kg)

5 tablespoons butter (70 g)

1 tablespoon extra virgin olive oil

1⅓ cups milk (330 ml)

1 teaspoon fennel seeds, crushed

Salt and freshly ground black pepper

¾ cup freshly grated Parmesan cheese (75 g)

Finocchi, or fennel, is considered a strictly Roman vegetable, like artichokes, wild chicory, wild asparagus, and broccoflower. In truth, the Romans like to claim almost everything as their own. For this dish, choose the *femmine*, or female, fennel, which is narrower and longer, if you can find it. The round larger fennel bulbs are better eaten raw.

1 Remove and discard the rough external leaves from the fennel, if they have not already been removed. Cut away the stems but reserve any feathery green fronds. Slice the fennel lengthwise about ½ inch thick. Wash rapidly in cold water and drain well.

2 Preheat the oven to 375°F (190°C).

3 Melt 4 tablespoons of the butter in the olive oil in a 15-inch (25-cm) oval gratin dish or shallow flameproof casserole.* Add the drained fennel slices and the feathery green leaves if there are any. Cook over moderately high heat, stirring often, for 7 to 10 minutes, or until the fennel is slightly softened.

4 Pour in the milk and cook over moderately high heat, stirring often, until the fennel is tender but still al dente and the milk is absorbed, 10 or 12 minutes. Season with the fennel seeds and salt and pepper to taste. Arrange the fennel in the prepared gratin dish. Cut the remaining tablespoon of butter into bits over the fennel. At this point the dish can be held at cool room temperature for 1 hour.

5 When ready to finish the dish, sprinkle the Parmesan cheese evenly over the fennel. Bake for 15 to 20 minutes, or until the top is light brown. Serve hot.

*If you don't have a gratin dish the right size, cook the fennel in a large skillet and then transfer it to a baking dish to finish off in the oven.

SIMPLE GRATINEED FENNEL

Finocchi al Forno Semplice

SERVES 4 TO 6

2¼ pounds fresh fennel bulbs (1 kg)

3 tablespoons butter

3 tablespoons flour

⅓ cup plus 2 tablespoons freshly grated Parmesan cheese (45 g)

Large pinch of crushed fennel seeds

Salt and freshly ground white pepper

This simple but elegant dish uses the cooking water from the fennel as the base for its sauce, which makes it flavorful but light, since the only dairy is the cheese. A variation with a little more heft reduces the cheese to 3 tablespoons and calls for an equal amount of bread crumbs to sprinkle on top before baking. Serve with roast pork or chicken.

1 Preheat the oven to 350°F (180°C). Butter an 11-by-7-inch (20-by-17½-cm) gratin or baking dish.

2 Clean the fennel without detaching the leaves and slice into wedges ½ inch thick. Put into a saucepan with 5 cups lightly salted water and bring to a boil. Simmer until the fennel is half cooked, about 5 minutes. Using a slotted spoon, remove the fennel wedges and arrange them in the prepared baking dish. Reserve the water in which the fennel was cooked.

3 Melt 2 tablespoons of the butter in a medium saucepan over moderate heat. Whisk in the flour, 1 tablespoon at a time. Whisk in 2 cups of the reserved hot fennel cooking water and bring to a boil, whisking constantly to prevent lumps from forming. Reduce the heat and simmer, whisking occasionally, for 8 minutes; remove from the heat. Stir in the Parmesan cheese and fennel seeds and season with salt and white pepper to taste. Pour this sauce over the fennel and dot the top with the remaining 1 tablespoon butter cut into small pieces. At this point the dish may be refrigerated; let return to room temperature before baking.

4 Bake for 20 minutes, or until the fennel is light brown. Serve hot.

SWEET-AND-SOUR PEARL ONIONS ROMAN STYLE

Cipolline in Agrodolce alla Romana

SERVES 4 TO 6

½ cup raisins (75 g)

⅓ cup extra virgin olive oil (80 ml)

1½ pounds large pearl onions, small white boiling onions, or cipolline, trimmed and peeled (675 g)

Salt

¼ cup white wine vinegar (60 ml)

2 tablespoons sugar

For years, *cipolline* — those wonderful small, flat sweet onions — were not available in America, so I became used to calling for pearl onions automatically as a substitute. Now, thanks largely to Frieda Kaplan, who has introduced so much exotic produce into supermarkets, *cipolline* are all over. Soon maybe I will change the name. For now, however, use whatever small sweet onion is easiest for you to get, as long as it is 1 to 1½ inches in diameter.

These tart and tangy onions are more like a condiment or garnish than a vegetable; a spoonful goes a long way. They are excellent with roasts and grilled meats. This dish is even better made a day in advance. Serve at room temperature.

1 In a small bowl, soak the raisins in tepid water to cover to plump them. Drain before using.

2 Heat the olive oil in a large nonreactive skillet and add the onions in a single layer. Cook over moderate heat, carefully turning the onions one by one as they brown. When they are golden all over, season with salt.

3 Stir together the vinegar and sugar and 1 tablespoon water to dissolve the sugar; pour over the onions. Bring to a simmer and cook for 10 minutes.

4 Add the raisins, distributing them evenly among the onions. Cover the skillet, reduce the heat to low, and simmer until the onions are soft, 30 to 40 minutes, turning once. Serve the onions at room temperature.

SWEET PEAS WITH PROSIUTTO

Piselli al Prosciutto

SERVES 6

3½ pounds fresh peas in the pod
(1.575 kg)

2 ounces prosciutto, coarsely
chopped (60 g)

1 small white onion,
thinly sliced

¼ cup extra virgin olive oil
(60 ml)

Salt and freshly ground
black pepper

The famous green, tender peas that grow around Rome are the most delicate and sweet peas in all of Italy. They are usually cooked simply, as they are here with only a little onion and a bit of prosciutto for richness and depth of flavor. The only difficulty at all is in shelling the peas; I suggest you call for volunteers.

1 Shell all the peas. You should end up with about 4½ heaping cups shelled peas.

2 Chop together the prosciutto and onion, using a mezzaluna or a food processor. (If using the processor, pulse to chop very finely but do not puree.)

3 Heat the olive oil in a medium saucepan. Add the prosciutto and onion and cook, stirring, for about 10 minutes over low heat, until the onion is soft and just beginning to color.

4 Add the peas to the pot, season with salt and pepper to taste, and pour in ¼ cup hot water. Raise the heat to moderately low, cover, and cook, stirring occasionally, for about 15 minutes, or until the peas are just tender but still bright green. If necessary, add a few more tablespoons of water. Serve hot.

NOTE: If you end up with any leftover peas, they are perfect for one of the pasta and peas recipes.

PEAS WITH LETTUCE AND CREAM

Piselli e Lattuga

SERVES 8

5 pounds fresh peas (2.25 kg) or
2 bags (1 pound each) frozen
small peas (900 g)

6 tablespoons butter (90 g)

2 white bunching onions or
3 large shallots, finely chopped

1 heart of romaine lettuce,
finely shredded

4 sprigs of parsley

Pinch of sugar

Salt and freshly ground
black pepper

¼ cup heavy cream (60 ml)

In Rome, this dish is strictly a seasonal event. Fresh peas are in season in the spring, usually around Easter. They are so sweet that they are delicious even eaten raw like candy. Peas with Lettuce and Cream is classic, reserved for special occasions, and is served with everything. It is especially good with veal, eggs, chicken, and roasts of all kinds. Of course, fresh is the preferred choice, but because of the quantity this serves, tiny frozen peas make an acceptable substitute, and they entail a lot less work. Plus it allows you to make the dish at other times of the year.

1 Shell the fresh peas, if you are using them. If you are using frozen, it is not necessary to defrost them.

2 Melt the butter in a large saucepan over low heat. Add the onions or shallots and cook they are until soft and translucent, 4 to 5 minutes, adding a tablespoon of water to prevent browning, if necessary. Add the peas, lettuce, parsley, and sugar; season with salt and pepper to taste. Cover and cook the peas on the lowest heat, stirring occasionally, until they are just tender, not wrinkled and still bright green: 10 to 15 minutes if fresh, 15 to 20 minutes if frozen.

3 Just before serving, remove and discard the parsley, add the cream, and simmer for 3 minutes. Serve hot.

NOTE: Without the cream, this is called *piselli jeuda*, peas as prepared in the Italian Jewish kitchen.

SWEET PEPPERS STEWED WITH TOMATOES

Peperonata

Serves 4 to 6

⅓ cup extra virgin olive oil
(80 ml)

2 cloves of garlic, peeled and
crushed

1 peperoncino, or hot red
pepper flakes to taste

2 medium onions, thinly sliced

6 large red and/or yellow bell
peppers, seeded and cut into
1-inch strips

1 pound ripe tomatoes, peeled,
seeded, and coarsely chopped
(450 g)

1½ teaspoons tomato paste

Salt and freshly ground
black pepper

2 tablespoons coarsely chopped
fresh basil, or 1 tablespoon
fresh oregano leaves

In his book *Roma in Cucina*, the great Italian cookbook writer Luigi Carnacina says that Romans have now made a cult of fresh, tender vegetables. If they had not, they surely would have after a visit to almost any Roman market in the spring or summer season. The peppers alone are worth worshipping.

1 Heat the olive oil in a large deep sauté pan or flameproof casserole. Add the garlic and whole peperoncino, if using, and cook over moderately low heat until the garlic is brown; then discard the garlic. Add the onions and cook, stirring occasionally, until lightly colored, 10 to 12 minutes.

2 Add the bell peppers, raise the heat to moderately high heat, cover, and cook for 5 minutes. Remove the lid and continue cooking, stirring often, for 5 minutes longer. Add the fresh tomatoes and the tomato paste. If using hot pepper flakes, add them now. Season with salt and black pepper to taste.

3 Reduce the heat to moderate and cook for 15 more minutes, stirring every now and then, until thickened. Check the seasoning. Serve hot or, preferably, at room temperature, with the basil or oregano sprinkled generously on top.

NEW POTATOES COOKED IN OLIVE OIL WITH ROSEMARY

Patate Novelle con Rosmarino

SERVES 3 OR 4

1 pound small new potatoes, preferably organic (450 g)

⅓ cup extra virgin olive oil (80 ml)

Coarse salt

3 tablespoons fresh rosemary leaves

Roman families, restaurants, and trattorias serve these potates often when they are in season. Choose small round new potatoes, as much as possible of the same size. They are sometimes called creamer potatoes in the United States. Easy and quick, they almost cook themselves, and they need only to be timed for dinner.

1 Scrub the potatoes but do not peel them; dry them thoroughly. Put the potatoes into a large skillet, about 9½ inches (24 cm) wide, where they will fit in a single layer. Pour the olive oil over the potatoes and shake the pan to coat them all over. Season generously with salt and add the rosemary leaves.

2 Cover the pan with a lid and cook the potatoes over the lowest heat for 40 to 45 minutes, a little more or less according to the size of the potatoes. During the cooking time, shake the pan often without removing the lid and turn the potatoes once or twice to ensure their browning all over. Test the potatoes with a kitchen needle or the tip of a small knife to be sure they are done. Serve hot.

POTATO CHIPS

Patate Fritte

SERVES 4

1 pound Idaho or all-purpose
potatoes (450 g)

About 1½ cups good-quality
vegetable or olive oil, or ¾ cup
peanut oil and ¾ cup lard
(360 ml)

Coarse salt

Crisp, hot potato chips are often served in Rome as an accompaniment to roasts and other simple meats. You can prepare them ahead of time and reheat them briefly in the oven, watching carefully, because they burn easily. For absolutely the best flavor, you should fry the potato chips in half peanut oil and half lard.

1 Peel the potatoes and rinse them. Fill a large bowl with cold water. Lay a mandoline on top and slice the potatoes directly into the cold water. Alternatively, slice them in a food processor. Soak the slices in the water for about 20 minutes. Drain and pat dry.

2 In a deep-fat fryer or large heavy saucepan, heat the oil to hot but not smoking over moderately high heat. Fry the potatoes in batches without crowding, watching carefully and pushing them around in the pan with a slotted spoon, until they are crisp and light brown. If the potatoes brown too fast, reduce the heat slightly.

3 Remove the potato chips with a skimmer or slotted spoon and drain on paper towels. Salt while hot. Keep the chips warm in a turned-off warm oven while frying the other batches. Serve hot.

ITALIAN POTATO SALAD WITH EGGS AND CAPERS

Insalata di Patate

SERVES 6 TO 8

2¼ pounds potatoes (1 kg)

6 eggs

½ cup capers, preferably salt-packed

2 cups celery ribs and tops, chopped fine

1 cup very thinly sliced small white onion

¾ cup extra virgin olive oil (180 ml)

1 tablespoon dry mustard, preferably Colman's

1½ tablespoons fresh lemon juice

½ teaspoon white wine vinegar

2 dashes of Tabasco sauce, or to taste

Salt and freshly ground black pepper

Y ou can see that Italians like plenty of eggs in their potato salad — roughly 1 per person — and plenty of celery. On the other hand, we dress the salad with a vinaigrette rather than mayonnaise. Yellow waxy potatoes are best for this salad. Sometimes salt-packed anchovies, well rinsed, are added as well. Leftovers should be refrigerated and are good the next day.

1 Scrub the potatoes. Put them into a large pot of cold water and gently boil until they are tender when tested with the tip of a small knife; do not overcook. Let cool, then peel off the skins; cut the potatoes into chunks about ¾-inch square.

2 While the potatoes are cooking, prepare the eggs. Put them in a medium saucepan, cover with cold water, and bring to a boil. When the water boils, cover the pan with a lid and remove it from the heat. Let stand for 20 minutes; then pour off the hot water and fill the pan with cold water. Tap the eggs just hard enough to crack them and leave them in the cold water. When ready to use the eggs, peel them. Cut 5 of the eggs into ¾-inch pieces; cut the remaining egg into 6 wedges.

3 Put the rinsed capers in a small bowl and cover them with cold water. Leave for 20 minutes; then drain them and dry them on paper towels.

4 In a large bowl, combine the potatoes, the 5 cut-up eggs, the capers, celery, and onion, separated into rings. Toss lightly to mix.

5 To prepare the dressing, put the olive oil in a small bowl. Whisk in the powdered mustard, lemon juice, vinegar, Tabasco, salt and pepper until the dressing is smooth and amalgamated. Pour the dressing over the salad and toss thoroughly but gently. Arrange the egg wedges on top like spokes. Cover and refrigerate until slightly chilled before serving.

OVEN-BAKED RADICCHIO

Radicchio al Forno

SERVES 4 TO 5

3 heads of radicchio,
about 1½ pounds (700 g)

5 tablespoons extra virgin
olive oil

Salt and freshly ground pepper

12 thin slices of bacon or
pancetta, any rind removed

Roasting brings out the nuttiness in this lovely bitter vegetable, which is particularly good with roast meats. Although the radicchio takes about half an hour in the oven, this dish can be put together in about 5 minutes.

1 Heat the oven to 375°F (190°C).

2 Trim the radicchio, leaving the leaves attached to the root. Rinse well and drain thoroughly. Cut each head of radicchio lengthwise into 4 pieces.

3 Use 1 tablespoon of the olive oil to grease a baking dish that will hold the radicchio in a single layer. Arrange the radicchio in the dish, cut side up. Drizzle 1 teaspoon of the oil over each piece of radicchio. Season well with salt and pepper and lay a slice of bacon or pancetta over each piece.

4 Bake for 25 minutes, or until the radicchio is wilted and light brown around the edges and the bacon is crisp. Serve hot.

THE TAXI DRIVER'S TOMATOES

I Pomodori del Tassista

SERVES 6

5 or 6 ripe but firm medium tomatoes, about 2 pounds (900 g)

3 cloves of garlic, peeled and chopped coarse

2 packed cups flat-leaf parsley sprigs

1 salt-packed anchovy, rinsed and dried, or 3 anchovy fillets packed in oil

½ cup dry bread crumbs (25 g)

Salt and freshly ground black pepper

About 6 tablespoons extra virgin olive oil

This recipe is from a driver who kept me in his cab for an extra ten minutes telling me how to prepare these tomatoes and several other recipes. He says his grandmother taught him these and many more.

1 Preheat the oven to 375°F (190°C).

2 Wash and dry the tomatoes and cut them horizontally in half. Using a small teaspoon, remove as many of the seeds as you can. Using the spoon again, cut out and reserve the center pulp of the tomato, being careful not to tear the tomato shell.

3 Put the tomato pulp, garlic, parsley, anchovy, and bread crumbs on a large cutting board. Chop all together finely, using a mezzaluna or a large chef's knife.* Season with salt and pepper to taste.

4 Spread 2 tablespoons of the olive oil over the bottom of a 14-by-9-inch (35-by-23-cm) gratin dish or heatproof glass baking dish. Fit the tomato shells into the dish and divide the parsley mixture among them. Drizzle 1 teaspoon olive oil over each tomato half. Salt again lightly and season with a grind of pepper.

5 Bake the tomatoes for 55 to 60 minutes, or until no more liquid is released and the tomatoes are soft but still hold their shape. Serve hot, warm, or at room temperature.

* All the ingredients can be pulsed in a food processor to chop, but do not puree.

THREE GREEN VEGETABLES A LA ROMANA

The Roman way of rendering greens richer in taste is unique. The vegetables are cooked al dente, squeezed by hand to remove excess water, and then stir-fried with olive oil, garlic, and peperoncino until the flavors blend. They are mixed constantly with two forks as they cook over high heat, until their remaining liquid evaporates and the vegetable wilts. This particular way of preparing vegetables can be done with chicory, broccoflower, spinach, broccoli rabe, Swiss chard, and what in Rome is called "Sicilian broccoli," our regular green broccoli.

WILD CHICORY IN A PAN

Cicoria Strascicata

SERVES 4 TO 6

4½ pounds chicory, preferably wild, trimmed and well rinsed (2 kg)

½ cup extra virgin olive oil (120 ml)

2 cloves of garlic, peeled and crushed

1 or 2 peperoncini, or hot red pepper flakes to taste

Salt

Freshly ground black pepper

For a simple meal, serve this with good bread and fried pancetta or sausages. Accompany with a rustic red wine, such as chianti.

1 Cook the chicory in a large pot of boiling salted water until it is just tender. Drain in a colander. As soon as the vegetable is cool enough to handle, squeeze it dry with your hands.

2 Heat the olive oil in a large skillet with the garlic and peperoncino over moderate heat. When the garlic is light brown, add the chicory and season with salt and black pepper. Turn up the heat to high — allegro, the Romans say — and cook the chicory, stirring and mixing it with 2 forks, about 8 minutes, or until the chicory seems to have shrunk a little. Pick out and discard the garlic and peperoncino and serve the chicory hot.

SAUTEED BROCCOLI WITH GARLIC AND HOT PEPPER

Broccoli Siciliani Strascicati

SERVES 4

2 pounds broccoli, washed and drained (900 g)

⅓ cup extra virgin olive oil (80 ml)

2 cloves of garlic, peeled and crushed

Peperoncino to taste

Salt and freshly ground black pepper

1 Cut off the tender broccoli shoots and cut the stems into strips vertically.

2 Heat the olive oil over moderate heat and add the garlic and peperoncino. When the garlic is brown, add the broccoli, stems first and after a minute or two the florets. Turn up the heat to high. Season the broccoli with salt and pepper and cook, stirring it often with 2 forks, for about 5 minutes.

3 Discard the garlic and peperoncino and serve the broccoli hot.

SAUTEED SPINACH ROMAN STYLE WITH RAISINS AND PINE NUTS

Spinaci Strascicati alla Romana

SERVES 4 OR 5

2¼ pounds fresh spinach (1 kg)

2½ tablespoons lard or butter (40 g)

Salt and freshly ground black pepper

2 tablespoons seedless dark raisins, plumped in warm water

2 tablespoons pine nuts

1 Wash the spinach thoroughly in cold water and cook it in a pot with only the water clinging to its leaves. Drain and, when the spinach is cool, squeeze it tightly to remove as much water as possible.

2 Heat the lard and add the spinach, separating the leaves with two forks as you heat it. Season with salt and pepper, mix, and add the drained raisins and the pine nuts. Cook over moderate heat for 4 minutes, mixing with the two forks every now and then.

3 Serve the spinach hot.

MIXED SUMMER VEGETABLES

Le Verdure Miste

SERVES 8 TO 10

⅔ cup extra virgin olive oil
(160 ml)

½ pound onions, thinly sliced
(225 g)

3 cloves of garlic, peeled
and crushed

1 teaspoon hot red pepper
flakes, or to taste

1⅔ pounds ripe red tomatoes,
peeled, seeded, and diced
(750 g)

2 tablespoons tomato paste

1½ pounds zucchini, sliced
¼ inch thick (675 g)

1⅔ pounds eggplant, cut into
1-inch pieces (750 g)

1⅔ pounds bell peppers,
cut into 1-inch strips (750 g)

Salt

In a hot climate like Rome's, one tends to cook in the morning for the entire day, before the heat makes it too difficult. This dish of fresh vegetables, which lends itself to advance preparation, goes well with fish or meat and is even good for picnics. It is eaten in all of southern Italy from Rome down. As is common with food for warm places, this dish is spicy and is customarily served at room temperature. If you like, you can stir in a handful of shredded fresh basil just before serving.

1 Heat the olive oil in a large flameproof casserole. Add the onions, garlic, and hot pepper flakes and cook over moderately low heat, stirring occasionally, until the onions are soft and translucent, about 7 minutes.

2 Add the tomatoes and tomato paste and cook, stirring, for 3 minutes. Add the zucchini, eggplant, and bell peppers, salting to taste, and cook over high heat for 10 minutes, stirring every now and then.

3 Now lower the heat to moderate, cover the casserole, and cook the vegetables, stirring occasionally, until they are tender but still firm, about 25 minutes. Serve at room temperature.

VEGETABLE PIE

Torta di Erbe

SERVES 6 TO 8

FOR THE PASTRY:

2⅔ cups all purpose flour
(300 g)

10 tablespoons cold butter,
cut into small pieces (150 g)

Pinch of salt

2 large egg yolks

FOR THE FILLING:

¼ cup plus 1 tablespoon extra
virgin olive oil (75 ml)

2 large artichokes, cleaned as
on page 211 and thinly sliced,
or 2 cups frozen artichoke hearts
(½ pound), partially thawed
and thinly sliced (225 g)

3 pounds garden-fresh peas,
shelled (1.35 kg), or 2½ cups
frozen peas (12 ounces) (340 g)

1 pound fresh spinach, cleaned
(450 g), or ⅔ pound frozen
spinach, coarsely chopped
(300 g)

In a book given to me by a Jewish friend, the preface quotes writer Lucia Levi: "In every country . . . the (Jewish) kitchen has adapted itself to the uses, local tastes, and to what the market offers. Culinary traditions have thus formed in every country, region, and family. Often these traditions are all that remains. . . ."

This *torta di erbe* from the Jewish kitchen is nearly *la vignarola* (see page 208), a *romanissima* dish made with almost the same vegetables — artichokes and garden-fresh peas, along with fava beans.

1 Make the pastry: If using an electric mixer, put all the ingredients in the large bowl of an electric mixer and mix just until the dough masses around the paddle. If using a food processor, put all the ingredients in the work bowl and process until they are just mixed. If mixing by hand, mound the flour and make a well in the center. Beat the egg yolks. Put the butter, salt, and beaten yolks into the well in the flour and mix the ingredients together rapidly. When the pastry is ready, leave it in a cool place covered with a tea cloth while you prepare the vegetables.

2 Heat ¼ cup of the olive oil in a large sauté pan and add the artichokes, peas, spinach, and parsley. Cover and cook over moderately high heat, stirring every now and then, for about 20 minutes, until the vegetables. Uncover the pan to dry the vegetables if necessary, and season well with salt and pepper. Add the remaining 1 tablespoon oil to the cooked vegetables, stir, and set aside to cool.

3 tablespoons chopped parsley

Salt and freshly ground pepper

2 large eggs

⅓ cup freshly grated pecorino Romano cheese, (35 g) (optional), or 2 tablespoons capers, rinsed and dried (optional)

3 When ready to make the pie, preheat the oven to 350°F (175°C).

4 Divide the pastry into 2 parts, one a little larger than the other. On a lightly floured marble or wooden work surface, roll out the larger piece of pastry and fit it into the pie tin. Beat the eggs and add the pecorino Romano cheese, if using it, to the eggs, or add the capers, if using them, to the vegetables. Mix the eggs and cooled vegetables together and spoon the mixture into the pastry-lined pie tin. Roll out the top crust and press it into place over the top of the *torta*, trimming the excess and crimping the edge.

5 Bake the *torta di erbe* for about 40 minutes. If desired, the *torta* can be painted with a yolk beaten with a little cold water before baking. Let the pie cool slightly before serving.

NOTE: Swiss chard greens, without the white center, can be used instead of spinach.

ZUCCHINI IN SAUCE

Zucchini Brodettati

SERVES 4 TO 6

1/4 cup extra virgin olive oil
(60 ml)

1 medium white onion, very
thinly sliced

2 pounds fresh small zucchini,
sliced about 1/4 inch thick
(900 g)

Salt and freshly ground
black pepper

1 whole egg

1 egg yolk

2 tablespoons freshly grated
Parmesan cheese

3 tablespoons fresh lemon juice

2 tablespoons finely chopped
fresh marjoram or parsley

The zucchini here are prepared in the same manner as
brodettati, with lemon juice and egg, easy to prepare. The
zucchini must be small and fresh and the cooking time, 20 to
25 minutes, planned so that they can be eaten when ready.

1 Heat the olive oil in a large skillet over moderately low heat. Add
the onion and cook until soft and translucent, 3 to 5 minutes.

2 Add the zucchini, raise the heat to moderately high, and cook,
stirring almost constantly, untl the zucchini are tender but still
firm, about 20 minutes. Season with salt and pepper to taste.

3 In a small bowl, beat together the whole egg, egg yolk, Parmesan
cheese, and lemon juice. Over low heat, pour the egg mixture over
the zucchini in the skillet, tossing and mixing rapidly. As soon as
the eggs begin to solidify, remove the zucchini from the heat and
arrange on a serving platter. Sprinkle the marjoram or parsley on
top and serve at once.

SALADS

Ce vorebbe l'insalata de Sisto Quinto.
He needs Pope Sixtus' salad.

This Roman proverb means "You need money." The reference is to Pope Sixtus V, who had a friend, fallen into want, who was so dejected over his poverty that he became ill. Having heard of his friend's misery, Pope Sixtus sent him a basket full of salad, which contained an abundant layer of gold coins on the bottom underneath the greens.

We have a quantity of lettuces in our markets, each a little different from its neighbor. *Cappuccio,* a round but loose head of lettuce, is usually used raw in salads. Romaine can be found everywhere in Rome, also in the Roman Jewish kitchen, as a salad or stuffed with olives, anchovies, and capers. It is braised alone or with other vegetables or added as an ingredient to other dishes. Radicchio is served as an uncooked salad or is baked with pancetta and olive oil. And we have a slightly bitter escarole, *lattughella,* which is a relative of lettuce, and *indivia* (endive), a curly topped green salad with a distinctive taste, all three to use either cooked or raw. Salads are an essential part of the Roman diet, so it's not too surprising that we even turn it into a risotto.

For dressing all salads there is a very popular saying here in Rome: *Pe' condi' bene l'insalata ce vonno quattro persone: un sapiente pe' mettece er sale, un avaro l'aceto, uno spregone l'ojo, e un matto che la mischi e la smucini.* "To dress salad well you need four people: a wise man for the salt, a miser for the vinegar, a waster for the oil, and a madman to toss it wildly."

ROMAN MIXED GREEN SALAD

Misticanza

*M*isticanza is one of Rome's famous salads and is never or very rarely found outside of the Eternal City. *Misticanza*, which means "mixture," is a Roman word for the extraordinary salad that originally was made up of about 20 different kinds of herbs, mostly wild, and largely impossible to find these days. But *misticanza* is still sold made up of five or more herbs in the markets, and even though "reduced in circumstances," it is still delicious. If you should have the good fortune to find arugula, wild chicory, wild watercress, and other small salad greens, wash them, clean them, dry them, and dress them with a simple oil and vinegar dressing. But the dressing must be prepared properly:

First, dissolve a good pinch of salt in 1 tablespoon of vinegar. Put this in a small bowl with 2½ tablespoons of extra virgin olive oil and a little freshly ground pepper. Toss the salad vigorously, like a madman as the proverb on the previous page advises.

Following are the local names of some of the wild greens that would be gathered for a real *misticanza*. I have translated the names, sometimes literally.

Barba dei frati . . . Monks' beard

Borragine . . . Borage

Caccialepre . . . Repel rabbit

Cicoria dolce . . . Sweet wild chicory

Costa del somaro . . . Donkey's rib

Crescione selvatico . . . Wild watercress

Crispigno . . . no translation

Denti di leone . . . Dandelion greens

Finocchio selvatico . . . Wild fennel

Grugno . . . no translation

Lattucella . . . Wild lettuce

Ortica (used cooked) . . . Nettle

Paparà . . . Wild poppy (papavero)

Pimpirinella . . . no translation

Porcacchia . . . (a succulent)

Raponzolo . . . (a root; the green part is discarded)

Rughetta selvatica . . . Wild arugula

Sugamele . . . (this absorbs the oil in the dressing)

PUNTARELLE SALAD WITH ANCHOVIES AND GARLIC

Le Puntarelle

SERVES 4 TO 6

2 pounds puntarelle, cleaned, washed, and soaked in cold water (900 g)

2 cloves of garlic, peeled

6 salt-packed anchovies

3 tablespoons white wine vinegar

½ cup extra virgin olive oil (120 ml)

Salt and freshly ground black pepper

Puntarelle is one of Rome's favorite salad greens. It is a kind of culivated chicory found in the vegetable gardens in and around Rome, highly seasonal, and very expensive when it is available. The greens are cleaned by slicing down the middle of the individual small stems, which will curl up after they are washed and placed in cold water. In the markets, puntarelle can be purchased already cleaned, washed, and curled. It should be drained thoroughly before being dressed. Of course, the vinaigrette can be altered to taste, and also used with other salads.

1 Drain the puntarelle and dry it thoroughly, using a salad spinner, if you have one.

2 Clean the anchovies, rinse them under cold water, and drain them on paper towels.

3 The dressing for the puntarelle should be prepared in a mortar with a pestle and not in a blender. Cut the garlic and anchovies into pieces, put them into a mortar, and pound them until they are thoroughly mashed. Then scrape into a small bowl and add the vinegar, olive oil, salt, and pepper, beating with a fork. Taste and correct the seasoning if necessary. If possible, allow the sauce to rest for about 1 hour before serving.

DESSERTS

Semel in anno licet insanire.

Once a year it is permitted to go mad.

At my cooking school, Lo Scaldavivande, I was always asked to produce *dolci al cucchaio*, "spoon sweets" — semifreddos, ice creams, creams, and ricotta desserts are Roman favorites. But so are all the sweets tied to religious feast days: Christmas, Easter, the Feast of Saint Joseph, Carnival, etc. Today, on Sundays, it is still common to see families with large packages of sweet pastries bought for the Sunday dinner after the family has attended Mass. Because Romans usually end their meals with fruit, sweets are still special and therefore are a cause for celebration.

Except on special occasions, Italians like to finish their meals with fresh fruit. They make delicious mixtures, for example:

Ripe peaches and cantaloupe cut into large bite-size pieces

Strawberries rinsed in wine and served with sweetened whipped cream

Mixed bite-size fresh fruits in season with walnuts or almonds

Orange sections with a little Grand Marnier poured over them . . . or:

   1 orange per person, peeled, pith removed, and sliced

   1 tablespoon confectioners' sugar per person

   1½ tablespoons white rum per person

   Put the orange slices in a bowl. Mix together the sugar and rum and pour over each layer of orange slices. Refrigerate for 2 hours before serving

Honeydew melon with raspberries

Mixed berries with sweetened whipped cream

Melon with port wine in the center

Ripe pineapple cut into bite-size pieces

SWEET ALMOND COOKIES

Fave dei Morti

MAKES 75 TO 80 SMALL COOKIES

½ pound natural almonds, skins on (225 g)

½ pound sugar (225 g)

1¼ cups all-purpose flour (175 g)

1 teaspoon ground cinnamon

3½ tablespoons butter, at room temperature (50 g)

Grated zest of 1 lemon

2 large eggs, at room temperature, beaten

These traditional Roman sweets used to be called *fave dei morti*, "fava beans of the dead," because they were prepared for the second of November, the Day of the Dead. This is a national holiday in Italy, and everyone goes to the cemetery to carry flowers to their family tombs. It is not at all a sad day; people remember their ancestors and, if they have their own chapel in the cemetery, will have Mass said there with all the extended family present, adults and children. These almond cookies are eaten as dessert with a glass of sweet wine. Today they are more often called simply *fave dolci*.

1 Preheat the oven to 350°F (175°C).

2 Working in batches, chop the almonds with the sugar very finely, but do not puree them to a paste or you will bring out the almonds' oil. (I have found that a spice grinder does this job best.) As you chop each batch, sieve it into a bowl, using a sieve that is not too fine. When all the sugar and almonds have been sieved, sift the flour and cinnamon into the bowl and mix all together.

3 Cut the butter into the almond mixture. Add the lemon zest and the beaten eggs, mixing until all is blended.

4 Flour a work surface, preferably marble, and turn out the almond mixture onto it. Quickly roll the mixture into ropes 1 inch in diameter. Cut small almond cookies from them about ½ inch thick. Flatten the cookies slightly and place on buttered and floured cookie sheets, leaving 1 inch of space between them.

5 Bake the cookies for 18 to 20 minutes, until they are lightly colored. Using a small spatula, remove the cookies from the sheet gently before they cool, and let cool on racks. When they are completely cool, store them in tightly covered containers. They keep for weeks.

HAZELNUT BISCOTTI

Tozzetti

MAKES ABOUT 36 HARD COOKIES

¾ cup superfine sugar *(150 g)*

Grated zest of 1 large lemon

2 large eggs, at room temperature, beaten

1 teaspoon baking powder

1½ tablespoons rum

2 cups flour (½ pound) *(225 g)*

½ pound whole hazelnuts *(225 g)*

Our friend Craig Claiborne came to spend a weekend with us in our hunting lodge near Barbarano Romano some years ago, and later he published an article in *The New York Times* about the food at our place. He mentioned, without giving the recipe, *tozzetti*, the biscotti he ate with a glass of *vin santo* there. On the strength of that mention, I received about ten letters from former American soldiers who remembered kind Italians giving them biscotti and sweet wine during the Second World War. I was unable to send them the recipe then because we baked *tozetti* outdoors in a wood-burning oven. Now we use an electric oven. These biscotti keep for months in a tin box. *Tozzetti* are found in Lazio, Umbria, and Tuscany, but they must be at their best near Rome because of the delicious locally grown hazelnuts.

1 Preheat the oven to 375°F (190°C).

2 Put the sugar into a bowl with the grated lemon zest. Add the eggs, baking powder, and rum. Mix these ingredients together and add the flour in 2 or 3 batches. When the flour has been incorporated, add the hazelnuts and stir all together.

3 Divide the mixture into 2 parts and, with the help of a metal spoon, put it onto the prepared cookie sheet in 2 rolls about 10 inches long. It will be sticky, so use a fork to help give a rounded form to the rolls, leaving a space of 3 inches between the rolls.

4 Bake the rolls for about 20 minutes, or until they are beginning to brown. Reduce the oven temperature to 350°F (175°C) and bake for another 10 minutes. Take the cookie sheet out of the oven but do not turn off the oven.

5 Carefully remove 1 roll at a time (I use a long spatula) to a cutting board and, using a very sharp knife, cut each roll into slices a little less than ½ inch thick to make the *tozzetti*. Lay the *tozzetti* flat on the cookie sheet and return them to the oven for about 8 minutes to dry.

6 Let them cool before you serve them. Store in a tin box; these biscotti keep for ages.

THERE IS USUALLY a terrible racket in the popular coffee bars, and you wonder how they keep all the orders straight. But they do, and they even have a greeting, usually ironic, for the regulars. The better bars, famous for their quality, often sell coffee beans for the home. Not too long ago most all of them did, but everybody seems to be rushing around these days and as a result they now buy their coffees from the shop for "staples." It is a pity, because these special bars toast their own beans and usually have various kinds of coffee that they grind while you wait. (Which reminds me: Romans once toasted their own coffee at home, and here again was a demonstration of their individualism, of which they are very proud, because everybody had their private way of toasting.) However, the commercial espresso coffee sold in Italy is excellent, and everybody swears by this or that coffee.

Coffee is usually drunk standing at the bar and the cup is drained at once. Cappuccino is drunk between meals, never after a meal.

The ways of preparing coffee in Roman bars are:

Macchiato	With a drop of milk
Caffé lungo	"Long" coffee (similar to American coffee)
Ristretto	Very concentrated
Cappuccino	With foamy milk
Con latte caldo	With hot milk
Con latte freddo	With cold milk
Caffé latte	More or less half milk, half coffee
Caffé corretto	With a liqueur or cognac
Con panna e cioccolata o cannella	With softly whipped cream and a shake of chocolate powder or a sprinkling of cinnamon
Con panna	With cream, whipped or plain
Caffé freddo	Iced coffee already sweetened, served without ice
Granita di caffé	Shaved iced coffee, served only in summer

This is not a complete list, but it certainly shows Italian individuality. To be added to this is the sweetening: in some bars the coffee maker puts in the sugar . . .

Amaro	Without sugar
Mezzo cucchiaino	Half a coffee spoon (very little)
Molto dolce	Very sweet

. . . or the number of teaspoons wanted.

These bars are generally considered to have the best coffee in Rome:

Camilloni a Sant'Eustachio, Piazza Sant'Eustachio 54/55, telephone 06 686 4995

Casa del Caffè la Tazza d'Oro, Via degli Orfani 84 (near the Pantheon), tele-phone 06 678 9792, 06 679 2768

TEA CAKE WITH PIGNOLI AND ALMONDS

Cake per il Té

4 egg yolks, at room temperature

1 whole egg, at room temperature

¾ cup superfine sugar (150 g)

Grated zest of 1 large lemon

1½ cups flour (180 g)

⅓ cup pine nuts (50 g)

10 tablespoons unsalted butter, melted and cooled (150 g)

¾ cup blanched whole almonds (100 g)

The tea cake is still popular in Italy, and tea parties are still given, with tables full of delicious things — sandwiches, hot hors d'oeuvres, open-face canapés with salmon, caviar, and so on. All kinds of sweet cakes, bonbons, and miniature fruit tarts are passed, and a granddaughter usually "pours," with another grand-daughter to help. After a certain hour, the spumante is brought out. It is a long affair but very pleasant. This is a tea cake recipe given me by a friend. It is her grandmother's special cake, with "1932" — the year she was given the recipe — written at the end. This is also a good breakfast cake, especially for children.

1 Preheat the oven to 350°F (175°C). Butter a 10-by-4-by-3-inch (25-by-8-by-6-cm) loaf pan. Line the bottom with waxed paper and butter the paper.

2 Beat the egg yolks and whole egg in an electric mixer. Gradually add the sugar and beat for 4 to 6 minutes, or until the mixture is a light lemon color. Add the lemon zest. Remove the mixer bowl and fold in the flour by hand together with the pine nuts. Now fold in the melted butter by hand, one-third at a time.

3 Pour the batter into the prepared loaf pan and sprinkle the whole almonds over the top.

4 Bake the cake for 50 minutes, or until it is browned on top and a cake tester inserted in the middle comes out clean. Let the cake cool for 10 minutes in the pan on a rack. Turn out the cake and remove the waxed paper. Let cool completely before cutting.

5 Store the cake in a tin or other cake box. Put a wedge of apple in the box to keep the cake fresh.

ROMAN CHERRY JAM TART

Crostata alla Romana

SERVES 8 TO 10

Sweet Pastry (recipe on page 256)

2 cups good cherry jam, wild if possible (300 g)

3 tablespoons cherry or berry liqueur

1 egg yolk

Whenever there is an outing or a country lunch or a big Sunday dinner, you can count on the Romans' most loved *dolce*, or sweet, being present. Wild cherries can be found all around the city of Rome, particularly in the Viterbese, and the marmalade made from them is a must for this *crostata alla romana*. Other marmalades may be used, of course, but it's just not the same thing.

1 Preheat the oven to 375°F (190°C). Butter and flour an 11-inch (28-cm) tart pan with removable sides.

2 Make the pastry as directed. Remove one-third of the pastry and refrigerate it while preparing the rest of the tart.

3 Roll out the remaining two-thirds of the pastry as thin as possible and fit it into the prepared tart pan. Fold the edges under and crimp them. Prick all over the bottom of the pan with a fork and refrigerate the unbaked shell while preparing the filling.

4 Put the jam into a small bowl, add the liqueur, and mix thoroughly. Pour the mixture into the prepared shell. Roll out the reserved pastry, cut it into strips, and make a lattice over the top of the tart, attaching the strips to the bottom crust. Crimp the rim of the tart. Beat the egg yolk with 1 tablespoon of water and use this glaze to paint the crust's rim and the strips.

5 Bake the tart for 30 minutes, or until it is light brown. Transfer the pan to a rack and let cool for 10 minutes. Gently remove the pan's rim and cool the tart. When the tart is cool, run a sharp knife around it and, using large spatulas, slide it onto a serving dish. Serve at room temperature.

SWEET PASTRY FOR PIES, TARTS, AND TIMBALLOS

Pasta Frolla

5 tablespoons cold unsalted
butter, cut into pieces (75 g)

5 tablespoons cold lard,
cut into small pieces (75 g)

2⅔ cups all-purpose flour
(300 g)

⅔ cup sugar, better if superfine
(130 g)

2 large egg yolks, at room
temperature

1 whole egg

Grated zest of ½ large lemon

This is the recipe most Italians use to make a thin pastry (*pasta frolla*) for pies, tarts, and *pasta timballi*. It can be made by hand or prepared in a food processor or electric mixer. The Romans have their own way and tend to make up the pastry by hand; it is allowed to rest under a clean tea cloth in a cool place, not the refrigerator, for about 30 minutes before using. But there are certain rules for *pasta frolla* all over Italy; most of them derived from Ada Parasiliti, my Roman/Milanese/Sicilian friend, who is an expert on *pasta frolla*. Lard makes the tastiest pastry, but if you don't want to use it, increase the butter to 10 tablespoons.

The ingredients for the various techniques are always the same. This quantity of pastry can be used for a 10-inch (25-cm) pie pan or springform pan or for an 11-inch (27-cm) tart pan. *Pasta frolla* is easily mended: simply press a piece of the pastry over the tear and gently press in place. Any leftover *pasta frolla* can be cut into biscotti (cookies) and baked for about 10 minutes in a 375° (173° C) oven, or an entire recipe made into biscotti. Sift confectioners' sugar over while still warm.

IF PREPARING BY HAND:

1 Remove the butter and lard from the refrigerator 5 minutes before using them. Sift the flour directly onto a work table, preferably of marble, hollowing out the center to make a well. Cut the cold butter and lard into small pieces into the well and quickly mix into the flour, using your fingertips. When the butter and lard are incorporated, again make a well in the center.

2 Beat the yolks in a small bowl with the sugar and lemon zest and pour into the center of the well. Work rapidly to amalgamate the yolks with the flour mixture, using your fingertips. Press with the palm of your hand two or three times. Wrap the *pasta frolla* in waxed paper and allow to rest in a cool place for at least 30 minutes before using it.

IF USING A FOOD PROCESSOR:

Put the flour in the work bowl and add the cold butter and lard, just removed from the refrigerator, cut into small pieces. Pulse until the mixture is crumbly. Beat together the yolks, sugar, and lemon zest and add to the bowl while the processor is in motion, pulsing just until the mixture forms a ball around the blade. Remove the dough from the bowl and gather together into a ball, then press into a disk rapidly. Wrap in waxed paper and refrigerate for a minimum of 1 hour, or overnight.

IF USING AN ELECTRIC MIXER:

Use the paddle or bread hook. Put the flour and the cold butter and lard cut into small pieces into the bowl of the mixer. Holding a tea towel around the bowl to keep the flour from scattering, mix until the butter, lard, and flour are crumbly. Beat together the eggs, sugar, and lemon zest. With the mixer on, add to the bowl, 1 tablespoon at a time. When the pasta is ready, it will form a ball around the paddle or hook. Wrap in waxed paper and refrigerate for a minimum of 1 hour, or overnight.

ROMAN RICOTTA PIE

Crostata di Ricotta alla Romana

SERVES 8 TO 10

⅓ cup raisins

2 tablespoons dark rum

Sweet Pastry (recipe on page 256)

1 pound 2 ounces fresh ricotta, drained (510 g)

1 cup plus 2 tablespoons sugar (250 g)

1 whole egg

2 egg yolks

Grated zest of 1 lemon (washed)

2½ tablespoons diced candied orange peel, optional (50 g)

1 tablespoon diced candied citron (optional)

⅓ cup pine nuts, lightly toasted (45 g)

The fresh ricotta in Lazio is considered the best in Italy, and not only by the Romans. *Ri* means "again" and *cotta* means "cooked"; the name refers to how ricotta is made, "cooked again." The fresh sheeps' milk is heated, almost to boiling, with a small piece of lamb's intestine for the rennet. Pecorino cheese is formed from this first heating. (The cheeses will be eaten fresh with olive oil and freshly ground black pepper or aged for several months for grating.) The whey is then reheated again almost to boiling, and the curds are put into the small willow baskets that allow the residual whey to seep out.

There is nothing better than fresh ricotta eaten as is or with very little accompaniment (see page 297). It was once a usual break-fast dish in Rome but now is more often eaten as a dessert. This *crostata* is the most Roman of all the Roman desserts. The pastry recipe is a little different from others in that it uses only lard.

1 In a small bowl, soak the raisins in the rum. If the raisins are hard, warm the rum slightly.

2 Preheat the oven to 350°F (175°C). Butter and flour a 10-inch (25-cm) springform pan. Make the pastry.

3 While the pasta is resting, make the filling: Either sieve the drained ricotta or pass it through a food mill. Put the ricotta into a bowl, add the sugar, and mix well. Add the whole egg, egg yolks, and lemon zest; blend well. Stir in the raisins with the rum, candied orange peel, and citron, if using, and pine nuts.

4 Set aside about one-quarter of the pastry to make lattice strips for the top of the pie. Dust the work surface with a little flour and roll out the remaining pastry as thin as possible. With the help of a spatula, drape the pastry over the rolling pin, and unroll it onto the prepared springform pan. Trim the sides.

5 Pour the filling into the pastry-lined pan. Roll out the reserved pastry, cut it into strips 2 inches wide, and make a lattice over the top of the pie. Crimp the edges.

6 Bake the pie for 40 to 45 minutes, or until the crust is light brown. Let cool on a rack for 15 minutes before removing the rim of the pan. Let cool completely before removing the bottom. Serve at room temperature. Refrigerate any leftover pie.

CHRISTMAS CAKE

Panpepato

MAKES 2, SERVES 8 TO 10 EACH

¼ pound pine nuts (110 g)

2½ ounces semisweet chocolate, coarsely chopped (70 g)

⅓ pound raisins (150 g)

⅔ pound hazelnuts, skins on (300 g)

6½ ounces whole almonds, skins on (180 g)

¼ pound mixed candied fruit (110 g)

¾ cup all-purpose flour (90 g)

9 ounces honey (250 g)

¼ pound walnuts (110 g)

Fresh bay leaves (optional)

Panpepato, which literally translates as "peppered bread," comes from Capranica, a small Etruscan town thirty minutes from Rome. It is a country dessert, full of whole nuts — especially the delicious hazelnuts that grow all about this part of northern Lazio — dried fruits, and honey. The sweet was originally spicy with black pepper, but modern recipes omit the pepper. This is clearly an "antique" recipe. It uses whole nuts — not chopped — and the finished cake even looks old, particularly when it is presented wreathed in laurel leaves. These panpepati are made in grand quantity at Christmas and given to friends as gifts, but they are often kept until Easter and added to the Easter sweets. A small glass of Italian dessert wine, vin santo, would be the perfect accompaniment.

1 Preheat the oven to 350°F (175°C). Butter and flour a large cookie sheet.

2 Put the pine nuts, chocolate, raisins, hazelnuts, and candied fruit in a bowl and mix with your hands. Add the flour, mixing well to coat the nuts and candied fruit. Pour in the honey and mix until all is covered with the honey. Now add the walnuts, again mixing so that they too are covered with honey.

3 Wash your hands and put a dish of cold water nearby. Wet your hands and divide the mixture in half. Form 2 balls, pressing to remove all air. Put the balls onto the prepared cookie sheet, making each into a dome shape, flat on the bottom and rounded on top.

4 Bake the *panpepati* for 1 hour, watching so that they do not color too much. If necessary, cover them loosely with foil. The cakes should be a deep golden brown. After an hour, test with a cake tester. If the cakes are sticky at the end of the cooking time, turn off the oven and leave them in the oven to cool. When they have cooled completely, wrap them in aluminum foil or waxed paper.

5 Present the *panpepato* encircled with fresh bay laurel leaves, if you have them. To serve, cut it into thin slices.

CRUMB AND RICOTTA PIE

Torta di Briciole e Ricotta

SERVES 10 TO 12

FOR THE FILLING:

¼ pound pine nuts, lightly toasted (110 g)

1 lemon, washed, for flattening the pine nuts

1¼ cups sugar (250 g)

3¾ cups ricotta (30 ounces), drained (850 g)

2 ounces bittersweet chocolate, cut in tiny dice (60 g)

2 tablespoons rum

FOR THE CRUST:

3½ cups all-purpose flour (500 g)

13 tablespoons butter, plus butter for the pan (200 g)

3 teaspoons baking powder

¾ cup firmly packed brown sugar (150 g)

My friend Ada Parasiliti, born in Sicily, reared in Naples and Rome, now living in Milan, gave me this recipe. I use it often, and taught it in my cooking school, where it was very successful, particularly in Rome where ricotta is so good and so popular. If possible, the dessert should be timed so that it does not have to be refrigerated before serving.

1 Preheat the oven to 350°F (175°C). Line a 10½-inch (27-cm) cake pan 2 inches (5 cm) high with aluminum foil and butter the foil generously.

2 Caramelize the pine nuts: Butter a marble surface or a large platter and place the lemon nearby. Heat ¼ cup of the sugar until it is a tawny brown. Add the pine nuts and mix well. Turn out the pine nuts onto the buttered surface and press with the lemon to flatten them. Leave the pine nuts to harden. When ready to use them, break them up with your hands.

3 Sieve the ricotta or pass it through a food mill, and mix it with the remaining 1 cup sugar, stirring with a wooden spoon. Stir in the pine nuts, chocolate, and rum and set the filling aside.

4 Using the dough hook of an electric mixer or your hands, mix together all the ingredients for the crust, the egg last of all. The mixture will be slightly damp.

1 cup finely chopped almonds
(110 g)

1½ teaspoons vanilla

1 egg

Confectioners' sugar to dust
the finished torta

5 Sprinkle half of the crumb mixture over the prepared cake pan, pat it against the pan, building it up around the sides to hold the ricotta filling. Pour in the filling and smooth with a spatula. Sprinkle the remaining crumb mixture evenly over the top to cover the ricotta completely.

6 Bake the *torta* for 45 minutes. Cool on a rack before turning out. Sift confectioners' sugar over the top just before serving. If there is *torta* left over, it should be refrigerated.

CHOCOLATE-ALMOND VARIATION

Substitute the same amount of peeled toasted almonds for the pine nuts and caramelize them with ¼ cup of sugar. When they have hardened, chop finely by hand. Do not pulverize. Add them to the drained ricotta together with the same amount of sugar as in the main recipe, the same amount of chocolate, the grated zest of a lemon, and 3 tablespoons of limoncello (a liqueur made from lemon peels) instead of rum. The cooking time and crust are the same.

CUSTARD PIE

Crostata alla Crema

Serves 6 to 8

FOR THE PASTRY:

2⅔ cups all-purpose flour (300 g)

10 tablespoons cold unsalted butter (150 g)

⅔ cup granulated sugar (130 g)

1 whole egg, at room temperature

2 egg yolks, at room temperature

¼ teaspoon baking powder

Grated zest of 1 lemon

FOR THE CUSTARD:

2 cups milk (500 ml)

¼ cup cornstarch (25 g)

4 egg yolks, at room temperature

¼ cup granulated sugar (50 g)

Grated zests of 2 lemons

FOR THE ASSEMBLY:

¼ cup blanched, peeled almonds, coarsely chopped (40 g)

Confectioners' sugar

I had a favorite restaurant in Rome called Sora Cecilia, decidedly not chic. It had evidently been put together in the very early fifties and not touched since, but it had wonderful Roman food, particularly a cream tart that every home cook in Rome makes. Alas, it closed, and I never managed to get Sora Cecilia's recipe for her perfect *crostata alla crema*. Oh, she promised, but she never had the time, and now it's gone forever. This recipe is an elegant version of her *crostata*, given me by an excellent cook, known for her ability in the kitchen. In spite of a kitchen gleaming with marble and full of machines, she does everything by hand, "as Mother used to do."

1 Preheat the oven to 325°F (165°C). Butter and flour a 10-inch (25-cm) springform pan.

2 Make the pastry: In a food processor or an electric mixer with a paddle, or by hand, mix together rapidly all the ingredients for the pastry. Divide the pastry dough into 2 parts, one slightly larger for the bottom crust. Dust a marble or wooden work surface lightly with flour and roll out the larger piece of dough for the bottom crust. Drape the dough over the rolling pin and unroll it on the prepared pan. Fit it into the pan and trim away the excess. Refrigerate the prepared crust and the dough for the top while preparing the custard.

3 Make the custard: Put the milk, cornstarch, egg yolks, and sugar in a blender and blend for 30 seconds. Pour into a small saucepan and add half the grated lemon zest. Cook, stirring constantly, until thickened. If lumps appear, simply stir energetically until they disappear. Remove from the heat and cover the surface with plastic wrap to prevent a skin from forming. Cool slightly.

4 Assemble the pie: Pour the cooled custard into the prepared crust. Sprinkle the remaining grated lemon zest on top. Roll out the top crust and place on the pie. Cut away the excess and crimp the edges. Prick the top of the pie with a fork. Sprinkle the almonds on top of the pie.

5 Bake for 1 hour and 5 minutes, or until the crust is light brown. Let cool before serving. Sprinkle with confectioners' sugar when ready to serve.

ZUPPA INGLESE

SERVES 6

4 egg yolks, at room temperature

½ cup plus 2 tablespoons sugar (125 g)

1 teaspoon vanilla

2 cups milk (500 ml)

⅓ cup cornstarch (40 g)

Grated zest of 1 lemon

2 tablespoons white rum

1½ ounces diced semisweet chocolate, or 3 tablespoons diced candied fruit, orange peel, or citron

Simple Italian Sponge Cake (recipe opposite), or use a store-bought sponge cake

1 cup cold heavy cream (250 ml)

This is a simplified version of *zuppa inglese*. When made at home, it is most often covered in whipped cream.

1 Beat together the egg yolks, ½ cup of the sugar, and the vanilla until the mixture is thick and lemon colored. Blend the milk and cornstarch in a blender and pour it into a medium saucepan. Warm over low heat, stirring often.

2 Gradually whisk the hot milk and cornstarch into the egg yolk mixture. Mix in the lemon zest. Return to the saucepan and cook, stirring constantly, until the pastry cream thickens; it may form lumps. Whisk energetically for 1½ to 2 minutes, then remove from the heat.

3 Continue stirring until all lumps have disappeared. Put plastic wrap directly on the surface of the pastry cream to prevent a skin from forming. Cool the cream. Refrigerate it if not using immediately.

4 Simmer the remaining 2 tablespoons of sugar with 2 tablespoons of water in a small saucepan for 4 minutes. Cool the syrup and add the rum. Set aside.

5 When ready to assemble the dish, stir the diced chocolate into the pastry cream. Slice the sponge cake into thin slices. Beat the heavy cream until stiff. Fold half of the whipped cream into the cooled pastry cream and set aside.

6 Line a medium-size serving bowl with slices of cake, on the bottom and around the sides. Sprinkle the sugar syrup and rum over the sliced cake, dividing the syrup among the slices, reserving a little for the slices that will cover the *zuppa inglese*. Spoon in the cream,

mounding it higher in the center. Cover the cream with more slices of cake, trimmed to fit, sprinkling the remaining sugar syrup over the slices. Spread the remaining whipped cream over the cake, like icing. Cover with plastic wrap and refrigerate until ready to serve.

SIMPLE ITALIAN SPONGE CAKE

Pan di Spagna

SERVES 6 TO 8

4 eggs, at room temperature, separated

⅔ cup sugar (150 g)

Grated zest of 1 lemon, washed

1 cup less 2 tablespoons cake flour (100 g)

A simple sponge cake, *pan di spagna* is used all over Italy, usually for desserts with pastry cream. It is simple to prepare. Just remember to fold in the flour sifted over the beaten eggs; do not be tempted to use a mixer.

1 Preheat the oven to 325°F (165°C). Butter and flour a 9-inch (23-cm) cake pan with sides 2 inches high.

2 Beat the egg yolks and sugar together in an electric mixer until thick and lemon colored, about 3 minutes Add the lemon zest.

3 In a clean bowl, with clean beaters, whip the egg whites until stiff but not dry. Fold into the yolks. Sift the flour over the beaten eggs, one-third at a time, and fold in gently. Turn the batter into the prepared cake pan.

4 Bake the sponge cake for 45 to 50 minutes, or until a cake tester comes out clean. Turn the cake out onto a rack and let cool completely before using. (It is easier to slice if kept for 1 day before using.)

PASTRY KNOTS

Frappe

SERVES 6 TO 8

1 pound all-purpose flour
(450 g)

2 extra-large whole eggs

1 egg yolk

Grated zest of ½ small lemon

Pinch of salt

1 scant teaspoon vanilla

3 tablespoons unsalted butter, at
room temperature (45 g)

2 tablespoons granulated sugar

2 tablespoons grappa or dry
white wine

Lard or peanut oil, about 2 cups
(240 ml)

Confectioners' sugar

Frappe are the special sweet for Carnival, made in all the pastry shops and bakeries. They are absolutely delicious, and "one calls the other," as the Romans say. They are only to be found at Carnival. Since the dough contains little sugar, be generous with the confectioners' sugar.

1 In a food processor, combine the flour, whole eggs, egg yolk, lemon zest, salt, vanilla, butter, granulated sugar, and grappa or white wine. Process until thoroughly mixed. Knead the dough by hand for a minute on a floured surface until it is smooth, then divide it in half. Put the 2 pieces of dough under an inverted bowl for 15 minutes to rest.

2 Divide each half of the dough into 4 pieces.

3 If using a pasta machine, put each piece of dough through the largest opening 10 times, folding the dough in half each time. (Sprinkle with flour if sticky.) Move the wheel down a notch and continue rolling the dough through on successive notches until the third/last notch.

4 Put the dough on a lightly floured board and cut each strip in half; trim the edges. Divide the pasta pieces into 5 strips. Tie each strip with a loose knot in the center, like a bow tie, and put on the floured board. Repeat with all the dough.

5 Heat the lard or oil in a large, deep frying pan until hot. Cook the frappe, without crowding the pan, until they are a dark golden color. Drain on paper towels and sprinkle generously with confectioners' sugar. Arrange the frappe on a large serving plate, piled up in a pyramid.

NOTE: If rolling out the dough by hand, divide into 2 pieces as above and roll out on a lightly floured marble work surface or wooden pastry board until it is about ⅛ inch thick. Cut the dough into strips as above.

AUNT NANNINA'S SWEET FRITTERS

Le Frittelle di Zia Nannina

SERVES 4 TO 6

½ pound ricotta, well drained
(225 g)

5 tablespoons all-purpose flour
(50 g)

3½ tablespoons granulated
sugar (50 g)

Pinch of salt

Grated zest of 1 large lemon

2 eggs, at room temperature

2 tablespoons grappa or
aqua vitae

Oil, for frying

Confectioners' sugar, for dusting

The first time I saw Aunt Nannina was when her grandnephew took her for a ride on his brand-new motorbike. She sat sidesaddle on the back, as Roman girls did if they were wearing dresses. She was eighty-five years old and very independent. She was fiercely reprimanded by her niece, Anna Maria Cornetto. Anna Maria and I were working on our cookbook then and wanted to use her kitchen, which was nearby. She refused, saying we were messy. This is her mother's recipe for *frittelle di ricotta*.

1 Pass the ricotta through a sieve into a bowl and add the flour, sugar, salt, grated lemon zest, eggs, and grappa, mixing thoroughly with a fork or a whisk. If the batter is too liquid, add more flour, a little at the time. Refrigerate the batter for 3 or 4 hours.

2 When ready to serve the fritters, heat the oil to moderately hot, not smoking.

3 Using an oiled spoon and knife, take up tablespoons of the batter and push them into the hot oil with the knife. Turn the fritters once or twice, or until they are a golden brown. Drain them on paper towels. Keep the finished fritters warm while preparing the rest.

4 When all the fritters are ready, sift confectioners' sugar over them and serve hot.

FROZEN CHESTNUT CREAM WITH CANDIED CHESTNUTS

Semifreddo con Marrons Glacés

SERVES 8 TO 10

6 tablespoons sugar

2 tablespoons best-quality unsweetened cocoa

1½ cups (1 pound) sweetened chestnut puree (I use Clément Faugier) (450 g)

1 heaped cup crumbled candied chestnuts (6 large marrons glacées)

4 egg whites, at room temperature

6 egg yolks, at room temperature

Pinch of salt

2 cups cold heavy cream (500 ml)

Extra marrons glacés; candied violets, if available; and softly whipped cream to decorate the semifreddo

This recipe is from my first cookbook, *Italian Cooking in the Grand Tradition*, written with Anna Maria Cornetto, published by Simon & Schuster.

This semifreddo was one of the desserts best loved by the Roman princesses at my cooking school. It makes the necessary *bella figura* and can be prepared and frozen several days ahead. It is festive and elegant and an excellent sweet to have around during the holidays. It is one of Rome's favorite desserts. Instructions are given here for unmolding and decorating the semifreddo, but if you are pressed for time, the cream can be frozen in a decorative bowl that can go right to the table.

1 Dampen the inside of a 2-quart (2-liter) mold or a 2½-quart (2½-liter) glass bowl and line with plastic wrap, allowing plenty of overhang on either side.

2 Using an electric mixer, or by hand, beat the egg yolks and sugar together until thick and lemon colored. Sift in the cocoa and mix well. Fold in the chestnut puree and the crumbled candied chestnuts by hand.

3 Beat the egg whites with a pinch of salt until stiff but not dry. Whip the cream until just stiff. Fold 1 large tablespoon of whites into the chestnut mixture thoroughly and then fold in the rest of the beaten whites. Now fold in the whipped cream. Do not overblend; the chestnut cream should be slightly marbled.

4 Spoon the chestnut cream into the prepared mold and cover with plastic wrap placed directly on the surface. Cover again with aluminum foil and freeze overnight.

5 When ready to serve, unmold the semifreddo onto a platter and let stand for about 5 minutes. Gently pull the overhang of the plastic wrap and ease the semifreddo onto the serving platter. Decorate, alternating marron glacé halves with small spoonfuls of whipped cream, interspersed with candied violets, if you have them.

6 Allow the semifreddo to soften at room temperature before serving, about 20 minutes, or according to the room's temperature.

HOW TO PREPARE CHESTNUTS

SHELL THE CHESTNUTS and cook them in a saucepan of boiling water until they are just tender. Test by piercing with a kitchen needle. Remove the skin while the chestnuts are still hot, using rubber gloves and working with a cupful at a time. (As they cool, the chestnuts become difficult to peel, so it is best to work with a small amount at a time.) Put the chestnuts into a saucepan, cover them with milk, and simmer them until they are well done, crushing them with a wooden spoon as they cook, if you wish.

FROZEN CHESTNUT CREAM WITH HAZELNUT PRALINE

SERVES 8 TO 10

Butter for the work surface

---

1 lemon or orange, washed,
for flattening the praline

½ cup sugar (100 g)

⅔ cup toasted hazelnuts (100 g)

---

4 eggs, at room temperature,
separated

Pinch of salt

1½ cups (1 pound) sweetened
chestnut puree, Clément Faugier,
if available (450 g)

---

2 tablespoons best-quality
unsweetened cocoa

---

2 cups cold heavy cream (450 ml)

---

6 marrons glacés, halved, or one-half
more of the hazelnut praline,*
chopped very coarse, for decorating
the base of the chestnut cream

---

*Prepare the praline with extra sugar and hazel-
nuts when you make the other praline and wrap
it tightly in buttered foil until it is needed.

Since marrons glacés are sometimes expensive or hard to find, I offer this variation of the preceding recipe.

1 Dampen the inside of a 2-quart (2-liter) mold and line with plastic wrap, leaving plenty of overhang on both sides. Alternatively, butter a marble work surface or a large platter where you will turn out the praline, and place a lemon or an orange nearby.

2 Melt the sugar in a small, heavy saucepan and, when it has dissolved and turned a tawny color, add the hazelnuts, stirring to coat them all with caramel. Turn out the praline onto the buttered surface and flatten it with the lemon or orange. When the praline has hardened, chop it coarsely. This may be prepared well in advance and stored, tightly covered, at room temperature.

3 In an electric mixer, or by hand, beat the egg yolks for 1 minute; add the chestnut puree and cocoa, mixing well. Beat the egg whites with a pinch of salt until they are stiff but not dry. Beat the cream until stiff. Fold half the praline into the chestnut mixture with the beaten egg whites (in 2 batches). Reserve 2 heaping tablespoons praline and fold the remaining praline into the chestnut cream together with the whipped cream. Do not fold in too thoroughly; the dessert should be marbled. Spoon the mixture into the prepared mold, cover tightly with plastic wrap, and freeze overnight.

4 Allow the semifreddo to soften for about 25 minutes, according to room temperature, before serving. Sprinkle the reserved praline over it, or decorate the dish with marrons glacés, if you have them, or use very coarsely chopped extra hazelnut praline around the edge of the semifreddo.

A VARIATION:
INDIVIDUAL CHESTNUT CREAMS
WITH HAZELNUT PRALINE AND
CHOCOLATE SAUCE

1 Prepare the semifreddo with the hazelnut praline, reserving 3 tablespoons of the hazelnut praline instead of 2. Put the bowl in the freezer.

2 To prepare the dessert, remove the semifreddo from the freezer and let soften for about 15 to 20 minutes.

3 Take as many small individual molds as needed, dampen them, and line them with plastic wrap. Spoon 2 tablespoons of the semifreddo into the bottom of each mold, put a small marron glacé on top of this, and fill the rest of the mold with semifreddo, covering the marron glacée on all sides. Put plastic wrap on top. Return the molds to the freezer until serving time.

4 Prepare a chocolate sauce: In a double boiler, melt 3 ounces bittersweet chocolate with 1/3 cup heavy cream. When the chocolate has melted, add 1 tablespoon rum. Cool the sauce. Pour a little chocolate sauce onto individual plates or into bowls and turn out the semifreddos on top of the sauce. Sprinkle the very coarsely chopped extra hazelnut praline over the semifreddos and serve at once.

FROZEN CREAM WITH HAZELNUTS

Semifreddo con Nocciole

SERVES 8

Vegetable oil or butter for
the work surface

1 lemon, washed, for flattening
the praline

1⅓ cups sugar (265 g)

1 cup hazelnuts, lightly toasted
(150 g)

4 eggs, at room temperature,
separated

3 tablespoons rum

Pinch of salt

2 cups cold heavy cream
(450 ml)

Hot Chocolate Sauce
(recipe opposite)

The excellent hazelnuts that grow near Rome can be bought directly from the grower. They are used for hard cookies, called *tozzetti*, meant to be dipped into sweet wine (see page 250), and for *panpepato*, a Christmas cake made almost exclusively of hazelnuts (see page 260). This delicate semifreddo uses hazelnuts and is also a specialty of Rome, like the cookies and *panpepato*.

1 Dampen the inside of a 2-quart (2-liter) domed or ring mold (a glass serving bowl will do) and line with plastic wrap, leaving plenty of overhang on both sides. Oil a marble work surface or a large platter with vegetable oil or butter and place the lemon nearby.

2 Put ½ cup of the sugar in a small, heavy saucepan. On low heat, cook the sugar to a light brown caramel, stirring to avoid burning. The sugar will form lumps at first, but then will melt gradually. When the sugar is a tawny color, add the hazelnuts, stirring to coat them evenly. Turn the hazelnuts out onto the oiled surface and flatten them with the lemon. Leave the praline to harden. (If preparing in advance, wrap the hardened praline in buttered foil and store it in a tightly closed tin.) When ready to use the praline, chop it coarsely by hand. Reserve one-third of the praline to decorate the top of the semifreddo at serving time.

3 Using an electric mixer, or by hand, beat the egg yolks, adding 1 cup of the sugar, a little at the time, until thick and lemon colored. Mix in the rum. Beat the egg whites with a pinch of salt until foamy, then add the remaining ⅓ cup of sugar slowly, beating until the whites stand in peaks. In a separate bowl, beat the cream until stiff. Fold the cream into the egg yolks and then fold in the whites.

4 Spoon one-third of the semifreddo mixture into the prepared mold or bowl and sprinkle part of the praline on top. Repeat 2 more times, spooning; do not pour. Cover the mold tightly and freeze the semifreddo overnight.

5 When ready to serve the semifreddo, turn it out onto a platter and let stand for a few minutes. Then ease out the dessert with the help of the plastic wrap overhang. If using a serving bowl, remove it from the freezer; the semifreddo must soften for 20 minutes, more or less, depending on your kitchen's warmth. It needs less time than an ice cream.

6 Sprinkle the reserved hazelnut praline on top. Serve with hot chocolate sauce.

HOT CHOCOLATE SAUCE

MAKES ABOUT 2 CUPS

½ pound best-quality bitter-sweet chocolate (225 g)

1 cup heavy cream (250 ml)

2 tablespoons dark rum

Melt the chocolate in the top of a double boiler. Stir until it is smooth and free of lumps. Gradually stir the cream into the chocolate. Add the rum and cook over low heat for 2 minutes. Remove from the heat, but leave the sauce in the double boiler until serving time and reheat when it is needed.

FROZEN CREAM WITH ALMONDS AND CHOCOLATE SAUCE

Semifreddo con Mandorle e Salsa di Cioccolata

Serves 6 to 8

4 egg yolks

⅔ cup sugar (150 g)

2 scant cups peeled, toasted chopped almonds (200 g)

¼ cup whiskey, plus extra to rinse the mold (60 ml)

3 egg whites

1⅔ cups cold heavy cream (400 ml)

8 ounces best-quality bitter-sweet chocolate (225 g)

Any Italian will tell you that frozen desserts such as this and *gelato*, or ice cream, are aids to digestion, and therefore good for you. But, typically, the Romans also like them because they look good — an absolute necessity when Romans entertain.

1 Dampen a 9-by-5-by-3-inch (18-by-10-by-6-cm) loaf pan or other 5-cup (1,150 ml) mold; line it with plastic wrap.

2 Put the egg yolks in the bowl of an electric mixer and beat for 30 seconds. Gradually add the sugar and beat until the mixture is light and lemon colored. Remove the bowl from the mixer and add the almonds and 2 tablespoons of whiskey to the yolks.

3 Beat the egg whites until stiff but not dry. Whip the cream until stiff. Fold the whipped cream and then the beaten egg whites into the egg yolk mixture. Rinse the mold you are using with whiskey and spoon the semifreddo into the mold. Cover tightly and freeze overnight.

4 Prepare the chocolate sauce when ready to serve the semifreddo: Chop the chocolate into large pieces and melt it in a double boiler over simmering water. Stir until the chocolate is smooth and free of lumps. Add the remaining 2 tablespoons whiskey and leave the sauce in the double boiler until serving time.

5 At serving time, remove the semifreddo from the freezer about 25 minutes before serving. Unmold onto a dish with a rim by tugging gently on the overhang of plastic wrap. (The rim is to contain the chocolate when it is poured over the semifreddo.)

6 Just before serving, reheat the chocolate sauce in the double boiler, whisking until smooth. Pour the hot chocolate evenly over the top of the dessert. If there should be any chocolate sauce left over, serve it in a sauceboat.

SIMPLE FROZEN CREAM

Semifreddo Semplice

SERVES 6 TO 8

6 egg yolks

⅔ cup sugar (150 g)

3 tablespoons white rum

4 ounces semisweet chocolate, cut in tiny dice (120 g)

1⅔ cups cold heavy cream (400 ml)

⅔ cup lightly toasted hazelnuts, chopped coarse (70 g)

Coarsely grated chocolate for decorating the semifreddo

This is a quick semifreddo, easy to prepare. It can be strewn with the grated chocolate, or you can sprinkle both chocolate and extra hazelnuts over it and maybe even serve a hot chocolate sauce, too.

1 Dampen a 6-cup (1,400-ml) ring mold and line it with plastic wrap, leaving plenty of overhang.

2 Beat the egg yolks with the sugar until thick and lemon colored. Add the rum and stir in the chocolate.

3 Whip the cream until stiff and fold it into the yolk mixture. Stir in the chopped hazelnuts. Spoon into the mold, fold over the extra plastic wrap to cover, and freeze overnight.

4 When ready to serve, turn the semifreddo out on a round plate and sprinkle the grated chocolate on top.

FROZEN CREAM WITH STRAWBERRIES AND ALMOND PRALINE

Semifreddo con Fragole

SERVES 6 TO 8

FOR THE PRALINE:

Vegetable oil or butter

1 lemon or orange, washed

½ cup sugar (100 g)

⅔ cup peeled, lightly toasted almonds (100 g)

FOR THE SEMIFREDDO:

1 pound fresh strawberries (450 g)

1 tablespoon fresh lemon juice

3 tablespoons white rum

4 eggs, at room temperature, separated

¾ cup sugar (150 g)

Pinch of salt

1 cup cold heavy cream (250 ml)

A semifreddo with fruit, fresh and pretty. Surrounded and filled in the center with strawberries, it too makes a Roman *bella figura*. Remember that a semifreddo needs time to soften before serving, but less than an ice cream.

1 Dampen a 2-quart (2-liter) ring mold and line it with plastic wrap, leaving an overhang. Oil or butter a marble work surface or a large platter for the praline and place the lemon or orange nearby.

2 Make the praline: Put ½ cup of sugar in a small, heavy saucepan. Place the almonds nearby. Put the pan on low heat and let the sugar melt, stirring occasionally. The sugar will form lumps, which will gradually melt. When the lumps have melted completely and the sugar is a golden brown, pour in the almonds, stirring to coat the almonds evenly. Be careful that the sugar does not burn. Turn out the praline onto the prepared surface and flatten it with the lemon or orange. During the preparation of the praline, be very careful not to touch the hot sugar. Leave the praline to harden. (This can be prepared in advance and wrapped tightly in buttered foil.) When ready to use the praline, chop it medium fine.

3 When ready to finish the semifreddo, wash the strawberries rapidly in cold water. Drain and stem them. By hand, chop the strawberries and mix them with the lemon juice and rum. Set aside. (Do not use a food processor: it turns the strawberries to juice.)

For serving:

*Extra fruit, about ¹/₂ pound
(225 g)*

———

*Fresh mint, if available
(it looks very nice around the
base of the dessert)*

———

4 Beat the egg yolks with the ¾ cup of sugar until thick and lemon colored. Fold in the fruit. Beat the egg whites with the pinch of salt until stiff but not dry. Beat the cream until stiff. Fold the whipped cream into the whites and then into the fruit, together with half the chopped praline, sprinkling the praline over the mixture as you fold it. Spoon the semifreddo mixture into the prepared mold, cover tightly, and freeze overnight.

5 When ready to serve the semifreddo, turn the mold over onto a platter and let stand for a few minutes. Ease the semifreddo out of the mold with the help of the overhang of plastic wrap. Surround the semifreddo with the extra fruit, and mint leaves if you have them. Sprinkle the remaining praline over the top.

NOTE: 1¼ pounds (570 g) of ripe peaches, plus ½ pound (225 g) for garnishing, may be used instead of the strawberries. Or 1 pound (450 g) of raspberries, plus ½ pound (225 g) for garnishing, may be used.

CHESTNUT ICE CREAM

Gelato di Castagne

SERVES 10 TO 12

1⅔ cups (18 ounces) sweetened chestnut puree (500 g)

1 teaspoon vanilla extract

3 tablespoons dark rum

1 tablespoon unsweetened cocoa

7 egg yolks

¼ cup plus 2 tablespoons granulated sugar (90 g)

3 cups heavy cream (700 ml)

2 cups milk (500 ml)

1½ tablespoons confectioners' sugar

Marrons glacés, grated chocolate or chocolate curls, or coarsely chopped almond praline, for decoration

An easy, easy chestnut ice cream that looks elaborate and complicated. This is better made the day before serving and decorated at the last minute. A ring mold makes serving the ice cream easier but any 6-cup mold will do.

1 Dampen a 6- or 8-cup ring mold and line it with plastic wrap, leaving an overhang. Pour the chestnut puree into a bowl and add the vanilla, rum, and cocoa, mixing well.

2 With an electric mixer, or by hand, beat the egg yolks. Gradually add the granulated sugar, a little at the time, beating until the mixture is light and lemon colored.

3 Scald 2 cups of the cream with the milk. Gradually pour the hot liquid over the yolks, beating constantly. Mix in the chestnut puree. Set the bowl in cold water with ice cubes and stir to cool the custard.

4 Process the mixture in an ice cream machine, following the manufacturer's instructions. When the ice cream is ready, spoon it into the prepared mold. Cover tightly with more plastic wrap and store in the freezer.

5 When ready to serve the ice cream, remove the top wrap, fold back the overhang, and turn the mold over on a serving plate. Leave the ice cream for about 5 minutes, or until it can be removed from the mold by pulling gently on the overhang of plastic wrap. (If you are not serving the ice cream at once, store it in the freezer on its plate. It will need time to soften before you serve it.)

6 Beat the remaining 1 cup cream with the confectioners' sugar until stiff; spread it all over the ice cream. (If you prefer, this extra cream can be omitted.) Arrange halved marrons glacés around the

base of the dessert, or decorate with chocolate or the almond praline.

NOTE: If you should want to make your puree from fresh chestnuts, to make 1 pound 2 ounces (500 g) of fresh chestnut puree you will need approximately 1²/₃ pounds (750 g) unshelled chestnuts. Shell the chestnuts and cook them in a saucepan of boiling water until they are just tender when pierced with the tip of a small knife. Remove the skins while the chestnuts are hot, using rubber gloves and working with a small amount at a time. Simmer the chestnuts in milk to cover, stirring occasionally, until they are tender. Puree them in a food processor. While the chestnuts are boiling, make a sugar syrup of 1 scant cup (200 g) sugar and ½ cup (120 ml) water. Simmer the sugar and water for 5 minutes. Add the syrup to the pureed chestnuts.

THE BEST ICE CREAM

THE LOCAL MANIA in Rome is ice cream, which we call *gelato*. Everybody knows where to get the best, even if it means driving through the Roman traffic. I have two children who keep me informed; they find the *best* in the oddest places. My son swears by a shop in the Roman Termini train station, of all places, and he must be right, because the owner has been so successful that he opened three more shops, all called La Gradisca. My daughter's favorite is near the Cestius Pyramid in Testaccio, a part of Rome known for its market and organic food shops. Instead, I am just down the street from San Crispino, probably the most famous ice cream shop in Rome, with wonderful flavors of all kinds of ice creams and sherbets — too many to name, but creams are their speciality. They do not serve their ice creams in cones but in little cups, and there are places where you can sit while you eat your gelato. They also have ice creams with liqueurs, and everything!

Il Gelateria di San Crispino, Via della Panetteria 42, Roma 00187, telephone 06 679 3924

GINGERED ICE CREAM

Gelato allo Zenzero

SERVES 8 TO 10

2 cups heavy cream (500 ml)

2 cups milk (500 ml)

1¼ cups sugar (250 g)

1 tablespoon grated fresh ginger

6 egg yolks

1 cup coarsely chopped
crystallized ginger, plus more
for garnish (175 g)

This simple ice cream was invented for an Indian dinner I did in my cooking school, and it turns up all over Rome now. It was inspired mainly by the bags of dried candied ginger sold in one of my favorite shops in Rome, Banane. They had all kinds of exotic fruits long before anyone else, and the fruit was usually ripe, which was unusual. As we all know, ice cream can also be made in ice trays in the freezer, but it is so tedious to do that I think the money for a machine is well spent. This ice cream keeps very well in the freezer and can be made up to 10 days ahead of time.

1 Put the cream, milk, sugar, and fresh ginger in a heavy stainless-steel saucepan and heat without boiling. Beat the egg yolks thoroughly in a large bowl. Gradually whisk in the hot cream mixture, straining it through a sieve and pressing on the ginger with the back of a spoon to extract all the liquid. Return the cream mixture to the saucepan and cook over low heat, stirring constantly, until the cream is slightly thickened and veils the spoon. (It may look curdled.) Do not allow it to boil. Remove the cream from the heat, stir, and let cool slightly. Add the chopped crystallized ginger to the cream and let cool completely.

2 Process the mixture in an ice cream machine, following the manufacturer's directions. Spoon the ice cream into a covered container and store in the freezer until ready to serve.

3 If you like, garnish each serving of the ice cream with more crystalized ginger.

HAZELNUT ICE CREAM

Gelato di Nocciole

SERVES 6 TO 8

Hazelnut Praline (recipe
follows)

———

2 cups milk (460 ml)

———

¾ cup hazelnut paste (180 g)

———

1 teaspoon vanilla

———

3 large egg yolks

———

⅔ cup sugar (150 g)

———

1 cup cold heavy cream
(250 ml)

———

This ice cream is made with Lazio's large hazelnuts, famous all through Italy. They are used in many Christmas sweets and in hard, sweet biscuits like *tozzetti* (see page 250). Serve this gelato with sweet biscuits and a glass of *vino dolce*.

1 Make the praline. This can be done several days in advance.

2 Dampen a 6-cup ring mold and line it with plastic wrap, leaving an overhang.

3 To make the ice cream, pour the milk into a small flameproof casserole with the hazelnut paste and vanilla, mixing well. (The paste is a little oily.) Bring just to a simmer over moderate heat. Remove from the heat and let stand for 30 minutes.

4 Beat the egg yolks and sugar in an electric mixer. Gradually beat in the hazelnut-infused milk in a slow stream. Pour into the casserole and cook on low heat, stirring, until the mixture is slightly thickened. Do not boil. Set the pan into a sink of cold water to cool. When cold, stir in the cream.

5 Process the mixture in an ice cream machine, following the manu-facturer's directions. When the ice cream is ready, spoon it into the prepared mold and store, tightly covered, in the freezer.

6 When ready to serve the ice cream, chop the hazelnut praline coarsely. (You will not need all the praline; store the remainder in the tin for another time.) Turn out the ice cream onto a platter by tugging gently on the plastic wrap overhang. Allow it to soften for 15 to 20 minutes, according to the room's temperature. Sprinkle the hazelnut praline generously over the ice cream before serving.

RICH ICE CREAM WITH HAZELNUT PRALINE

Gelato di Crema con Praline di Nocciole

SERVES 8 TO 10

8 egg yolks

¾ cup sugar (150 g)

1 cup milk (250 ml)

3 cups heavy cream (700 ml)

¼ cup limoncello or other liqueur (60 ml)

Hazelnut Praline (recipe opposite)

A rich "company" ice cream, flavored delicately with limoncello and with toasted pralined hazelnuts sprinkled over the top. It is a perfect ending for a Roman dinner.

1 Dampen a 2½-quart ring mold and line it with plastic wrap, leaving an overhang. (Or choose an attractive serving bowl and spoon out the ice cream at table instead of molding.)

2 Beat the egg yolks, add the sugar, and beat until thick and lemon colored. Meanwhile, heat the milk and cream in a heavy saucepan to hot but not boiling and pour slowly over the yolks and sugar while beating. Return this mixture to the saucepan and cook over low heat, stirring constantly, until it has thickened slightly and coats the back of a metal spoon. Do not allow it to boil. Place the saucepan in a sinkful of cold water to cool.

3 Process the mixture in an ice cream machine, following the manufacturer's instructions. Add the limoncello to the ice cream after it begins to harden.

4 Coarsely chop three-quarters of the hazelnut praline and add it to the ice cream just before it is ready. Wrap the remaining praline in buttered aluminum foil until it is needed.

5 Spoon the ice cream into the mold, cover with plastic wrap, and store in the freezer. Soften it at room temperature before serving. When ready to serve the ice cream, chop the remaining praline. Turn out the ice cream onto a round platter and sprinkle the praline over and around it. If some ice cream remains, store it in the freezer.

HAZELNUT PRALINE

Makes about 1¼ cups

Butter

———

1 lemon

———

1 cup shelled and peeled hazelnuts (140 g)

———

½ cup sugar (100 g)

———

1 Butter a marble work suface or a large platter. Place the lemon nearby.

2 Toast the hazelnuts very lightly.

3 Put the sugar in a small saucepan large enough to contain the hazelnuts. Heat the sugar slowly, stirring to avoid burning it. Lumps will form at first; when they have melted and the sugar is a tawny brown color, pour in the hazelnuts, stirring to coat them evenly. Turn out the praline onto the buttered surface and flatten it with the lemon. Leave the praline to harden. When it is hard, it may be wrapped in buttered foil and stored in a tin.

LEMON ICE CREAM

Gelato di Limone

SERVES 6 TO 8

3 large ripe lemons, preferably organic

¾ cup sugar (150 g)

4 large egg yolks

1 cup milk (250 ml)

1 tablespoon vanilla extract

Pinch of salt

2 cups cold heavy cream (500 ml)

Candied lemon slices, chocolate curls, or lemon leaves for garnish

Luciano Arcangeli, a very well-known art historian, is also famous for his ice creams and marmalades, which are never too sweet and always keep their fruit taste. I ate this lemon ice cream on his terrace full of roses in bloom, just across the river from Castel Sant'Angelo. Luciano is very generous with his recipes, insisting only that the lemons used be ripe.

1 Dampen a 4- to 5-cup container and line it with plastic wrap, leaving an overhang. Remove the outer zest (without the pith) from the lemons and chop the peel with the sugar in a food processor for about 3 minutes, or until the zest and sugar are well mixed.

2 In a bowl, using an electric beater, beat together the egg yolks, sugar and lemon zest, milk, vanilla, and salt. Put this bowl into a larger bowl full of hot water (or use a large double boiler over hot water) and beat the mixture until it is thick and has doubled in volume. (You can also use a whisk for this.) Remove the bowl with the lemon mixture and put it into a larger bowl with cold water and ice cubes, continuing to beat until the mixture is cold. Add the heavy cream. Put the mixture into an ice cream machine and process according to the manufacturer's instructions.

3 Spoon the ice cream into the prepared mold, cover tightly, and store in the freezer. This is best after 1 day in the freezer but can be kept for 1 week longer.

4 When ready to serve, turn the mold over on a platter and turn out the ice cream by tugging gently on the plastic wrap overhang. Decorate the ice cream with candied lemon slices, chocolate curls, or lemon leaves. Allow to soften for about 20 minutes at room temperature before serving.

RICOTTA CREAM

Gelato di Ricotta

SERVES 4 TO 6

3 egg yolks

⅔ cup superfine sugar (125 g)

1 pound ricotta, well drained,
preferably overnight in the
refrigerator (450 g)

¼ cup white rum (60 ml)

1 cup cold heavy cream
(250 ml)

Blackberries, strawberries,
raspberries, or sweet cookies
as an accompaniment

Although called an ice cream in Italian, this never goes into
the freezer. The ricotta cream does, however, require at least 6
hours in the refrigerator to chill and set before serving. Berries
are an excellent accompaniment—Romans like blackberries
with this when they are in season—but they serve sweet cookies
with it more often. Before the base is prepared, it is essential
that the ricotta be drained really well, preferably overnight. The
cream can be molded, or simply served from a dessert bowl.

1 If you want to mold the cream, dampen a 7-inch (18-cm) springform or a 1½-quart bowl and line with plastic wrap, allowing plenty
of overhang. (Or choose an attractive serving bowl and simply spoon
out the ricotta cream at the table.)

2 Beat the egg yolks and add the sugar slowly. Sieve the ricotta and
stir into the egg yolks. Mix in the rum.

3 Whip the cream until stiff and fold into the ricotta mixture, not
too thoroughly.

4 Spoon the ricotta cream into the prepared pan or in the bowl,
cover with plastic wrap, and refrigerate for 6 hours. Turn out onto
a platter or serve from the bowl. Offer berries or cookies, or both
on the side.

ORANGE ICE

Granita d'Arance di Luciano

SERVES 6 TO 8

10 oranges

2 lemons

Sugar, to taste

4 to 6 tablespoons orange-flower water, to taste (60 ml to 90 ml)

1 tablespoon lightly beaten egg white

Orange ice offers a wonderful light finish to a substantial Roman meal. This can be garnished with orange slices or sections. Chocolate cookies or brownies are good as an accompaniment.

1 Grate the zest from 2 of the oranges. Squeeze all the oranges and the lemons. Strain the juice to remove any pulp. Mix the grated zest with the juice.

2 Add sugar to taste to the juices and zest; it is impossible to give a quantity as oranges vary in their sweetness. Add the orange-flower water and put the sweetened juice in an ice cream machine.

3 Process according to the manufacturer's instructions until the ice is mushy. Add the egg white and continue processing until the ice is frozen. Transfer the ice to a container or pack it in a mold or bowl lined with plastic wrap. Keep it in the freezer, tightly covered, until serving time.

GRANITAS

AT CAFÉ DU PARC in Piazza Porta San Paolo there is an unassuming 1960s kiosk at the edge of the park, with outdoor seating under a corridor-long canopy. It is close to the gastronomic neighborhood of Testaccio and very close to the Cestius Pyramid. The ice creams are average, but they serve first-rate lemon and coffee granita — what you think of as Italian ices. But their cremolati, granitas made with fresh fruit, are worth the trip just for them. The flavors vary with the seasons, although pineapple, strawberry, and banana can be had all year-round. In the spring they have pear; in the summer, peach, melon, and fig; and in the fall, persimmon. They serve these granitas also as *affogati*, "drowned," doused with alcohol, melon cremolato in port, fig cremolato in whiskey, and so on. The man who makes them uses only fruit and sugar with sometimes a little lemon to enhance the strawberry flavor, or pineapple for the banana. This kiosk has been in operation for 62 years, and it is my daughter's number-one choice for cremolatos.

Café du Parc, Piazza Porta San Paolo (no precise address; it is at the edge of the park, near the Cestius Pyramid), telephone 06 574 3363

PERSIMMON ICE

Sorbetto di Cachi

SERVES 6

⅓ cup water (80 ml)

⅔ cup sugar (150 g)

2½ pounds ripe persimmons
(1.125 kg)

¼ cup fresh lemon juice (60 ml)

Persimmon ice is one of the trendy flavors that abound in Rome. It is a pretty pale-peach color and is very refreshing. Be sure the persimmons are soft and overly ripe.

1 Make the sugar syrup: Put the water and sugar into a small, heavy saucepan and bring to a gentle simmer, stirring to dissolve the sugar. Simmer for 5 minutes. Remove from the heat and let cool.

2 Rinse off the persimmons under cold running water. Remove the stem part and peel the persimmons carefully, discarding the seeds if there are any. In a blender or food processor, combine the persimmon pulp, the syrup, and the lemon juice. Puree until smooth.

3 Process the persimmon puree in an ice cream machine, following the manufacturer's instructions. When the ice is ready, transfer it to a covered container or pack it into a 6-cup ring mold lined with plastic wrap. Cover with the wrap directly on the surface of the ice, and wrap again in plastic wrap. Store the ice in the freezer until needed. This is best after a few days.

NOTE: This ice depends on the persimmons for its sweetness. If desired, more sugar can be added.

MONT BLANC

Montebianco

SERVES 8

1½ pounds chestnuts in the shell (675 g)

1⅔ cups milk (400 ml)

¼ cup plus 3 tablespoons confectioners' sugar (75 g)

1 teaspoon vanilla extract

1 square (1 ounce) bittersweet chocolate, grated, plus more for decoration (30 g)

2 cups cold heavy cream (450 ml)

During the chestnut season, men and women can be seen on the small back roads gathering the chestnuts that have fallen onto the roads, out of the owners' jurisdiction. There the chestnuts are on free territory and can be collected by anyone. Montebianco is the deliciously rich chestnut dessert made in Rome during this time of year. The Romans say that *la morte delle castagne è montebianco*, meaning that *montebianco* is the way for chestnuts to die. It is best prepared at the last minute, but the chestnut part can be done in advance and the dessert assembled when it is time to serve it.

1 Shell the chestnuts and cook them in a saucepan of boiling water until just tender. Test by piercing them with a kitchen needle. Wearing rubber gloves and working with a few at a time, remove the skins while the chestnuts are still hot. (As they cool, the chestnuts become difficult to peel.) Put the chestnuts into a saucepan, cover them with the milk, and simmer until they are well done, crushing them with a wooden spoon as they cook.

2 Cool the chestnut mixture slightly and pour into a bowl. Add the confectioners' sugar, vanilla, and grated chocolate, mixing well.

3 Pass the chestnuts through the largest disk of a food mill, directly onto a serving platter, shaping the chestnut puree into a cone with the help of a small spatula. At this point the puree may be refrigerated, covered tightly, but do not flatten the cone.

4 When ready to serve the dessert, whip the cream until just stiff. Spread the whipped cream all over the cone-shaped chestnut puree and sprinkle the extra grated chocolate over all. Serve at once.

FRUIT IS OFTEN SERVED as dessert: cooked fruit, *macedonia* (fresh fruit salad), cherries in season, oranges, pineapples, and other exotic fruits. But these never completely satisfy the Roman sweet tooth, particularly if there are guests. For company, there are always chocolates after dinner, along with digestifs, often whiskey. The absolutely best chocolates in Rome — they are handmade — come from Moriondo and Gariglio. It is a family concern. All the candy is handmade, and they and their extended family all work in the shop. It is a madhouse at Christmas and Easter; you must order well in advance, because sometimes on those holidays they are so busy, they lock the door and won't let you in. Their Easter eggs are a marvel and your husband can get the diamond bracelet he just bought you enclosed in a chocolate egg, as big as you like. When you go for your chocolates, be sure to see the huge marble foot lying at the beginning of the next street from Moriondo. It was dug up where you see it and is a remnant of a colossal statue of Roman times, about 2,000 years old.

Moriondo e Gariglio, Via Pie' di Marmo 21/22, Roma, telephone 06 6990 856

When you leave Moriondo you are about two blocks from the Pantheon. The fountain in front of the Pantheon was where farmers used to meet every Saturday to sell their produce. Being farmers, they dressed all in black, as was the custom then for people from the country. I remember seeing them there on Saturday mornings. It's hard to believe, with all the cafés and strolling musicians around the fountain now.

AUNT IRENE'S ORANGE RICE PUDDING

Budino di Riso all'Arancia di Zia Irene

SERVES 6 TO 8

1½ cups risotto rice, preferably vialone nano (300 g)

Peel of ½ large lemon, cut in long strips

6 tablespoons unsalted butter, at room temperature (90 g)

1 cup freshly squeezed orange juice (250 ml)

½ cup superfine sugar (100 g)

Grated zest of 1 large orange

½ cup pistachio nuts, peeled and halved (75 g)

½ cup diced candied orange peel (65 g)

Orange Sauce (recipe opposite), or 1 cup orange marmalade mixed with 2 or 3 tablespoons white rum

Orange slices, for decoration

My husband's aunt Irene studied cooking with the famous Italian culinary authority Ada Boni, a *romana di Roma* (having at least five generations of Roman ancestors), who taught her lessons from Palazzo Odescalchi, which was designed by the famous Gianlorenzo Bernini. It was rather unusual to take cooking lessons at that time, about seventy-five years ago, but Zia Irene had a professor husband who made a cult of the dining room table. This is her rice pudding recipe.

1 In a large saucepan of lightly salted boiling water, cook the rice with the lemon peel until the rice is just tender. Drain thoroughly and discard the lemon peel.

2 Return the rice to the pan. Mix in the butter, orange juice, sugar, and grated orange zest. Bring to a simmer over moderate heat. Cook, stirring, for 1 to 2 minutes.

3 Remove the pan from the heat and let cool slightly, stirring every now and then. Mix in the pistachios and the candied orange peel. Dampen a 6-cup mold and pour the rice into it. Let stand until tepid, then cover and refrigerate until serving time.

4 Turn the pudding out onto a platter and surround with orange slices. Serve the sauce separately in a sauceboat.

ORANGE SAUCE

Salsa d'Arancia

MAKES ABOUT 4 CUPS

1¾ cups fresh orange juice
(410 ml)

———

2¼ cups sugar (450 g)

———

5 ounces white rum (140 ml)

———

This sauce is precious to have on hand for puddings, ice creams, and other desserts. It keeps for a year stored in a dark, dry place, in a glass jar with a lid. Do not refrigerate it.

Cook the orange juice and sugar together in a stainless steel saucepan over low heat for 30 minutes. Add the rum and simmer for 30 minutes longer. Remove from the heat and let cool overnight. The sauce should be the consistency of fluid marmalade. If it is too thin, cook a little longer. If it is too thick, gradually add more juice, a little at a time.

STUFFED PEACHES

Pesche Farcite

SERVES 4

4 large, ripe peaches, preferably white ones

3 tablespoons almonds

1½ cups white wine (360 ml)

8 teaspoons apricot preserves

4 teaspoons brown sugar

½ lemon

These are the peaches we serve in the summertime in Rome. They are a snap to make and actually are eaten all over Italy, in our hot summers. For baking, the fruit should be ripe but unblemished. The dessert is best served tepid or at room temperature. Accompany the peaches with *amaretti di Saronno* cookies, if they are available.

1 Preheat the oven to 350°F (175°C).

2 Rinse and dry the peaches; halve them with care. Remove the pits, break half of them open with a hammer, and remove the kernels. Chop the peach kernels together with the almonds.

3 Pour ¼ (60 ml) cup of the wine into a small baking dish. Arrange the peach halves in the dish in a single layer, cut side up. Pour ¼ teaspoon wine into the center of each peach half and spoon 1 teaspoon preserves into each half. Divide the chopped peach kernels and almonds among the peaches. Sprinkle ½ teaspoon brown sugar over each peach half.

4 Pour the remaining wine into the dish and bake for 45 to 60 minutes, or until the peaches are very tender. Halfway through the baking time, baste the peaches carefully with the wine in the dish. Serve tepid or at room temperature. Just before serving, squeeze a little lemon juice, about ¼ teaspoon, over the center of each peach.

RICOTTA PUDDING

Budino di Ricotta

SERVES 6

2½ heaped tablespoons raisins

2½ tablespoons white rum

Butter and granulated sugar, for the soufflé dish

1 pound fresh ricotta, drained (450 g)

½ cup superfine sugar (100 g)

4 large eggs, separated

2½ tablespoons citron or zuccata,* in tiny dice

Grated zest of 1 large lemon

3 tablespoons all-purpose flour

Hot Chocolate Sauce (page 275)

*Zuccata is Sicilian candied gourd.

Ricotta is used as a filling, or in cake batters, or drained and eaten on its own with a little condiment. Of course, the fresher the ricotta the better. Lazio has the best ricotta in Italy (in the world, the Romans say), and it has been made here since 1000 B.C. — a fact confirmed by the tools for making ricotta that archeologists have found in Rome. No wonder that Rome's preferred desserts are made of ricotta. This "pudding" will not seem like one; it is more like a soufflé. But it is called a pudding here in Rome, and is often served with a hot chocolate sauce.

1 Put the raisins into a small bowl or cup and pour in the rum. Soak for as long as possible, even overnight.

2 Preheat the oven to 350°F (175°C). Generously butter an 8-inch (20-cm) porcelain soufflé dish. Dust the dish with granulated sugar and tap out any excess.

3 Beat the drained ricotta in an electric mixer until smooth. (Or sieve the drained ricotta and then beat it by hand.) Beat in the superfine sugar a little at a time until the ricotta is smooth. Add the egg yolks and beat thoroughly. Stir in the raisins and their rum, the citron or *zuccata*, and the grated lemon zest. Sift the flour over the ricotta and fold in carefully. (This can be prepared 30 minutes ahead and kept in a cool place, not the refrigerator.)

4 When you are ready to bake the pudding, beat the egg whites until stiff but not dry. Fold into the pudding very gently. (It doesn't matter if a little egg white shows.)

5 Bake the pudding for 25 to 30 minutes, or until lightly colored. It can wait 5 or 10 minutes in the oven, but it will fall a little. Serve with hot chocolate sauce.

BEATEN RICOTTA

Ricotta Battuta

SERVES 6 TO 8

1 pound ricotta, well drained (450 g)

¼ pound mascarpone (110 g)

¼ cup freshly squeezed orange juice, strained (60 ml)

¼ cup Cointreau or other liqueur (60 ml)

1 cup cold heavy cream (250 ml)

2 tablespoons confectioners' sugar, or more to taste

Grated or shaved semisweet chocolate

Ricotta can be eaten as is, as well as in dishes of all kinds, and it can be fried. Drained thoroughly, dredged in flour and then in egg, and fried in hot oil, it is delicious. The sheep give birth twice a year, so we have ricotta all year-round. It is soft and a little watery when first made. For this reason the ricotta is put into round baskets made of willow, loosely woven, to allow the liquid to drain. When the cheese is turned out, it has the lovely woven design of the basket all over it.

Ricotta is one of the Roman basic foods; you make it your business to know exactly when it arrives fresh in the store and who has the best. Ricotta is a favorite dessert here, and these simple recipes use the best, freshest ricotta with what you have in the pantry. Biscotti are usually served with these ricotta dishes. Remember to drain the ricotta, even overnight, if necessary.

1 Either sieve the ricotta or pass it through a food mill. Mix the ricotta and mascarpone together thoroughly. Add the orange juice and the liqueur, beating to incorporate them into the ricotta mixture.

2 Whip the cream until frothy, adding the confectioners' sugar while beating. When the cream is stiff, fold it gently into the ricotta.

3 Divide the ricotta among 6 or 8 small bowls. Sprinkle 1 generous tablespoon of the chocolate over each bowl before serving. Refrigerate any leftover ricotta battuta, covered.

VARIATIONS

If you have really good ricotta, these are the simplest and best ways to serve it:

- Sweeten the drained ricotta to taste with superfine sugar and mix in good rum to taste. This is called *alla burina,* or "the peasant's way."

- Sieve the ricotta, put it into a bowl, and add a few tablespoons of finely ground espresso coffee, superfine sugar to taste, and a little good cognac. Mix all together and serve from the bowl.

- Slice the ricotta about $1/2$ inch thick. Top with a sprinkling of cinnamon and sugar.

ZABAGLIONE

SERVES 8 TO 10

6 large fresh egg yolks

6 tablespoons sugar

⅓ cup dry Marsala (60 ml)

1½ cups cold heavy cream (375 ml)

3 ounces good-quality semi-sweet chocolate, diced (85 g)

6 ounces chocolate-covered torroncino (nougat), chopped coarse (See note below for an alternative.) (170 g)

Zabaglione is what mothers give to their little children when they look peaked — and they make it for their older children after a night on the town. Zabaglione gives you back your strength and puts roses in your cheeks. Halve this recipe if you like.

1 Remove the eggs from the refrigerator ½ hour before using them. Measure out all the ingredients, but wait until you need it to whip the cream.

2 Put the egg yolks in the top part of a large double boiler, or a saucepan that can be used as one. Over barely simmering water, beat the yolks for 1 minute with a wire whisk (or a handheld electric beater); add the sugar gradually and beat until the mixture is light and fluffy. Add the Marsala, 1 tablespoon at a time, beating constantly, until the zabaglione holds a small peak when the beater is withdrawn. Put the top of the double boiler in a sinkful of cold water with a few ice cubes and continue beating until the mixture is cool.

3 Whip the cream until it is just stiff. Fold 2 tablespoons of whipped cream into the zabaglione, then fold in the rest of the whipped cream, alternating with the diced chocolate and chopped torroncino. Do not overblend.

4 The zabaglione can be served at once in glasses, or refrigerated for 2 or 3 hours and served cold. It can also be frozen, spooned into a glass bowl and covered with plastic wrap and foil. If frozen, it must be allowed to soften before it is served.

NOTE: If nougat (preferably chocolate covered) is not available, use almond praline, chopped fairly coarse, and another ounce of chocolate. You will need ⅓ heaping cup (75 g) sugar and ⅓ pound (150 g) lightly toasted almonds for the praline. See the method on page 285.

THE BEST LIMONCELLO

MAKES ABOUT 1 QUART (1 LITER)

8 lemons, preferably organic

1 quart alcohol for liqueurs (100 proof vodka can be substituted) (1 l)

3 cups (1½ pounds) sugar (700 g)

3½ cups water (820 ml)

In our book, *Italian Cooking in the Grand Tradition*, Anna Maria Cornetto and I gave a recipe for limoncello liqueur (it is all over Italy), which we thought very good. But I now have a better one, truly the best, extorted from a friend in Vietri on the Amalfi coast. The Romans pour limoncello over plain ice cream or sherbet, just a little, or serve it as a digestif, directly from the freezer. It is absolutely delicious but very potent.

1 Wash the lemons well in warm soapy water; rinse and dry them well. Use a potato peeler to remove the yellow part of the peel — the zest — without any white pith.

2 Put the lemon zest in a jar with 1 cup of the alcohol or the vodka. Seal tightly and leave for 30 days in a cool, dark place, shaking every now and then.

3 When ready to complete the limoncello, combine the sugar and water in a stainless steel saucepan. Bring to a simmer, swirling the pan or stirring just until the sugar dissolves. Allow to simmer for 10 minutes. Remove from the heat and let cool.

4 Remove and discard the lemon zest. Mix together the lemon-flavored alcohol, the cooled sugar syrup, and the remaining unflavored alcohol or vodka. Using a funnel, pour the limoncello into bottles and seal tightly. Store the limoncello in a cool, dark place for 20 days before tasting it. After 20 days, transfer to the freezer. Serve ice cold in very small glasses.

INDEX